FINAL CUT

THE POST-WAR B-17 FLYING FORTRESS: THE SURVIVORS

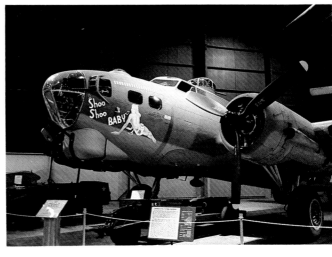

FINAL CUT

·······

THE POST-WAR B-17 FLYING FORTRESS: THE SURVIVORS

·······

by SCOTT A. THOMPSON

PICTORIAL HISTORIES PUBLISHING COMPANY

LIBRARY OF CONGRESS CATALOG CARD NO. 90-60027

ISBN 0-929521-32-3

First Printing: August 1990
Second Printing: March 1992
Third Printing: August 1993
Fourth Printing: December 1995
PRINTED IN U.S.A.

Typography: Arrow Graphics
Layout: Stan Cohen
Cover Design: Kirk Johnson

For Lisa, my silent partner,
who shows me forests when all I see are trees.

Photo Credits:
Title page: top left—Randy Walker, top right—Tim Hade, middle left—Tim Hade,
middle right—D. Truax via AAHS, bottom left—Paul Snider, bottom right—Ross via Eric Parrow.
Facing page: National Warplane Museum.

PICTORIAL HISTORIES PUBLISHING COMPANY
713 South Third West
Missoula, Montana 59801

INTRODUCTION
■ ■ ■ ■ ■

The saga of the Flying Fortress has been thoroughly documented through the years. Its story has been told and retold, particularly with emphasis on the air war it fought over Europe nearly a half century ago. The development and utilization of the B-17 was nearly synonymous with that of American military airpower; the laboratory became the great raging air battles fought across western Europe in 1943 and 1944. The many accounts of the gestation and maturation of the airplane, as well as the young aircrews which took it into combat, are gripping and thorough.

But it seemed apparent to me that a final chapter was yet missing. Most historical records about the B-17 gave quick overviews about its post-war activity and generally commented upon the type's versatility. I felt that a more in-depth treatment was in order, particularly with regard to the few surviving examples of the Fortress.

The post-war use of the B-17 was unique both in its longevity and diversity. Though its use as an American bomber ended in May 1945, the B-17 remained in the military inventory in large numbers long after contemporaries such as the B-24 and even the B-29 had been relegated to the scrapyard. Even the grandmother of longevity, the DC-3/C-47 series, was rivaled by the Fortress but, with several notable exceptions, rarely saw general utilization much beyond its designed use of passenger and cargo transport. The Fortress, on the other hand, finished its role as the heavyweight bomber of World War II to segue into roles which included air-sea rescue, weather and photo reconnaissance, test-beds for engines and electronic equipment, cargo and administrative transport, drone and drone controller use, covert activities with the CIA, and airborne radar platforms. Leaving military service, surplus B-17s were put to wide use as air tankers, sprayers, transports, test-beds, and film production, among others.

The era of the B-17 is finally drawing to a close over fifty years after the Boeing Model 299 first left the drawing board.

Those remaining in the U.S. are the survivors of several decades of combat, military, and civil use. For the most part they have now become pampered queens – especially those owned by private individuals and museums. They shine and glisten, with re-mounted gun turrets and other combat gear, often wearing precisely authentic paint and running better than the day they were built. They deserve pampering, for they are the literal end of the line.

But chances seem good they will continue to survive. The thoughtless destruction of seemingly worthless machines has ended. Those tucked into museums are now only threatened by hangar fires or freak accidents. The flying examples are exposed to pilot error and mechanical failure, as serious accidents in 1987 and 1988 demonstrated. Even the victims of such will probably be painstakingly rebuilt to better than new condition. Unfortunately, destructive accidents with operating airplanes are always possible, as occurred in England in July 1989 with the loss of a French-operated B-17. Such is the price if we are to continue to see living, breathing B-17s return to their element.

So, this is the story of the survivors. Their trial of fire was German flak, military scrapyards, smelters, atomic explosions, air-to-air missiles, Bolivian density altitude, unthinking vandals, Southern California brush fires, and the economic bottom line. These, then, have made the final cut.

Notes about the Text

Throughout the text aircraft that currently exist are flagged with an asterisk. Several of the airframes that are included are incomplete or badly damaged. They are listed because they are identifiable and may be eventually used to build up complete aircraft.

ACKNOWLEDGMENTS
■■■■■■

The sources for some of this material are official records obtained from the military and Federal Aviation Administration. By their nature many of these records, particularly the military record cards, contain errors and are often difficult to decipher. Wherever possible dates and usage have been confirmed by those involved in the operations of these B-17s.

Many people provided a great deal of help in assembling this book, but I wish to give specific thanks to those below for the assistance, photos, and information provided. Photos have been credited to the original photographer, if known, and/or the collection it was drawn from. My apologies for any omissions or errors which may have occurred.

TECHNICAL ASSISTANCE
Cliff Bowman
Tim Stroud
Mark Thompson

PHOTOS
American Aviation Historical Society
R.F. Arnold
Brian Baker
Roger Besecker
Peter Bowers
David Campbell
Gary Criss
Jim Farmer
Robert Fitzgerald
Harry Gann
Leo Geis
Bruce Gowans
A. Kevin Grantham
Malcolm Gougon
Tim Hade
Jim Hale/Vintage Aircraft
Chuckie Hospers
Gene Kanary
Tom Hennion
Michael Kellner
Art Krieger
William Larkins
Steve Leon/Reynolds Electrical
    & Engineering Company
John Lindquist
Edward Louria
R.A. McLauglin
Ed Maloney
Peter Marson
Dave Menard
Robert Mikesh
Military Aircraft Photographs
Robin Mitchell
National Air and Space Museum

Merle Olmsted
Eric Parrow
Ev Payette
Milo Peltzer
Richard Schultz
Chuck Self
Paul Snider
Sam Taber
Maurice Taylor
Norman Thompson
Ray Wagner/San Diego Aero-Space Museum
Randy Walker

INFORMATION
Jim Farmer
Jim Fausz/Lone Star Flight Museum
Art Lacey
Jim Miller
Robin Mitchell
Milo Peltzer
Tom Reilly/Vintage Aircraft
Bob Sturges
Sam Taber/Weeks Air Museum
Kermit Weeks/Weeks Air Museum
Gustavo Wetsch

United States Air Force:
    Office of History, Air Force Logistics Command,
        Wright-Patterson AFB
    Reference Division, Historical Research Center,
        Maxwell AFB

United States Navy:
    Naval Historical Center, Aviation Branch
    Office of the Chief of Naval Aviation,
        Naval Aviation History and Archives

National Air and Space Museum
    Archival Support Center

Federal Aviation Adminsitration
    Office of Aircraft Registry

CONTENTS

■■■■■

XPB-1 77258 shortly after conversion in 1945. It was assigned to the Navy Research Laboratory in Boston as a running prototype and replaced the original PB-1 prototype, BuNo 34106.

Important in the post-war engine development tests of Wright engines was this JB-17G, shown here in 1957 with a late version of the R-3350 turbo-compound engine installed. Carter Collection

One of the first USAF B-17s preserved was this ex-DB-17P drone controller shown here at the Air Force Museum in August 1965. This aircraft is now displayed at the Dover AFB Historical Center in Delaware. Carter Collection

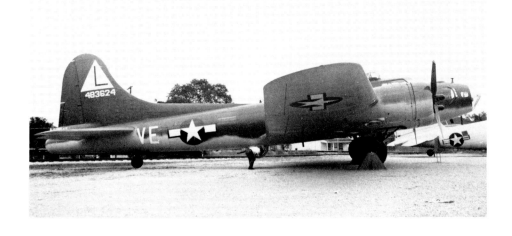

PART ONE:
THE DUST SETTLES
......

A veteran of over 75 combat missions, "Fearless F" awaits an undignified end at Kingman in 1947. Larkins

CHAPTER ONE:
FROM THE FIRE INTO THE FRYING PAN
■■■■■■

It was May 1945, and the English countryside was quiet for the first time in seven years. The war in Europe was finally over. Huge Allied armies spread across the broken continent as a tide of invincible military might. The mainstay of the American Eighth Air Force Bomber Command, the mighty Boeing B-17 Flying Fortresses, were parked; their job was finished. 2,800 of the B-17s were in Europe, the largest component of what had become the most destructive force in the history of the world. The Americans, true to their heritage, were eager to get back home.

Nine B-17 groups were slated for occupation duty on the Continent, and they were dispatched in June and July. Some of the Eighth Air Force bomb groups equipped with Consolidated B-24 Liberators were scheduled to return to the U.S. for transition training into the new Boeing B-29 Superfortresses, to be followed by deployment to the still raging war against Japan. As it happened, none would see any Pacific action. The atomic bomb abruptly ended prospects of that.

In Great Britain, tired B-17s, some veterans of 150 combat missions, waited with new B-17s still in replacement depots. The Army Air Force faced a rapid demobilization but needed to regroup its widely dispersed air forces from around the world into a peacetime force. Hundreds of thousands of airmen and tens of thousands of warplanes slowly began making their way back home, the first group for discharge, the second for dispersal and an uncertain future.

The British fields slowly emptied of the American bombers as eager aircrews took them back across the Atlantic into vast storage yards being established around the country. The first of the bombers left in late May and through the summer and fall of 1945 an aluminum migration occurred. The far-flung Army Air Force was coming home for demobilization. The 2,200,000 men and women of the USAAF shrank to 500,000 personnel by April 1946 and 303,000 by mid-1947. The 78,750 aircraft on hand in 1944 was reduced to only 25,000 by the end of 1947 and 16,800 by 1950.

The combat aircraft pouring into storage yards posed no particular logistical problems. Tentative plans had been made by the civil administration toward the demobilization as early as 1943; the only surprise came at the quickness of the victory over Japan, not expected until early 1946. Plans called for a substantial number of the surplus bombers and fighters entering long-term storage as, indeed, over 700 B-29s and lesser numbers of other types would actually be placed. Many of the planned storage centers would, however, become disposal sites administered by Reconstruction Finance Corporation.

Stories abound to this day of cheap surplus airplanes going begging for buyers. Douglas A-26s could be had for $2,000. New P-38s for $1,000, and B-17s for $13,750. Prices were

Line-up of B-17s at the Ontario Auxiliary Air Field near Chino, California, in 1946. The scrapping of these B-17s was featured in the concluding scenes of the film "Best Years of Our Lives." Carter Collection

B-17F-DL 42-2970 in flight. Note that wartime censors removed the serial from the photo. Peltzer Collection

even less in most cases; one particular B-17 went to a civil owner for $750. Combat aircraft had no readily applicable civil use, however, and the relatively few single-sales of surplus military aircraft to civil users were usually of transports or single-engined trainers which could economically be converted to a civil role. In any event, the vast majority of the surplus aircraft were eventually disposed of in large lots, sold only for their scrap value.

Probably the best known of all the disposal sites was Storage Depot Number 41, located in western Arizona near Kingman. At one time Kingman Army Air Field was home to flexible gunnery and B-17 copilot schools. The field was idled at the war's conclusion but the Reconstruction Finance Corporation decided to take advantage of the favorable climate and available expanse, and initiated plans to bring 20,000 warplanes to Kingman for storage.

They began arriving in October 1945 and by December, were landing at the rate of one a minute. Most of the arrivals were well-worn combat veterans, many having seen in excess of a hundred combat missions over Europe. Some of the scarred planes limped into Kingman with one or two engines shut down, sliding down that final, final approach to an inglorious end. Many factory-fresh B-17s made it to Kingman with nothing but a few ferry flights on the logbooks, but they too took their places next to their well-worn brethren in the growing rows of B-17s. Kingman's warplane population never approached the planned levels, but in excess of 6,000 military airplanes of all types from Curtiss P-40s to Convair B-32s, including 1,800 Flying Fortresses, were soon parked wingtip to wingtip across ten square miles of desert scrub.

Ironically, even as plans establishing the storage yards were finalized, new Fortresses continued to roll off production lines. Though Boeing built their final B-17, B-17G-110-BO 43-39508 on 11 April 1945, Douglas didn't complete theirs, B-17G-95-DL 44-83885 until 28 June (though their last delivery, 44-83882 was accomplished on 31 July). Lockheed continued building well into the summer, their last example, B-17G-110-VE 44-85841, being delivered to the Army Air Force on 28 July.

The factory-fresh examples would, almost exclusively, become the source for both civil and military B-17s to survive into the post-war period, but in the summer of 1945 they too would be flown to storage depots as the Army Air Force began to sort out its post-war requirements.

With so many zero-time B-17s in storage the days of any heavily used B-17s were numbered. The Army Air Force soon decided it had no further need for the worn airplanes and they were declared surplus. The jurisdiction of the aircraft was transferred to the Reconstruction Finance Corporation, designated by the Surplus Property Board as the disposal outlet for the aircraft. Most of the storage depots were offered for sale by sealed bids under the auspices of the RFC's Office of Surplus Property. An air force was for sale.

Thus, with nary a thought for sentimentality (or, for that matter, post-war equipment needs), fleets of B-17s with dramatic combat heritages were auctioned to the highest bidders. Only a very few of them made it past the scrapper's blade. Someone thought to make a famous B-17D, the "Swoose" (40-3097*) into a war memorial for Los Angeles, so possession of the tired bird was transferred to the city for $300. The "Memphis Belle," B-17F-10-BO 41-24485*, held so high three years earlier for being the first Fortress to complete twenty-five combat missions over Europe, was found languishing in the weeds at Altus, Oklahoma, and as an afterthought, someone from Memphis thought to save the

Rollout at Long Beach of B-17G-15-DL 42-38113, the thousandth B-17 built by Douglas. McDonnell-Douglas via H. Gann

Nighttime production at the Douglas-Long Beach plant in the summer of 1944. McDonnell-Douglas via H. Gann

old bomber. But lost were so many veterans of hundreds of dramatic and crucial missions on battlefields that had disappeared with the first breeze. No one could ever visit the places where these battles were fought, no landmarks to pour over, no maps from which to study intricate combat tactics. No memorials could be erected upon the expanse of European skies where decisive warfare occurred and quick, terrifying death claimed thousands. The airplanes were all the memorial left from that air war, but few remembered those carcasses of battle parked on the Arizona desert and now deemed junk.

Paul Mantz, the famed Hollywood movie pilot, bought

B-17s and B-24s await their fate on the Arizona desert in February 1947. Larkins

Though most of the B-17s at Kingman were combat veterans, several hundred were factory fresh examples with just ferry time. Larkins

one field of 475 airplanes, including 78 B-17s, at Stillwater, Oklahoma for $55,000. His intent was to take the best of the lot for future use in what he knew would be a rush of war-related film productions. Unfortunately, he had no takers on financing the logistics of moving his fleet to the west coast, so he took a few of his airplanes, including a pair of Mustangs soon to become famous on the post-war racing circuit, a B-25 he would rebuild for use as a camera ship, and B-17F-50-DL 42-3360, to his west coast base in Burbank and had the rest of his "junk" scrapped.

At Kingman, the idled B-17s and their compatriots spent 1946 bleaching under the hot Arizona sun. But late that year, 5,400 of them were sold to the Wunderlich Contracting Company for $2.78 million, barely $500 apiece. Wunderlich took over the field and organized a great smelting operation. Three huge furnaces were constructed to take the airplanes. Engines were stripped from the bombers in preparation for their transformation into molten aluminum. By mid-1947 the process was well under way, consuming the final formation of parked planes. As each plane was towed or pushed to the smelter, it was met by a giant chopping blade which neatly sliced the airplane into manageable pieces. Then cranes would lift the scrap, still bearing the intricate nose art once lovingly applied a world away, still showing the scars of combat, and still carrying the bloodstains from forgotten battles, and drop it into the consuming fire to emerge as neat ingots of aluminum for 1948 model pots and pans.

To an extent, one can understand this massive destruction. From the perspective of the Army Air Force, it had no need, nor personnel, to maintain even a fraction of what had essentially become obsolete equipment. The Army Air Force was quickly shrinking to pre-war levels and was beginning to have difficulty maintaining any sort of readiness with even its meager remainder. Beyond that, it would be difficult to encourage a peace-time Congress to appropriate money for new aircraft like the B-36 and the on-the-drawing-board B-52 when there were thousands of bombers and fighters rotting on various fields across the nation.

The civilian administration, flush with victory and looking for opportunity, was eager to put the war firmly behind it and gave few thought about destroying the implements of that war. The country was too busy with the future to think of the past. The United States had emerged from World War II as the only complete victor. The cost in men and money had been large, but the U.S. held an intact industrial base, was easily the most powerful nation on earth in terms of military, financial, and political might, and could look forward to shaping the world in the mold of the American century. Fleets of junk had no place in a nation with its eyes so brightly fixed on the future.

In retrospect, it seems incredible that more combat veterans like the "Swoose" or the "Memphis Belle" were not earmarked for preservation. In actuality, it was only quirks of fate that saved any at all. Sentimentality held no charge in a nation busy with a readjustment to peace, and the aircraft which had so dramatically driven the war into the heartland of Nazi Germany were quickly forgotten. The scrapper's blade worked unceasingly along the countless rows of B-17s, and when it came time for second thoughts about what was melted away on the Arizona desert, it was decades too late.

Congratulations all around at the ceremonies marking the end of Douglas' production of the Flying Fortress. Pictured is 44-83884, which wasn't delivered until 15 July 1945 and went to the Navy for conversion to a PB-1W. The last serialed Douglas B-17 was 44-83885, delivered two weeks earlier on 28 June. NASM

PART TWO:
POST-WAR MILITARY
USE OF THE B-17

......

Flight of drones over the New Mexican desert in April 1946, six weeks prior to their deployment to Eniwetok Atoll. View clearly shows individual markings developed to enable quick identification of drones from a distance. USAF

OVERVIEW
■■■■■■

While the majority of B-17s surviving the war were beginning to pour into vast storage lots dotting the country, new B-17s rolled from still-active production lines through the summer of 1945. Some of them would be flown from the factories directly to Naval Air Station (NAS) Johnsville in Pennsylvania for conversion to PB-1Ws and a Navy future. Some would be placed in temporary storage at places like Patterson Field, Ohio, to be pulled for use as CB-17s, staff transports, or experimental test-beds. Most of the factory-fresh Fortresses, however, were placed in large storage lots, among them Syracuse, New York and South Plains, Texas. This group of B-17s was then declared excess to military use in October 1945.

The majority of the Syracuse Fortresses were flown to a Reconstruction Finance Corporation lot at Altus, Oklahoma in November 1945 for disposal. A large number of these would be scrapped, but a few would survive to become war memorials or be purchased by civil users. Other Syracuse Fortresses were flown to Kingman, Arizona for scrapping (though most of the B-17s at Kingman were actual combat veterans).

Conversely, most of the B-17s at South Plains would remain in long term storage. Apparently, someone deep within the paperwork bowels of the Pentagon foresaw a need for the new B-17s in the post-war Air Force and, a month after being declared excess, returned them to the inventory. That is not to say that the aircraft were put to any immediate use, however. Most remained at South Plains until early 1947, then transferred to Pyote, Texas for additional storage. The new B-17s were pulled when needed, usually to become DB-17s or VB-17s. The B-17Gs slated for assignment to the Coast Guard as PB-1Gs were pulled from South Plains in early 1946.

Several dozen new B-17s were withdrawn from storage and sent to the Aberdeen Proving Grounds in Maryland for various test programs. The fate of these aircraft has not been verified, but it can be presumed they were destroyed in the process, or damaged and then scrapped.

A large number of the several hundred new B-17s in replacement depots in Britain when the war ended were sent on to European storage depots, particularly in Germany, during the summer of 1945 to serve as part of the occupation forces. Most of the B-17s which remained in storage in these depots into 1948 were scrapped overseas and never returned to the U.S., although some were eventually pulled for conversion to VB-17s and assigned to Air Forces Europe.

One lone B-17 was earmarked for preservation by the Army Air Force. B-17G 44-83504 was set aside on 20 February 1946 for a future, but unplanned, Army Air Force Museum. The plans did not mesh, however, and the spared bomber was scrapped in August 1949.

It would be difficult, if not impossible, to document all the roles played by the B-17 in the post-war American military. Beyond the lack of detailed historical records on their more obscure uses, the Fortresses were involved in a multitude of research programs which resulted in configurations which continually changed and never assigned specific designations. The widespread use of the Fortress as drone controllers (and drones), as staff transports, for search and rescue, as well as Navy radar platforms, accounted for much of the post-war utilization, but other less prominent missions also found the B-17 an ideal vehicle. The virtues seen by the U.S. military (and, indeed, other military and civil users) lay in the range and payload carrying ability of the aircraft, general lack of complexity, availability in the post-war inventory, and easy adaptability to any number of roles would enable the 1934 design to soldier on well into the jet age and bridge to the space age.

The following two chapters contain a general discussion of specific post-war military uses of the Fortress, provided here to avoid repetition in subsequent chapters about individual aircraft. It should be noted that many of the operational roles assigned to the B-17 were never given a prefix designator, particularly before 1948 when the newly created United States Air Force modified the existing Army Air Force system of designators, developing more prefixes to denote specific operational uses. Also, the list that follows in no way attempts to give a complete account of all usage of B-17s, either as B-17s or under other military designations (C-108, PB-1, F-9, etc.). Even limited as such, the versatility and basic soundness of the design rapidly becomes apparent.

CHAPTER ONE:
USE OF RECONFIGURED FORTRESSES

■■■■■■

The B-17 series was built over a ten-year period beginning in 1935 with the Boeing Model 299. It was forged in the pre-war innocence of the mid-thirties but matured quickly under the onslaught of the Japanese Zero and the mighty Luftwaffe. The early versions of the Flying Fortress held the aesthetic attraction of a graceful beauty, sleek lines curving through polished aluminum, the aerodynamically tolerated defensive gun positions faired into the least obtrusive blisters possible. For the first five series of Fortresses built, from the Y1B-17 through the B-17D, it would seem beauty indeed conquered the beast.

But the Air Corps and Boeing heeded the lessons learned by the Royal Air Force over Europe in the early months of the war, and the B-17 design went through a metamorphosis. The casual observer could still see Fortress in the lines, but this was obviously a beefier variation of the type. The unobtrusive gun blisters had given way to massive power turrets bracing pairs of heavy machine guns. A huge vertical stabilizer and rudder assembly topped a redesigned tail section equipped with tail guns, replacing the petite tail of the early Fortresses. Beginning with the B-17E, which first flew three months before Pearl Harbor, the Fortress lost the innocence and assumed its inevitable role as the premier American heavy bomber in the European air war. When the final production series, the B-17G, first flew in 1943, it ably demonstrated the evolution undertaken by the design; the princess had become a hardened, no-nonsense combat veteran with function now demonstrated by every curve.

Army Air Force demands for the B-17 quickly outstripped the ability of Boeing alone to build their Fortress, and by 1944 Boeing was building Fortresses in Seattle, with the Douglas Aircraft Company and Vega, a subsidiary of Lockheed, building B-17s at their respective plants in Southern California. Together, they produced 12,731 B-17s.

Volumes have been written about the feats of the Fortress and its crews. Suffice to say, the airplane was a favorite among airmen, the public, the press, and the Army Air Force. The Fortress fairly reeked with charisma, but there was also substance behind the aluminum. The airplane was well-designed, well-built, and from the record it would seem many crews ascribed invincible faith in their bomber to carry them through the battle. Unfortunately, such faith could not always stand up to the iron thrown against it, and thousands of young men died in their chariots. Nonetheless, the B-17 would emerge from World War II as playing a pivotal, if not decisive, role in the victory.

B-17H and Beyond

The B-17G was the last Fortress series produced. Subsequent series suffixes, such as B-17H or B-17L, were modifications of existing B-17Gs. Following is a listing of assigned suffixes beyond the "G" series, all of which were either later dropped in favor of a newly created prefix (as the B-17H became the SB-17G in 1948), or were modifications to existing special prefix versions (as in QB-17G to QB-17N).

B-17H—lifeboat carrying Air-Sea Rescue series (see SB-17)

B-17L—drone derivative (see DB-17/QB-17)

B-17N—drone derivative (see DB-17/QB-17)

B-17P—drone controller derivative (see DB-17/QB-17)

Special-Use Prefixes as Applied to the B-17

The Army Air Corps and its later transformations (USAAF and USAF) developed a number of special-use prefixes to denote additional uses of a type beyond its primary role as indicated by its mission designator ("B" for bomber in the case of the B-17). Though not encompassing all special uses a type might be employed in, the method as applied to the Fortress gives some indication of the diversity of its use.

TB-17G-110-VE 44-85817. Note the buzz number on the tail and wing undersurface, instituted by the Army Air Force in 1945 to reduce buzzing incidents.
Krieger Collection

CB-17: Personnel Transport

A CB-17G on Guam in September 1945. Though lacking turrets, note the lone .50 caliber gun in the left cheek position. Peltzer Collection

The CB-17 was a derivative of the B-17 developed in 1943 when the Army Air Force was in need of troop transport capability. As initially envisioned, the CB-17 would retain some defensive armament but would have offensive equipment, such as bomb racks, stripped and replaced with provisions to seat as many as sixty-four armed combat troops. Apart from the obvious drawbacks of using the already cramped accommodations of the B-17 in such a way, the requirement of such a conversion was quickly negated by sufficient numbers of standard transport types. Subsequent wartime use of CB-17s was in administrative transport and usually utilized withdrawn-from-combat Fortresses. Armament was often removed and a few nicer amenities such as insulation, seats, and food provisions were installed. Postwar CB-17s were usually new Fortresses drawn from storage depots for conversion. No standard was ever established for the CB-17, and plushier post-war CB-17s more often resembled the staff-transport VB-17. CB-17s would often become VB-17s in the paperwork, and just as quickly revert to CB-17 status. In many cases, it seems the designation depended more upon to whom the aircraft was assigned rather than the actual configuration. CB-17s (and VB-17s) continued to serve through the Korean War as staff transports, and some would remain active into the late fifties before retirement to Davis-Monthan AFB.

DB-17/ QB-17 Drone Director/ Drone

The development of the DB-17 director and QB-17 drone occurred simultaneously as two components of the same system. A number of programs involved the conversion of B-17s to director/drones prior to the establishment of the specific mission prefixes in 1948. The early, wartime con-versions were redesignated as new types, the director version becoming the CQ-4 while the drone became the BQ-7.

The initial wartime projects using modified war-weary B-17s converted to flying bombs were largely failures. The control systems used, as developed at Wright Field's System Engineering Laboratory, were first generation technology which proved unreliable in operational use. Two azon (azimuth only) control units, first developed for use in early guided bombs, were connected to the B-17's autopilot to provide radio control inputs to the flight controls. The double-azon system was incorporated into "Project Aphrodite" and its successor, "Project Castor" which envisioned diving explosive laden BQ-7s into hard targets in France, particularly V-1 buzz bomb launch sites and hardened submarine pens. The technology available prevented radio-controlled take-offs, thus requiring a two man crew to fly the bomber until the explosives were armed and control transferred to the director aircraft. The crew then parachuted to safety. Control difficulties and inadvertent explosions which killed flight crews, as well as a general lack of demonstrated success in destroying selected targets, eventually led to the cancellation of the programs.

Post-war development of the control technology was dramatically accelerated by the drone requirements of Operation Crossroads, the first of a series of atomic tests undertaken in the South Pacific. Operation Crossroads called for the use of unmanned aircraft equipped with research instruments to be flown through and near the mushroom clouds of the two atomic explosions planned. This required radio control through the landing phase and, in initial planning meetings for Crossroads, the Army Air Force committed itself to providing B-17 drones to the project.

Under the direction of General Roger Ramey, commander of Air Task Group 1.5, the development of a refined control system took less than six weeks culminating on 19 February 1946 when a war-weary B-17 drone was controlled through all phases of a test flight undertaken at Clovis Field in New Mexico. Further developmental tests followed quickly, and by late May 1946 the group had drawn sixteen new B-17s from storage depots, developed ten (six primary, four back-up) into drones with several hundred pounds of radio, radar, television, and other experimental and research equipment installed in each. Much of the work was accomplished by the San Antonio Air Depot at Kelly Field in Texas. Also, six director B-17s (four mother ships, one supermother ship with the capability to control any drone, and one back-up mother ship) were developed, with the unit set to deploy to Eniwetok Atoll for the operation by 01 June 46. Operation Crossroads required extensive operational preparation to coordinate timing of the multi-faceted experiment, but both detonations were accomplished successfully in July.

The drones were flown near and through both mushroom clouds for sample collection and atmospheric research. Success of the program led to development of drone squadrons for use in the testing of a wide variety of air-to-air missiles, ground-to-air missiles, and numerous other programs. With the establishment of the USAF, the director aircraft became DB-17Gs while the drones became QB-17Gs.

Further deployments to the South Pacific for a succession of atomic tests occurred through 1952, by which time most DB-17s and QB-17s had been be assigned to the 3205th Drone Group at Eglin AFB in Florida, home of the Air Proving Ground Command. Squadrons from the 3205th Drone Group were deployed to provide drones at the Missile Test Center at Patrick AFB in Florida, the Holloman Air Development Center at Holloman AFB in New Mexico, and the Pacific Missile Test Range at Naval Air Station, Point Mugu on the California coast. Pt. Mugu drones were also utilized at the Air Force Flight Test Center at Edwards AFB and the U.S. Naval Ordinance Test Station at Inyokern, both in the nearby Mojave Desert.

Most B-17s slated for conversion to Directors came from storage depots and modification work was performed at the Middletown Air Depot at Olmsted AFB in Pennsylvania. A derivative of the DB-17G was the DB-17P which utilized different control systems as developed in 1955. Many Directors remained as DB-17Gs, however, until retirement in 1959.

Additional derivatives of the QB-17G were also developed, becoming the QB-17L and the QB-17N. The later series utilized sophisticated optical tracking equipment in detachable wing tip pods equipped with explosive bolts and parachutes for recovery of test data in the event of loss of the drone. Other modifications, beyond the installation of the Drone Stabilization Control System (DSCSE), included exterior lighting to assist external operators determine the

Ground control drone pilot Capt. R.M. Seldomridge demonstrating technique during development testing at Clovis Field in March 1946. USAF

Cockpit of B-17 drone developed for Operation Crossroads. Note servos for control of throttles and props, and the liberal amount of tape used to secure elevator and aileron trim wheels. USAF

Line up of B-17 'baby' drones at Roswell, New Mexico in March 1946 in preparation for Operation Crossroads. USAF

Detail of the insignia carried by the Crossroads B-17s. USAF

Crewman assigned to secure B-17 drone after unmanned landing at Eniwetok runs from the aircraft after determining unsafe radioactivity level. Minimal precautions were taken to protect personnel assigned to such duties. USAF

drone's configuration, heavier electrical system capacity, additional radio equipment, and numerous minor internal changes. Differences between the QB-17L and QB-17N lay in specific control and television transmitting equipment installed.

Sources for QB-17 conversion were new B-17s in storage, B-17s retired from other duties such as VB-17 staff transport, and DB-17s excess to requirements.

The typical DB-17/QB-17 mission as undertaken by the Air Proving Ground Command had QB-17 runway alignment, engine start, and pre-flight checks accomplished by ground crewmen. A ground control pilot, utilizing a mobile ground unit, would then assume control of the drone and fly it from the runway at which point the airborne DB-17 would take over. The QB-17 would often be the subject of intentional near-misses during missile tests to preserve the drone for as many missions as possible. If the QB-17 survived the test, the DB-17 would fly it back to the airfield for landing by the remote ground controller.

The utility of the DB-17/QB-17 combination ensured their use until the late fifties. By then, jet and rocket-powered drones had became available in sufficient numbers and more approximated the type of targets realistically envisioned for the equipment being tested.

All QB-17s were eventually expended in development tests, the last DB-17/QB-17 mission being flown on 06 August 1959 with QB-17G 44-83717 being blown from the New Mexican sky by a Falcon missile fired from an F-101 Voodoo. One last QB-17G was destroyed in a missile test in the summer of 1960 at the test range off Patrick AFB in Florida.

By then, most of the DB-17s had already been retired to Davis-Monthan AFB or farmed out to a myriad of museums. The last active USAF Fortress, DB-17G 44-83684* arrived at Davis-Monthan AFB for storage in August 1959, and an era that spanned three decades ended quietly in the stillness of the Arizona desert.

The end results of a mission flown by QB-17G 44-83556 from Holloman in 1956. Damaged suffered on some of these test missions was comparable to that of aerial combat over a decade earlier. Fitzgerald

An unidentified QB-17 with the 3225th Drone Squadron of the 3205th Drone Group at Holloman in 1956. Paint scheme was a bright red fuselage and natural metal wings. Both vertical and horizontal tail were badly damaged during this missile test. Fitzgerald

One series of tests conducted in 1948 involved using QB-17G 44-85648 to test ditching procedures. The program was based at Eglin AFB. USAF

EB-17: Exempt from Technical Order Compliance

EB-17s were usually aircraft loaned to organizations by the Air Force for test work. The prefix "E" specifically exempted the aircraft from all but urgent technical orders issued for the type. This was considered necessary because the EB-17s were often based away from Air Force installations in the course of their test work, and to insist on compliance with each new order would hinder test or research work in progress. Presumably, the orders were complied with upon return of the aircraft to the Air Force.

EB-17s were often lent to defense contractors for developmental projects. Two well known examples of this were B-17G-110-VE 44-85813*, loaned to the Wright Aeronautical Corporation for use as an engine test-bed, and B-17G-70-VE 44-8543*, loaned to the Federal Telecommu-

nications Corporation for research.

Other EB-17s included a number of SB-17Gs diverted to the Air Force Missile Test Center at Patrick AFB in Florida beginning in 1952. These EB-17s were equipped with loudspeakers and VHF radios to clear civil boats and aircraft from the missile ranges prior to test shots. They remained on duty at Patrick through 1958.

The "E" prefix was supplanted by the "J" and "N" prefix established in 1955. All EB-17s became JB-17s at that time, there being nothing in the records to indicate that any NB-17s were ever in the Air Force inventory.

After 1955, the "E" prefix was reassigned to designate aircraft used in an early-warning role. No USAF B-17s were used as such, though the Navy utilized PB-1Ws in that capacity through 1955.

Allison's engine test bed B-17. This Fortress, B-17G-110-VE 44-85747, was less well known than the other two radically modified B-17s which also performed as post-war test beds for Wright and Pratt & Whitney. Allison

EB-17G 44-85813 fitted with the XT35 engine in the radically modified nose structure. The cockpit was moved aft nearly four feet to accommodate the fifth engine. MAP

FB-17G 44-85514 in 1946 or 1947. Note the loop antenna forward of the cockpit. This aircraft later became a RB-17G when the designation system was modified in 1948. It was attached to the 9th Strategic Reconaissance Group at Fairfield-Suisun Army Air Base in California. Krieger Collection

Later designated as a JB-17G, 44-85813 is shown here flying under the power of its radial engines, though the powerful turboprop could also do the job alone. Curtiss-Electric propellers replaced the hydraulically powered Hamilton Standard props as evidenced by the different shaped hubs. Bowers Collection

FB-17: Photographic/Reconnaissance

The Army had originally redesignated photo-adapted B-17s as F-9s in 1944. In 1945 the designating system was revised, many F-9s becoming FB-17s. The system was again changed in 1948, with the remaining F-9s and FB-17s becoming RB-17s. From the record, it appears no FB-17s survive in the U.S. today.

JB-17: Temporary Test Role

The "J" prefix was established in 1955 to denote aircraft temporarily assigned to test work or temporarily converted for a test role, thereby replacing the "E" prefix. Several JB-17s (as EB-17s) were loaned to contractors for developmental-related work. As noted earlier, the most highly modified example was JB-17G 44-85813, loaned to the Wright Aeronautical Corporation and converted to an engine test bed by moving the cockpit aft several feet. The nose area of the B-17 was extensively reworked by Boeing to allow for the installation of a fifth engine for test work. The conventional landing gear configuration of the Fortress made the design ideal for such a conversion and, in fact, two additional B-17s were similarly modified, though never receiving the JB-17 designation. (One, B-17G-100-VE 44-85734*, was purchased outright by Pratt & Whitney in 1947 specifically for the conversion; the other, B-17G-105-VE 44-85747, was used by Allison but did not require the cockpit be moved aft and was retired prior to the establishment of the JB-17 designation.)

The extensive conversion of 44-85813 would suggest that it should have been designated an NB-17G, in keeping with the intended uses for the "J" (temporary test status) and "N" (permanent test status) prefixes. In fact, JB-17G 44-85813 was returned to a conventional configuration by an air tanker operator in the mid-sixties. Operating under the civil registration of N6694C, the tanker was nearly destroyed in an April 1980 crash.

MB-17: Missile Launcher

With the advent of guided bombs and missiles, the Army Air Force modified a number of B-17s to act as launchers. Initial efforts were directed toward the development and operational testing of glide bombs, equipped with "razon" (range and azimuth only) and "azon" (azimuth only) guidance systems during the period 1943-1945. Post-war tests included the launching of captured German V-1 buzz bombs, redesignated JB-2s by the Army Air Force. One JB-2 was mounted under each wing of the MB-17. MB-17s also were used to launch a series of drones used as gunnery targets.

The "M" prefix was reassigned the medical evacuation role in 1948, and MB-17s became TB-17s for lack of any other relevant designation (though several MB-17s retained the designation into 1953). At least one MB-17 survives, 44-83624*, on display at Dover Air Force Base.

QB-17: Drone

See DB-17/QB-17

RB-17: (Before 1948) Restricted By Obsolelscence

Prior to 1948, the "R" designation as applied to B-17s indicated obsolete aircraft which no longer would be used for their primary mission. All B-17D and earlier series were redesignated RB-17s in late 1942, with B-17Es redesignated as such in late 1943. RB-17s were usually relegated to training, transport roles, or scrapped.

The prefix was not generally applied after 1945 when the Fortress was withdrawn from use a bomber in favor of the B-29 Superfortress. By then, any B-17 not in storage or having a post-war assignment was well on its way to the scrapyard anyway.

RB-17: (After 1948) Reconnaissance

With the establishment of the USAF and a modified designating system in 1948, the "R" prefix came to be assigned to the reconnaissance role. Thus, any photo-version Fortress (F-9s or FB-17s) became RB-17s.

With the escalation of hostilities in Asia in the early fifties, the B-17 assumed a murky and still obscure role. Two RB-17s had been assigned to the 6204th Photo Mapping Flight based in the Philippines at Clark AFB when the Korean War began in 1950. At least one of the RB-17Gs, painted gloss black and with few markings, performed numerous missions from Clark for the Central Intelligence Agency. Purported targets of these missions, involving both reconnaissance and "agent insertion" were the People's Republic of China, Burma, North Korea, and North Vietnam. Little information is available to this day about the specific role of the RB-17 in Southeast Asia, though the CIA continued to use one B-17, 44-83785* (as N809Z), through the mid-sixties for a number of classified operations.

MB-17G 44-83641 was used as an aerial launching platform for JB-2 flying bombs. This particular aircraft, though based at Eglin, was deployed to the South Pacific in June 1946 for Operation Sandstone. Shipp

TB-17H 44-83722 in early post-war years. TB-17Hs and B-17Hs became SB-17Gs in 1948. Armament was deleted but note dorsal turret ring retained on this aircraft. Larkins

Also of note are the twenty RB-17Gs transferred from SAC squadrons to the U.S. Navy in the last month of 1949 and the first half of 1950. No Navy records have come to light regarding these aircraft, their use, or fate. (See Appendix 2)

SB-17: Air-Sea Rescue

Initially designated the B-17H or TB-17H, the Air-Sea Rescue version of the Fortress was developed to provide for air-dropped boats for downed flight crews in the English Channel and across the vast reaches of the Pacific. Initially conceived in mid-1943, it did not become operational until the war was nearly over. Nonetheless, the B-17H was instrumental in saving a number of B-29 combat crews during the air war against Japan.

B-17Hs were standard B-17Gs, retaining full defensive armament, but equipped with a self-righting motorized Higgins A1 lifeboat attached to the belly of the bomber via cables running to the bomb shackles in the bomb bay. The boat extended from just aft of the chin turret fairing to the ball turret and was contoured to mold to the fuselage of the belly. In the event of assisting a downed crew, the B-17H crew would drop the lifeboat, equipped with maps, food, provisions, and survival equipment sufficient to provide until a pick-up could be arranged. The boat would descend on three parachutes until contact with the water, upon which rocket-propelled string lines were automatically ejected to assist those in the water retrieve the boat.

Post-war use of the B-17H and TB-17H continued, though the aircraft were disarmed. The Air Rescue squadrons were organizationally assigned to the Military Air Transport Service. Radar installations replaced the deleted chin turrets. In 1948, with the amended designating system, all B-17Hs became SB-17Gs.

By 1950, SB-17Gs were organized into nine Air Rescue Squadrons, each consisting of a headquarters unit and four flights. Three of the flights were detached from the each headquarter unit to provide air-sea rescue services over the wide-ranging deployment of the USAF, from Weisbaden, Germany to Dhahran, Saudi Arabia.

During the Korean War, SB-17Gs were rearmed with flexible guns and, in some cases, top turrets. Thus, they became the last armed B-17 in U.S. service, administratively assigned to the world-wide Air Rescue Service (subordinate command of MATS) but under the command of local units deployed in Korea and Japan. The 2nd and 3rd Air Rescue Squadrons were attached to the Far East Air Forces which utilized the capability of the SB-17s as patrol and orbit aircraft for B-29 strikes against North Korea.

All SB-17Gs were retired by the mid-fifties, some being assigned to provide range control services at missile test centers. (See EB-17.) At least two examples of SB-17Gs survive in the U.S. today.

TB-17: Trainer Version and More

Though originally conceived as a trainer version of the B-17, the TB-17 eventually became the "catch-all" designation for numerous Fortresses in post-war roles.

Wartime TB-17s were usually war-weary Fortresses returned from overseas duty to ply out their last days training new crews for operational deployment. Towards the end of the war, new B-17s were available in sufficient numbers to allow them to also be assigned to training.

With the cessation of hostilities came the end of the B-17s use as a bomber, as well as a reduced demand for any type of training. Nonetheless, TB-17s would soldier on in the capacity of squadron hacks, recurrent trainers, or the designation would be assigned to a B-17 for which there was no specific prefix designation (such as the MB-17s became TB-17s when the "M" prefix was reassigned).

VB-17: Staff Transport

VB-17s were an evolution of the CB-17 derivative, the "V" prefix being established in 1945 to denote staff transports. Like the CB-17, no specific standard was developed for the VB-17, and custom modifications to suit the desires of individual commands were the rule. In general, however, VB-17s were more luxurious (using the term loosely) than the CB-17, with fullservice galleys, sound and temperature insulation, airline-type seats, and work space usually installed. Combat equipment was deleted.

VB-17s were utilized extensively for assignment to general officers, with many used as such during the Korean War while based in Japan. VB-17s were also assigned to major commands for staff transport or American embassies for diplomatic use. A number of VB-17s, deemed excess to the transport role, were converted to QB-17 drones and earmarked for destruction, but many of the staff transports served through the 1950s and were among the last of the Fortresses retired to Davis Monthan AFB.

WB-17G: Weather Reconnaissance

B-17s had been used during World War II for the specific role of weather reconnaissance over Europe. Beginning in 1945, additional aircraft were modified for the role, and were given additional fuel tanks, radios, and weather measuring equipment. In 1948 some of these aircraft were redesignated as WB-17Gs, though often as not B-17s assigned to the role retained the designation of TB-17G.

VB-17G 44-85774 in the late forties, probably photographed at Tinker AFB in Oklahoma. Unusual feature is the modified early-style tail stinger. Note the air-stair style main entrance door, common to most VB-17s.
R. Stachowiak via AAHS

CHAPTER TWO:
USE OF REDESIGNATED FORTRESSES

■■■■■

The diverse use of the Fortress and a tendency by the wartime Army Air Force to create new model designations for relatively minor changes in configuration or engines would cause the B-17 to be redesignated to a variety of types. Among bomber designations, B-17s became the B-38 (re-engined with Allison V1710-89 powerplants) and the B-40 (experimental bomber-escort gunship). A transport conversion was designated the C-108, and the wartime use of explosive-laden B-17 drones resulted in the BQ-7 designation, with the corresponding drone controller becoming the CQ-4. A photographic version became the F-9, while the Navy and Coast Guard operated Fortresses as PB-1s.

C-108: Cargo/Transport Conversion

In an effort to supplement the supply of transport-type aircraft, the Army Air Force initiated a program to evaluate various bomber designs converted to transports. The B-17 program resulted in the designation C-108 assigned to the conversion which, in many respects, paralleled the development of the CB-17 troop transport. The Fairfield Air Service Command, located at Patterson Field in Ohio, coordinated and evaluated the C-108 program, and their shops actually performed the conversion work on at least two of the C-108 aircraft. Another C-108 was developed by Boeing at Seattle.

Only four B-17s came to be redesignated as C-108s, and one of those, the XC-108 (B-17E 41-2393), was specifically converted for General Douglas MacArthur's use as a personal transport. The YC-108 (B-17F-40-VE 42-6036) was converted to a similar executive-type transport and used for a short time as a staff transport for General Frank Hackett in India. The XC-108A (B-17E 41-2595*) tested the cargo-carrying ability of the design and featured a cargo door on the port side of the fuselage aft of the wing. It also provided a hinged solid nose section for baggage stowage and tested the ability to install litters for evacuation of wounded personnel. The fourth C-108 was the XC-108B (B-17F-90-BO 42-30190), converted for fuel transport with all armor and armament deleted and additional fuel tanks installed in the fuselage.

41-2595 at McChord Field, Washington, in 1944. The XC-108A suffered from perpetual engine difficulties. Reported modifications included a solid, hinged nose cone though this photo does not depict this. The additional modification may have been completed at a later date. Army Air Force via Bowers Collection

XC-108 41-2593 was a Boeing modified B-17E. Program was begun in early 1943 and the sole XC-108 was modified as a transport for General Douglas MacArthur. Boeing

Navy PB: Service with U.S. Navy/ U.S. Coast Guard

U.S. Navy use of the B-17 saw the application of the PB designation to the Fortress. Under the Navy system, the primary role (in this case "P" for patrol) was followed by the manufacturer ("B" for Boeing), thus the PB designation. Successive series were indicated by numbers after the primary designation, with special use suffixes added if needed. In the case of the PB-1, two special use suffixes were assigned; the PB-1 became the PB-1W in USN service and the PB-1G in USCG service. It has been noted, with some irony over the years, that virtually none of the PBs were actually built by Boeing. All were either Douglas or Vega built examples, and should have been designated P4D-1W (Patrol, fourth Douglas built model accepted by the Navy) or P3V-1G, respectively. However, no one has ever accused the Navy of being entirely too consistent with their designations, and the general PB nomenclature simplifies the categorization of the type anyway. The Navy assigned the PB designation on 31 July 1945.

B-17s were generally transferred to the Navy for two purposes: to become PB-1W patrol aircraft with early warning radar installations aboard, or as PB-1G air rescue aircraft similar in configuration to the Army Air Force B-17H (later SB-17G). PB-1Gs had not yet entered service when the Coast Guard returned to the Department of the Treasury on 01 January 1946.

PB-1W

The Navy had recognized the utility using large, land based aircraft carrying search radar for anti-ship and anti-submarine duty during the last year of World War II. Though initially considering using the Douglas C-54, the Navy ultimately decided the aircraft needed defensive armament and selected the B-17 for use. Eventually, twenty-seven B-17s were transferred, most of which were Douglas-built aircraft flown directly from the Long Beach factory to the Naval Aircraft Modification Unit at NAS Johnsville in Pennsylvania during the summer of 1945. There, the Navy installed APS-20 search radar, the large scanning antenna protruding from the sealed bomb-bays and protected by a bulbous radome. The war ended before any PB-1Ws were operational and defensive armament was subsequently deleted.

The first few PB-1Ws went to VBP-101 (Navy Picket Squadron), four of them available by 01 April 1946. Deliveries were somewhat slowed by delays in obtaining a sufficient supply of the APS-20 radars. As operational experience was gained with the type, the mission gradually evolved to one of airborne early warning, broadening its scope to fully realize the potential of the radar equipment. By 1947 PB-1Ws were deployed in units with both the Atlan-

U.S. Navy utilized 25 Douglas-built B-17s as PB-1Ws. MAP

Two of the surplus PB-1Ws at Litchfield Park in 1958. The PB-1W had generally been retired by 1955 and all were stricken from the Navy inventory in 1956. A large group were sold together in late 1957, and these two were among that number. N5226V had been Bu77227, while N5225V was Bu77138. Neither aircraft survived past the mid-sixties. Baker

PB-1W at Litchfield Park in late 1958, shortly after being sold surplus. No civil markings have been applied, though the Fortress would shortly carry the civil registration of N5228V. Note the preponderance of additional antennas carried by the PB-1W and the retention of the dorsal turret mount even though the aircraft was disarmed many years earlier. All Navy markings, down to the the "NAVY" in the data block under the horizontal stabilizer, have been painted over. Baker

tic and Pacific Fleets. On the east coast, VPB-101 had been redesignated as VX-4 (Aircraft Development Squadron) on 15 May 46 and assigned to NAS Quonset Point, Rhode Island. VX-4 became VW-2 (Airborne Early Warning Squadron) on 18 June 1952 and assigned to NAS Patuxent River, Maryland. Aside from the primary mission of early warning, VW-2 also had secondary missions of anti-submarine warfare, hurricane reconnaissance, and developmental work assigned.

VW-1 was established as a new squadron also on 18 June 1952 with four PB-1Ws based at NAS Barbers Point, Hawaii. Elements of VW-1 were drawn from VC-11 at NAS Mirimar, California and VP-51 (Patrol Squadron) at NAS San Diego and attached to VW-1. VW-1 was assigned missions similar to that of VW-2.

PB-1Ws continued in service until 1955, gradually being phased out in favor of the Lockheed WV-2 (Navy version of the Lockheed Model 1049 Constellation, the WV later being designated as the EC-121 after 1962). PB-1Ws were retired to the Naval Aircraft Storage Center at Litchfield Park, Arizona. Stricken from the inventory in mid-1956, a number were declared surplus and sold in 1957, many making it onto the civil register. Thirteen were sold to a scrap dealer at Dallas-Love Field in Texas, where most of them sat for several years before civil operators purchased the by-then derelict airframes. Two of the Love Field PB-1Ws (Bu77240 and Bu77243) were used in the filming of the motion picture "The War Lover", shot in Great Britain in 1962, after which both were scrapped. Several ex PB-1Ws survive today.

As a peculiar footnote to the U.S. Navy use of the B-17 are the twenty RB-17Gs transferred from the Air Force to the Navy in the first half of 1950. Most were transferred from units attached to the Strategic Air Command. No Navy records have been revealed which indicate what, if any, Bureau numbers were ever assigned to these twenty aircraft and what their ultimate fate was. (See Appendix 2 for listing.)

PB-1G: USCG Air-Sea Rescue

With the success and utility found by the Army Air Force with the air-sea rescue B-17H, the Coast Guard decided to similarly equip its own squadrons. Designated the PB-1G, the Coast Guard obtained sixteen new Vega-built B-17Gs from Army storage depots beginning in early 1946 for conversion. The PB-1Gs were utilized primarily for long-range air-sea rescue, but other examples were used for iceberg patrol and high-altitude photo mapping. On 01 January 1946 the U.S. Coast Guard had left the jurisdiction of the Navy and returned to the Department of the Treasury, but the Navy nonetheless reworked their B-17s, equipping them with the droppable Higgins A-1 lifeboats and search radar along the specifications of the Army Air Force B-17H.

By 1953, PB-1Gs were stationed throughout the hemisphere, with five at Coast Guard Air Station (CGAS) Elizabeth City, North Carolina, two at CGAS San Francisco, two at Argentia, Newfoundland, one at Annette Isle, Alaska, and one at CGAS Port Angeles in Washington State.

The Coast Guard had the distinction of operating the last American military Fortress, ex B-17G-110-VE 44-85828* PB-1G Bu77254, in operational service. PB-1G 77254 had been assigned to the U.S. Coast and Geodetic Survey for photo mapping, and was retired to CGAS Elizabeth City in October 1959. The airplane was sold surplus, served as an air tanker for many years, and is now on display in Arizona.

USCG PB-1G 77254 configured for photo-mapping with camera installation in the ball turret location. Standard PB-1G was used for air-sea rescue and was equipped similar to the USAF SB-17G. Bowers

Freshly surplus N2873G at Phoenix-Sky Harbor in 1959. Ex PB-1G 77247 was later exported to Peru and its fate is uncertain. Peltzer

CQ-4/BQ-7: Drone Controller/Drone

See Chapter 2, DB-17/QB-17

B-38: Fortress with Allison Engines

As Lockheed's subsidiary, the Vega Corporation, was gearing up to build the B-17 at Burbank, they proposed to the Army that the Fortress be refitted with 1400 hp Allison V-1710-89 liquid-cooled engines. Lockheed's familiarity with the engine, as used in their P-38 Lightning fighter, ensured a smooth modification of B-17E 41-2401 to the XB-38. Utilizing the standard radial-engine mount hard-points on the firewalls, the Allison engines were encased with P-38 style cowlings with the oil cooler intakes beneath the propellers. The coolant radiators were installed between the engines on each wing.

No dramatic increase in performance was demonstrated before the XB-38, with twelve hours of test time, crashed after developing an uncontrollable engine fire. The crash, which occurred on 16 June 1943, plus the developing shortage of Allison V-1710 engines (used in the P-38, P-39, P-40, and early P-51) resulted in the cancellation of the program.

F-9: Photo-adapted Fortress

See Chapter 2, FB-17 and RB-17.

B-40: Bomber Escort

Conceived as a bomber-escort, the B-40 was developed to increase defensive capability in bomber formations. The XB-40 was B-17F-1-BO 41-24341 as rebuilt by Vega under contract with the Army. A Bendix chin turret, an additional dorsal turret in the radio compartment, and twin .50 caliber power-assisted flexible machine guns in the waist and tail positions brought defensive armament to fourteen heavy guns. In operational use no bombs were to be carried, replaced instead with additional ammunition.

After initial tests were completed in the fall of 1942 an additional thirteen YB-40s were developed by Douglas. Operational tests were undertaken in Europe beginning in May 1943 with mixed results. Deemed too slow to keep up with the lighter, post-bomb run B-17s, the YB-40 was found only slightly more effective in defensive ability than the normally configured B-17. Difficulties with some of the armament systems also plagued the operational testing and the program was eventually canceled. Nonetheless, the benefits of the Bendix chin turret and staggered waist gun positions, as developed on the B-40, were readily apparent and both were quickly phased into production lines and modification centers, appearing on late B-17Fs and B-17Gs entering combat.

XB-38 was developed by Lockheed from Boeing-built B-17E 41-2401. Program began in early 1942 and terminated in June 1942 when the sole B-38 was lost due to an engine fire. Allison

Converted from the second Boeing-built B-17F, the XB-40 was developed by Lockheed as a bomber escort. Photo, taken in late 1942, shows new paint applied where conversion work was performed.
L. Jones via AAHS

PART THREE:
CIVIL USE OF THE FLYING FORTRESS
■■■■■■

One well known civil B-17 was N5116N. Purchased from surplus stocks in 1947, 44-85507 was converted to executive configuration for use by Robert McCormick, owner of the Chicago Tribune. Photo taken in September 1950 in Chicago. Peltzer Collection

OVERVIEW

■■■■■

Civil use of the Flying Fortress ran a parallel course to its later military utilization; that is, the aircraft found diverse and, in some cases, extraordinary roles assigned which far differed from those envisioned by Boeing engineers in 1935. However, to be precise, civil use of Boeing's Model 299 actually began in 1935, for the first Flying Fortress was a civil aircraft and carried the Bureau of Air Commerce government registration of "X13372" prominently on its tail. It remained a civil aircraft through to its unfortunate destruction in October 1935, and never received a military designation.

The remaining 12,730 Flying Fortresses built between 1936 and 1945 were for the Army Air Corps and later, Army Air Force. At the conclusion of the World War II there were roughly 4,000 B-17s left, the others being expended in combat losses or accidents. Of the 4000 survivors, 2800 were in Europe and were either sent on to Germany as part of the occupation forces or returned to the U.S. for disposal. The B-17s fresh off the production line were left in marshaling depots or placed into indefinite storage. As noted elsewhere, several hundred found use in the post-war military. The rest were scrapped or trickled into the civil market.

After the first wave of post-war surplus sales, which generally had ended by 1948, the availability of B-17s directly from surplus stocks was limited. Three military sources remained, and each eventually made the aircraft available to interested civilians. The first group was sold by the U.S. Navy, which disposed of their PB-1Ws in sales beginning in 1956. The second group was placed up for auction by the U.S. Coast Guard in 1959, and consisted of their PB-1Gs. Finally, the remaining USAF Fortresses were retired beginning in 1954, but were not generally made available from Davis-Monthan AFB until 1959. All military surplus B-17s, save one lone exception at Davis-Monthan, were gone by 1961.

Since 1946, when a second Flying Fortress received its civil registration, seventy-seven B-17s have been assigned U.S. civil registrations. Over one hundred U.S. registration numbers have been assigned to B-17s, the numerous re-registrations comprising the difference.

In the immediate post-war period the Fortress floundered in search of a civil role. Though the aircraft could boast a great load carrying ability, the availability of interior space was limited. The B-17 had a relatively small cross section and the main wing spars ran through the bomb-bay, effectively blocking any attempts to open the fuselage up for bulky cargo. It was relatively expensive to operate, and government restrictions on carrying passengers prevented it from being used by commercial airlines, though demand for such conversions in the U.S. would have been minimal anyway. It did not boast great speed, thereby making it less attractive for the executive conversions being enjoyed by the B-25 and other faster twinengined bombers. The advantages of the Fortress were its range, payload, and stability; until its use as an air tanker secured a role in the post-war civil market, the B-17 was left a few oddball tasks and that of playing itself in post-war films.

Thus, a smattering of film work, followed by tentative use as aerial survey platforms, made up much of the utilization through the fifties. A few were put into unique roles, such as flying aquariums or vegetable haulers. Three civil examples reverted to their original designed use and were exported to Israel for their meager air force. Several were used as test beds for engines or other equipment. But by the early sixties many had ended up rotting on unused airfields or exported to South America where they were valued for their cargo hauling capability and high altitude performance.

The domestic civil B-17s hit their pace, however, with the rapid growth of air attack on forest fires. The old Fortress quickly settled into a familiar niche which enabled the B-17 to continue in a commercial role until the early eighties. Unfortunately, the nature of the work also resulted in the destruction of ten B-17 air tankers and sprayers.

In the past decade the B-17 finally transitioned from the asset end of the business ledger to the liability column, and the remaining few tankers either were the subject of trades with the Air Force Museum or sold to private individuals or museums with preservation a primary goal. Toward that end, there are twelve B-17s in the U.S. either operational or under restoration to airworthy condition. An additional three B-17s remain airworthy in Great Britain and France. All are civil examples.

One of a group of surplus PB-1Ws purchased by a broker in 1957, N5226V rots at the Dallas-Love airport in April 1960. The Fortress was later purchased by a cargo-hauler in Bolivia where, as CP-742, it was destroyed in a 1965 crash. San Diego Aerospace Museum

CHAPTER ONE:
DISPOSAL AND INITIAL CIVIL USES
■■■■■■

Though the material that follows centers on the B-17, much of it could also apply to any of the types which the U.S. military found surplus to requirements at the end of the war. Individual sales of aircraft which had obvious military application and limited use otherwise, such as the Douglas A-26 and other fast attack bombers, plus most advanced fighter aircraft, were controlled in an effort to prevent subsequent export to foreign military forces. Other aircraft, such as the numerous cargo and training types, were released in large numbers for post-war commercial use. The B-17 fell into a middle area, as the military utility of the type was well proven. However, it was also recognized that the B-17 had limited civil applications and they were sold into the civil market to meet the meager demand.

Surplus military aircraft became available to civilians in three different ways. They could be purchased in lots of several hundred with the stipulation that, with few exceptions, they were to be scrapped. Individual examples could be purchased for private or commercial use at an advertised price which, for the Fortress, was given at $13,750. Finally, the government made surplus aircraft available to educational institutions, communities, and individuals under varying agreements which usually included a requirement that the aircraft were not to be flown again and in which the government retained title.

A number of government agencies handled the disposal process and their jurisdiction and authority often overlapped. The U.S. government had made preliminary plans toward the conversion of the war economy and general demobilization in late 1943. As part of the planning, the Congress established the Surplus Property Board (SPB) when the Surplus Property Act of 1944 was passed in October of that year.

The Surplus Property Board was assigned the task of coordinating and delegating the disposal of surplus property through different agencies of the government. On 15 May 1945 the Board designated the Reconstruction Finance Corporation as the disposal agency for capital and producer goods, which included surplus aircraft and parts. The RFC established within itself the Office of Surplus Property, Aircraft Division, to handle the disposal of surplus aircraft. The Surplus Property Board recognized that surplus warplanes had few civil uses. Agreements drawn between the War and Navy Departments and the SPB established that surplus aircraft would not be sold to foreign nations for military use.

Any transfer of such equipment was to occur under the direction of the Munitions Assignment Board, which was a part of the Combined Chiefs of Staff, and the equipment was to be drawn from military stocks before they were declared surplus.

The SPB determined that the cost to dismantle aircraft exceeded the value of the parts. As an example, it was learned that it cost $3200 to dismantle a B-24, but the resulting assemblies were worth less than $2400. It was decided that the most practical and cost effective method of disposal of tactical aircraft was salvage and scrapping.

Five categories were established for surplus military aircraft. Class A was for tactical aircraft. Class B, C, and D were for other types, such as transports, light aircraft, and aircraft components. Class E was unabsorbed surplus, with the aircraft and components not useful for flight purposes. It was decided that Class A aircraft would be offered for sale for thirty days, afterwhich they would be declared Class E and only fit for scrap value.

One component of the regulations established by the Surplus Property Board was Regulation 4 entitled "Disposal of Surplus Aeronautical Property to Educational Institutions for Non-Flight Use" whereby commercially valueless property was to be distributed to eligible educational institutions. Recipients were required to certify that the material was not to be used for flight purposes. To administer this program, the RFC established the Educational Disposal Section in their Office of Surplus Property. The transfer process often included a nominal fee and authorized a one-time delivery flight to the receiving locality. The first aircraft distributed under the program was a B-17 sent to a small school in Williamsport, Pennsylvania in late 1945.

In September 1945 the Surplus Property Board was supplanted by the Surplus Property Administration. It drew a larger share of manpower and oversight, but essentially continued the work of the Board. The RFC continued as the designated agency for disposal of aircraft. However, the following January a general reorganization of the disposal process occurred. On 31 January Executive Order 9689 established the War Assets Corporation as a subsidiary of the RFC and transferred the functions of the Surplus Property Administration and many of the other agencies, divisions, and offices concerned with surplus disposal into the new Corporation. The Order also mandated that the War Assets Corporation was to become the War Assets Ad-

Rows of tired B-17s join other veteran B-24s, B-25s, and B-26s at Walnut Ridge, Arkansas after the war. Eventually the majority of these aircraft were broken up for scrap and smelted on the spot. NASM

Kingman also had its share of B-17s—over 1800 of them. Photographer William Larkins had the foresight to capture these veterans in February 1947. Larkins

B-17s destined for the scrapheap at Altus in 1946. Most B-17s at Altus were well-worn combat veterans, but hundreds were factory fresh examples with only a few ferry flights on the logbooks. G. Hale via Walker

B-24s also ended up at Altus, though this photo is included for the row of B-17s in the background. Several of the Fortresses were surplus from training squadrons. G. Hale via Walker

ministration on 25 March 1946 and removed from the Reconstruction Finance Corporation.

Thus, the War Assets Administration was established within the Office for Emergency Management and assumed all the functions of the Surplus Property Administration and disposal related agencies in other parts of the government, including the RFC. One final administrative reorganization occurred on 01 July 1947 when statutory authority was granted to the WAA. Essentially, the executively established WAA was abolished and its functions were transferred back to the Congressionally-established Surplus Property Administration which, in turn, was renamed the War Assets Administration. The War Assets Administration then continued until the expiration of the Surplus Property Act of 1944 and its functions were placed under the General Services Administration on 30 June 1949.

The Reconstruction Finance Corporation's Office of Surplus Property established twenty-seven storage centers located throughout the country to concentrate the surplus aircraft and components. It was decided to concentrate the material as an aid to marketing it to the aluminum scrapping industry when the scrapping operations began. As material was declared surplus by the military, it was dispatched to the centers for disposal. Salvage operations were eventually organized to strip the airframes of any usable items, such as engines, instruments, and any valuable military equipment. In the fall of 1945, the Army and Navy were declaring over 175 aircraft a day surplus to their needs. By the end of 1945, over 21,600 had been declared surplus, with over half of those declarations made in that last quarter of the year.

With the establishment of the storage lots, B-17s were primarily sent to depots located at Kingman, Arizona; Walnut Ridge, Arkansas; Altus, Oklahoma; Stillwater, Oklahoma; and Minneapolis, Minnesota. During the war Syracuse, New York, had been the location of a staging depot

Pair of B-17s in storage at Davis-Monthan in 1958 or 1959. Fate of these aircraft is unknown. USAF via Criss

One of four factory-fresh B-17s transferred from surplus stocks to the French Institut Geographique National in 1947, F-BEEB was B-17G-105-VE 44-85733 and is shown here still in the U.S. prior to it overseas ferry flight. Note the aircraft is complete down to turrets and gun mounts, with the sole exception of the machine guns.
Levy via Bowers Collection

The Navy stored their PB-1Ws in 1956 at Litchfield and most were sold in 1957. This example, BuNo 77236 (44-83873), went to Kenting Aviation in Canada in Toronto, Canada, for use as a parts source to keep other B-17s airworthy. MAP

PB-1G 77250 shortly after being sold surplus by the Coast Guard in 1960. It was later sold south to Bolivia where it was destroyed by a crash in 1963. MAP

The first post-war Fortress to receive a civil registration number was 44-85728 which was assigned the experimental certificate of NX4600 on 17 July 1946. It later was assigned NL1B when TWA received the converted B-17 and a limited type certificate from Boeing. NASM

for aircraft destined to overseas locations and, with the end of hostilities, it also was relegated to storage. South Plains, Texas; Garden City, Kansas; and Patterson Field, Ohio all handled new B-17s off the production line destined for storage. As it happened, most lots were eventually sold to scrap dealers who set up massive smelters and sought to squeeze every possible dollar from molten aluminum.

Initial efforts were made to place low time aircraft into long-term storage at the depots. At Kingman, for example, each aircraft went through a time intensive program of preservation. The engines were run with white gasoline to burn them clean of lead deposits, and then oil was injected into the cylinders as a protective coating. Props and landing gear were smeared with grease, and the engines were covered with canvas. The plexiglas was covered and sealed, and the aircraft were then towed off into storage. It took a crew of six men a full day to prepare each aircraft. This process continued through mid-1946 when the order came down to stop the preservation work and begin hacking the engines off to make each aircraft unairworthy. Soon lines of severed engines, complete with cowlings and accessories, joined the rows of aircraft. Eventually the whole lot was sold to a contractor for smelting. As the smelting furnaces were constructed each aircraft was stripped of all non-aluminum components, including such items as wiring junction boxes, stray shell casings, and instruments. They were then cut into smaller pieces, smelted, and shipped out as 1500 pound aluminum ingots. By 1948 the job was done, and quiet returned to the desert scrub.

General civilian utilization of the B-17 began with the issuance of Limited Type Certificate L-1 on 02 December 1946 by the Civil Aeronautics Administration. Though the CAA had previously licensed B-17s in the Experimental category, the issuance of the Limited certificate broadened the scope of operations beyond the highly restrictive Experimental license issued for ferry and test flights. The granting of the Limited airworthiness certificates enabled operators to carry passengers or cargo in private, restricted commercial, and corporate use.

The Limited Type Certificate was granted to Transcontinental and Western Air, Incorporated, precursor to Trans World Airlines. They obtained (and are still recorded as holder of) the LTC because of their efforts to convert B-17G-105-VE 44-85728 to executive use for development of new route structures on TWA's foreign runs. Boeing was hired to rebuild the Fortress at their Seattle facility, which Boeing saw as a opportunity to explore the post-war market for similar Fortress conversions. Boeing designated the conversion as Boeing Model 299AB, and obtained the registration of NX4600 for the aircraft after it was purchased in June 1946. Once the modifications were completed TWA deployed NX4600 to the Middle East and used it to transport TWA executives to the International Air Transport Association Conference held in Egypt in October 1946. With the issuance of the LTC, TWA reregistered NX4600 as NL1B, but the Fortress was transferred to the Shah of Iran in April 1947, afterwhich it was given the Iranian registration of EP-HIM. Eventual fate of the aircraft has not been determined, but it was most likely scrapped in the mid-1950s.

Several B-17s found their way to civil market after being sold for scrap. One of these was to make several film appearances in post-war productions. Paul Mantz, the movie pilot, arranged a consortium of partners and purchased 475 surplus fighters and bombers located at Stillwater, Oklahoma.

Of that number, 78 aircraft were B-17s. Mantz evidently had avoided scrap restrictions on his purchase as he envisioned using some of the aircraft in post-war films. He sought a studio to finance the movement of seventy-five of the best aircraft to the west coast, for which he offered cut-rate prices for his services and equipment in the forthcoming films. No studio stepped forward, so he picked a dozen of the best surplus aircraft and arranged with his partners to scrap the rest. He later bragged that he made enough from just the fuel drained from the tanks of this "air force" to bankroll the entire deal. At least four of the fortunate dozen survivors earned a place in the post-war era. Two were P-51Cs, registered NX1202 and NX1204, which Mantz used to win the 1946, 1947, and 1948 Bendix transcontinental air races. NX1202 was later used by Charles Blair to set several other speed records, and is now in the NASM collection. Another of the survivors was N1203, a B-25J Mantz rebuilt into a custom camera ship which was used through the 1970s to film a variety of motion pictures. Finally, Mantz saved B-17F-50-DL 42-3360. The B-17 was apparently operated without a certificate as the U.S. civil registration of N67974 was not issued until 17 March 1950 (shortly before Mantz sold the bomber). Mantz had saved the B-17 from Searcy in 1946 to use it for several of the post-war films headed toward production. As it turned out, film studios chose to use operational military B-17s which were still available in sufficient numbers to satisfy the needs of the film producers. N67974 was briefly utilized in "The Best Years of Our Lives" (1946), "Command Decision" (1948), and "Chained Light-

ning" (1949), but otherwise languished in disuse at Mantz's base at the Lockheed Air Terminal in southern California. Mantz subsequently sold the B-17 to Owen Williams of California-Atlantic Airways, who sold it south to Bolivia for cargo operations. It was destroyed in September 1955.

In 1946 and 1947 a total of ten B-17s were issued U.S. civil registrations. Most of these first civil B-17s had come from the large number in storage at Altus, Oklahoma, but were low-time aircraft recently declared surplus and ferried in from Syracuse, New York. Of this initial group of B-17s, two went to an engine-test program at Pratt & Whitney. Two of the B-17s were involved in aerial mapping programs, and two others were purchased for conversions similar to that performed on NL1B. Three B-17s were bought by a Miami pilot intent on starting a Caribbean cargo airline.

Six of the B-17s were indirectly bought from brokers or scrappers who had made the original purchase from the War Assets Administration, and in several cases subsequent arrangements were necessary to release the aircraft to the new civil operators.

As noted earlier, a fair number of surplus B-17s were also authorized one-time flights for delivery to communities or educational institutions for use as memorials or instructional aids, and the aircraft did not receive civil registrations. The RFC arranged these transactions in tightly worded contracts in which the government usually retained ownership. In cases where title was released, restrictions were added which prohibited export of the aircraft without a further release by appropriate authorities. The intent of the government was

A survivor of the Dallas-Love surplus PB-1Ws is ex-Navy BuNo 77138 (44-85679). As N5225V, it is shown here on the ramp at Long Beach Airport in February 1962. The civil operator was Von Carstedt (doing business as C 'Air) who modified it for use as a sprayer. It apparently was never used as such, however, and was later sold to the South Coast Canning Company in Florida. It was destroyed in a 1964 crash. San Diego Aerospace Museum

Over two dozen B-17s were employed in the Bolivian civil aviation fleet in the post-war years. This example, B-17E 41-9210, still exists in derelict condition in La Paz. 41-9210's first civil owner was the University of Minnesota to whom it was lent by the Reconstruction Finance Corporation in 1946. MAP

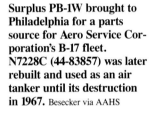

Surplus PB-1W brought to Philadelphia for a parts source for Aero Service Corporation's B-17 fleet. N7228C (44-83857) was later rebuilt and used as an air tanker until its destruction in 1967. Besecker via AAHS

to retain a measure of control to prevent the surplus warplanes from making their way into the hands of arms merchants.

This restrictive policy, though admirable, was not wholly successful. In a peculiar footnote to the combat utilization of the B-17 is the saga of three civil Flying Fortresses which were smuggled from the United States to Israel in 1948, to become the backbone of the new Israeli Air Force. Purchased illegally from U.S. civil operators by Jewish nationalists in June 1948, the B-17s were flown from Miami to Israel via Puerto Rico, the Azores, and Czechoslovakia, with the aircraft being armed and loaded with bombs at its last stop. Its delivery flight into Israel included bomb runs over Egyptian targets, the first of numerous sorties undertaken by the three bombers. There was an attempt to bring a fourth B-17 into Israel, but it was interned by Portugal after it landed in the Azores. The three Israeli B-17s survived through the 1948 war, were rearmed with power turrets and other military equipment, and served again in the 1956 war

as the predominant component of the Israeli bombing force. In the end, the three aircraft were retired in 1958 and scrapped two years later. Only a fuselage section would survive, and went on to form a studio prop for the production of the film "The War Lover" in England in 1961.

B-17s were also subjected to unusual conversions to meet the demands of a specific need. Such was the case with the conversion of B-17G 44-83439. Purchased from surplus stocks at Davis-Monthan AFB in 1959 by an aircraft broker, the Fortress was subsequently sold to Paramount Aquariums of Vero Beach, Florida. They had the B-17 rebuilt by Hamilton Aircraft in Tucson. It was modified with 4 inches of insulation in the fuselage skin. Bunk beds and other living accommodations were installed in the aircraft, and additional radio equipment was added. The Fortress was then used to transport tropical fish from South America into the the U.S. for eventual sale. Registered as N131P, the B-17 could carry as many as 500,000 tropical fish on the non-stop flights and was utilized for several years.

A mysterious Fortress. N39356 is B-17G-BO 43-39356. This photo was taken in 1958 at Van Nuys, California and shows a hybrid military/civil B-17 with all military markings intact save the civil registration which is a modified form of its military serial. 43-39365 had completed its military days as a VB-17 and the FAA holds no record of a B-17 registered as N39356.
W. Bodie via San Diego Aerospace Museum

Unique role given this B-17G (44-83439) was that of tropical fish transport. Bought surplus from the Air Force in 1959, Paramount Aquariums had the Fortress converted and used it for trips to South America. It was used through the mid-sixties. Photo taken at Oakland, California. Peltzer Collection

Unknown B-17 being removed from storage, probably at Davis-Monthan AFB in the late fifties. Several dozen B-17s were stored at the base through the latter part of that decade.
K. Rust via AAHS

CHAPTER TWO:
B-17s AS AIR TANKERS AND SPRAYERS
■■■■■■

Probably the best known civil use of the B-17 was its role in aerial fire-fighting. Beginning in 1960, no less than twenty-three B-17s were converted and utilized in the air-attack role. Over a dozen companies used the aircraft as part of their tanker fleets and operated them under contract with the United States Forest Service, state forest agencies, and lesser governmental agencies involved in the annual battles against destructive fires. The B-17s continued in the role through the early eighties, though the USFS effectively banned the use of the aircraft against its fires in 1980, finally considering the type too old and worn for the demands of the work.

To a lesser extent, the B-17 was also utilized as an aerial sprayer to combat infestations of insects. These efforts were particularly concentrated in the southeast and involved about six B-17s through the years. Generally, spray bars were attached to the trailing edge of the wings and were fed from bomb-bay tanks. Environmental concerns brought much of the spraying to an end in the mid-seventies.

The history of the air tanker begins in 1954. Though tentative experiments were conducted earlier on the possibility of using aircraft against forest fires, the first demonstration of the potential was conducted in 1954 by a Paul Mantz-owned TBM against a fire in Orange County, California. The dramatic effect of the water drops on the fire quickly led to the establishment of tanker fleets consisting primarily of TBMs, B-25s, and PBYs, though other types were utilized which ranged from the crop duster Stearmans to the venerable DC-3. Through the years, nearly 120 TBMs were converted for use as air tankers, as were 39 B-25s. A series of crashes in the late fifties led to a phase-out of the B-25s from the tanker fleets in the contiguous U.S. (Alaskan operations of B-25 tankers continued through 1973).

The need for a heavyweight air tanker and the availability of the B-17 led to its use beginning in 1960. Two operators simultaneously developed B-17 tankers. Abe Sellards, soon to be a partner in Aviation Specialties, converted N17W (under lease from Max Biegert) to a tanker and first employed it in a fire in August 1960. At the same time Fast Way Air Service of Long Beach, California converted N3702G to tanker configuration and put it to use the same month while based at Chino, California.

The U.S. Forest Service was the primary contractor for services of the air tanker companies. Through the period when the B-17s were employed as tankers, the Forest Service was organized into regions which established specific tanker requirements. They established tanker base locations,

tanker capacity needs, and time frames for availability based upon the local fire season. Individual tanker companies then bid to provide the tankers to meet the requirements, with the contracts generally running for three years. The contracts provided for a daily availability charge for the tanker to be on stand-by. When the tanker was called for fire work, an hourly rate was paid based upon the capacity of the tanker which, in the case of the B-17, was 2,000 gallons of fire retardant. From the contracted fees, the tanker companies would pay operating expenses, maintenance, and crew requirements.

There were several large air tanker companies which operated through the heyday of the B-17 tanker operations. The two major operators were Aero Union, based at Chico, California, and Aviation Specialties of Mesa, Arizona. Aero Union began as Western Air Industries and was based at Anderson, California. In the early sixties they changed their name to Aero Union and moved to Chico, where they remain to this day. They first obtained a pair of surplus B-17s in late 1960 for conversion, and in the subsequent years operated five B-17s.

Aircraft Specialties was established by three partners in the early sixties and was initially based at Phoenix, Arizona but moved to nearby Falcon Field in 1965. Aircraft Specialities was actually a holding company which owned a second company named Aviation Specialties. Aviation Specialties operated the air tankers, which included a vast array of many types, including TBMs, C-54s, DC-6s, and PV-1s. Abe Sellards, one of the partners, brought B-17F N17W into the company and Aviation Specialties eventually operated seven B-17s tankers. They also provided five B-17s for the film "Tora Tora Tora" in 1969, and one for "1000 Plane Raid" in 1968. The company encountered financial difficulties in the early seventies and was reorganized as Globe Air in 1973. Globe Air continued to operate the aircraft through 1985 when the owners decided to liquidate their holdings. Assets were sold off with much of the material being sold at a unique aviation auction held in October 1985. Two B-17 tankers were sold at that time.

Another major B-17 tanker operator was TBM, Incorporated, of Tulare, California. TBM had their main tanker base at Sequoia Field near Visalia, and operated two B-17s purchased from FastWay Air of Long Beach. They operated their B-17s through 1985 and were involved with several trades with the Air Force Museum and other operators which resulted in several B-17 going to museums. TBM is

One of the more imaginative paint schemes carried by a B-17 was the one worn by N66573. Dubbed the "Batmobile," it was destroyed a 1979 crash. This photo was taken in May 1962 at Porterville, California. Peltzer

N3702G as Tanker 61 at Chino in January 1970. There were several air tanker bases throughout Southern California which B-17s operated from, including Chino, Burbank, Ontario, and Hemet Airports. Matthews via Besecker

Dothan Aviation in Alabama operated this ex USCG PB-1G. N4710C once carried the Army serial of 44-85812. Note the spray bars under the wings. N4710C was destroyed in a 1976 crash. F. Hartman via AAHS

An ex PB-1W, N5233V operated with Aero Union based at Chico Airport for four years beginning in 1971. Larkins

N621L was one of two B-17s returned from cargo work in Bolivia in 1967. Both it and stablemate N620L were bought for use as air tankers by Aircraft Specialties of Mesa, Arizona. N621L was used in "Tora Tora Tora" but was destroyed in a July 1975 crash while operating on the fire lines. Peltzer

N1340N had the distinction of being re-engined with Dart turboprop engines in 1970. The new engines were its downfall, however, as forest fire generated smoke caused engine failure and the B-17F crashed in October 1970. This view shows the aircraft at Willows, California in 1963. Larkins via Peltzer Collection

PB-1W 77233 at Dallas-Love Field in April 1960. Part of a group of thirteen surplus Fortresses, N5237V was one of three which survived to become air tankers. N5237V spent much of its civil career being operated by Butler Aviation of Redmond, Oregon. The aircraft is now on display at he RAF Bomber Command Museum in Britain. San Diego Aerospace Museum

part owner of Butler Aviation of Redmond, Oregon, which also operated several B-17 tankers.

Arnold Kolb and his Black Hills Aviation operated seven B-17 tankers through the years, though not more than two or three at one time. Black Hills Aviation was originally based at Spearfish, South Dakota but moved to Alamogordo, New Mexico when the Spearfish airport lost part of its runway to a highway project.

There were also a number of smaller tanker operators which operated one or two B-17s. Among these were Aero Flite, Inc. of Cody, Wyoming; William Dempsey, who operated Central Air Services from Wenatchee, Washington; and Fast-Way Air of Long Beach, which operated a pair of B-17s in the early sixties.

The Fortress gained a substantial lease on life by its use as an air tanker but by the late seventies the shortage of parts and rising doubts about the structural integrity of the well worn B-17s caused its withdrawal from the tanker fleets. The FAA began to question the amount of unanticipated stress on structure by the concentrated load of fire retardant carried in the bomb bay. They eventually restricted the load to 1800 gallons of retardant which added a margin of safety. The Forest Service, however, effectively eliminated the Fortress from their contracts when they established 2000 gallon tanker requirements in 1980. Without coming out and say-

ing so, the USFS had decided the aircraft was no longer considered safe. The B-17 was primarily replaced by Douglas transport types, such as the C-54, DC-6, and DC-7. The B-17 continued to operate for state forest agencies, and California contracted for B-17 tankers until 1984 when they also determined the day of the B-17 tanker had passed.

Predating the use of the B-17 as an air tanker was its use as an aerial applicator. Max Biegert, as owner of B-17F N17W, had modified his aircraft with seven tanks in the mid-fifties, and employed it as an aerial sprayer with the installation of spray bars on the trailing edge of the wings. It was used in May 1957 to attempt to eradicate a gypsy moth infestation in Michigan by making low-level spray runs across affected areas.

On occasion air tankers were utilized as sprayers. Aircraft Specialties was contracted in one instance to provide B-17 sprayers for use in Maine against a spruce budworm infestation.

The major B-17 sprayer operator was Hugh Wheelless, owner of Dothan Aviation in Dothan, Alabama. He operated five B-17s as sprayers in the mid-sixties, primarily under contract with state agencies in their battles with the fire ant in several southeastern states. Those spray attacks ended in 1976, as did the B-17's use as a sprayer.

This B-17G, 44-83864, was purchased in 1963 from Mexico, where it had carried the civil registration of XB-BOE. It was returned to Grass Valley, California for overhaul and conversion to an air tanker. It later carried the U.S. registration of N73648. Larkins via Peltzer

N73648 as it later appeared. The Fortress was operated by Black Hills Aviation when it was destroyed in a 1972 crash.
A. Swanberg via AAHS

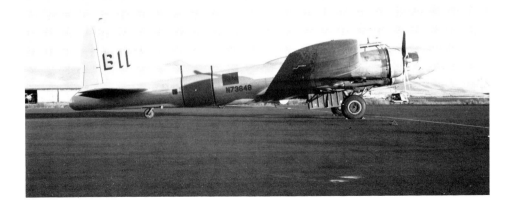

CHAPTER THREE:
MOTION PICTURE AND TELEVISION USE

■■■■■■

The B-17 was a natural for the silver screen. In the pre-war period of the late 1930s the B-17 epitomized the future of aviation and the dominance of American airpower. Through the war years it served as a rallying point for numerous stories based more on patriotic propaganda than fact. Through the early post-war years the B-17 played itself in a number of high-quality war dramas, and has since recreated its famous heritage for both motion picture and television productions. For the purpose of this volume, only the post-war productions will be covered as they relate to the post-war use of the Fortress.

The first post-war film to use the Fortress in a major role was RKO's production of "The Best Years of Our Lives" which was released in 1946. The story revolves around three veterans returning from the war to pick up their lives, their families, and their futures. The interweaving experiences of the three resulted in a film which won seven Academy Awards, including Best Picture of 1946. B-17s were used in two key segments of the film. The three veterans enjoy a cross-country trek in the nose of a Fortress, discussing their hopes, dreams, and fears of the impending homecoming. And in a key scene near the end of the film, actor Dana Andrews finds new courage in his old "office", the bombadier position of a war weary Fortress about to meet its fate in a smelter. The scene was reportedly filmed at the Cal-Aero field at Chino, California. Rows of B-17Fs, veterans of training squadrons, are awaiting the smelter as Dana Andrews heaves himself up into the nose of a discarded B-17. Engines stripped, one can see the dismantlers working in the background, making their way toward Andrew's B-17. Finally, a re-energized Andrews finds work breaking the old bombers apart for a new future.

Two back-to-back aviation classics were produced in 1948 and 1949. MGM's "Command Decision" was released first, and featured a fictionalized story about the early days of the Eighth Air Force in England. Starring Clark Gable, the film occasionally sank into conventional histrionics, but at it best the film takes an atypical cut at the military hierarchy. B-17 footage revolves around actual combat film, but two civil B-17s were leased for use in several scenes shot in the San Fernando valley. Paul Mantz provided his Fortress, 42-3360, and the other B-17 may have been N1212N which later enjoyed use over the skies of Egypt with the Israeli Air Force.

"Twelve O'Clock High" is probably the definitive aviation combat film. Produced by Twentieth Century-Fox in 1949, the story examines the exploits of the fictional 918th Bomb Group in England and the general who is sent in to restore the guts of the group. Most of the B-17 footage was shot for the film, utilizing a half dozen DB-17Gs and QB-17Gs from the 1st Experimental Guided Missile Group based at Eglin AFB in Florida and another six B-17s drawn from various depots. The QB-17Gs were veterans of Operation Crossroads conducted two years earlier and still showing some radioactive effect of the atomic testing. Location filming at an Eglin AFB auxiliary field and in Alabama at an abandoned Army field commenced in the late spring of 1949. The most famous, and borrowed, scene from the film was the crash landing performed by Paul Mantz for the

One of the most famous scenes ever produced for a aviation film is this showing Paul Mantz crash landing DB-17G 44-83592 for "Twelve O'Clock High" in 1949. Mantz flew the ex-drone controller, repainted as a Eighth Air Force B-17, solo for the scene.
Bowers Collection

cameras. Simulating a combat damaged B-17, Mantz brought a Fortress in on its belly and slid it through a row of tents for the scene. Mantz used a relatively new DB-17G, 44-83592, drawn from the Brookley depot and assigned to the 1st Experimental Missile Group for the spectacular landing. (A curious sidenote is the request sent from Eglin AFB Base Operations to Wright-Patterson for the proper 'code' to use in the aircraft paperwork to explain its demise. The resulting record indicates it was 'reclaimed' in September 1949.) The sequence later showed up in the TV version of the film, "The War Lover," and "Thousand Plane Raid," to name but a few.

The film, starring Gregory Peck as General Frank Savage, won critical acclaim from the film industry, Air Force, veterans, and general public as a serious look at the personal cost of advanced warfare.

Lesser attempts and less serious efforts also utilizing the B-17 emerged though the immediate post-war years, usually making liberal use of combat footage for the action shots. In these cases the use of the B-17 was incidental to the story line and rarely required an actual B-17 for the film production.

grueling formation flights before the cameras as they were beat up and damaged by enemy fighters and flak. Two of the B-17s were so badly damaged by the filming it was decided to avoid the expense of import duties and repair work and they were broken up at Manston, England at the completion of the filming. The film starred Steve McQueen and Robert Wagner as the two antagonists, with McQueen providing a particularly disturbed "Buzz Rickson" for the storyline.

Through the sixties, the B-17 made the occasional appearance on the wide screen, usually in a bit part or featured as an oddity. However, a pair of late sixties productions featured the type to prominence and remained the last major use of the B-17 in film work until "The Memphis Belle" was filmed in 1989. The first of the pair was "1000 Plane Raid" filmed on location at Santa Maria, California in early 1968. It employed three B-17s and a B-25 as a camera ship. As detailed in various chapters, the B-17s were drawn from the Air Museum at Ontario, the Tallmantz collection at Orange County, and Aircraft Specialties from Mesa, Arizona. Two weeks of location filming commenced on Monday, 15 January 1968 and utilized two of the B-17s and

It was not until 1961 that another serious effort to specifically portray the exploits of a B-17 group was attempted. Columbia Pictures in England produced John Hersey's novel "The War Lover" as a psychological investigation into a disturbed combat pilot. The film inevitably drops into a sticky morass of love affairs but emerges with a dramatic end. Though underrated, no doubt due to the aforementioned 'menage a trois', "The War Lover" remains vivid to this day due to attention paid to the hardware used in the film. The film makers produced uncharacteristically realistic combat scenes utilizing three B-17s rebuilt in the U.S. and flown to England in the fall of 1961. As detailed elsewhere (see 44-83563) the exploits of recovering two B-17s from scrapyards and flying a trio of Fortresses halfway around the world was remarkable in itself. Once on location, Film Aviation Services, under the direction of John Crewdson, returned the three Fortresses to external duplicates of wartime B-17s, complete with installed gun turrets and fixed gun positions. The B-17s were employed in

a B-25 in air-to-air filming. One B-17 (N17W) had its landing gear lowered into parallel trenches to simulate a belly landing and the wing of DC-4 was ignited nearby to complete the effect. A fair amount of effort went into the production work on location, but little of it ended up in the completed version released in the summer of 1968. The result was a grainy, obviously low-budget effort which quickly receded into film vaults everywhere.

The next film to use the Fortress in a central role was Twentieth Century-Fox's production of "Tora Tora Tora" in 1969. An epic in every sense of the word, the film utilized five Aircraft Specialties air tankers flown in from Arizona. Aircraft Specialties also provided all aircraft maintenance

Ex PB-1W 77243 (44-83883) carrying the U.S. civil registration of N5229V over the skies of England in the fall of 1961 during the filming of "The War Lover."
Bowers Collection

One of the three B-17s flown to Britain in September 1961 for "The War Lover." This B-17, ex PB-1W BuNo 77243, carried the civil registration of N5229V and was broken up at the completion of the filming. MAP

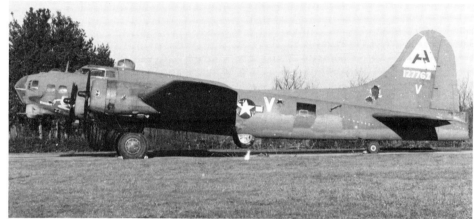

The same aircraft repainted for the film. Note the artificial combat damage on the tail and aft fuselage. MAP

Line up at Bovingdon Airfield in October 1961. First B-17 is N9563Z. Second aircraft is N5229V and carries dark gray and glossy undersurfaces. Obvious inaccuracies in paint scheme and other details occurred but overall authenticity was considerably better than most cinematic efforts.

San Diego Aerospace Museum

Operational scene from "The War Lover" showing all three B-17s utilized in the filming. First aircraft is N5229V. B-17 to right is N9563Z, while furthest Fortress is N5232V.

San Diego Aerospace Museum

Another scene from "The War Lover", depicting a particularly vicious buzz job by a half-crazed pilot. Note the latter day markings on the ambulances, a small oversight by the film crew. Bowers Collection

One of the stars of "The War Lover" out to temporary pasture at Tucson in February 1963. N9563Z was sold shortly afterwards and began a long utilization as an air tanker. Peltzer Collection

for the film studio fleet which numbered nearly fifty aircraft. Many of the aircraft were mock-Japanese types reconstructed from T-6 Texans and BT-13s, but several P-40s and other assorted types were also used. The B-17s were painted for the film while still in Arizona, and were finished in 1941 era combat colors with Army Air Corps markings added. They were ferried to NAS Barbers Point in Hawaii where turret shells and other armament was added. Dramatic license was taken with the use of a B-17F and B-17Gs in the film, as the actual aircraft involved during the raid were B-17Ds. Early shark-fin B-17s were portrayed, however, as full size two dimensional cutouts were erected in the background of filmed scenes. An added bonus was

realized when an in-flight malfunction of a landing gear provided N620L landing on one main gear before the cameras. The resultant footage ended up in the released film. "Tora Tora Tora" was released to mixed reviews, and with the trio of big-budget aviation combat films –"Catch22", "Battle of Britain", and "Tora Tora Tora" – released in the last two years of the decade all rolling over slowly in the box offices, it was evident they would be among the last for the foreseeable future.

The B-17 has made other, more sporadic, appearances on the wide screen. Most were as a short clip in the film "MacArthur" (1977) which merely depicted a discussion of wartime air operations with a B-17 on the set. (Actually, the

One of five B-17 tankers used in the film production of "Tora Tora Tora," N620L was painted in 1941-era Army colors for the 1969 film. MAP

N620L (44-85840) in its tanker colors. MAP

B-17 was to play a much bigger role in "MacArthur", with a depiction of the evacuation of MacArthur from the Philippines in 1942 a major part of the film. The leased B-17 (44-83525), however, experienced mechanical difficulties on the ferry flight to the location site, and had to be written out of the film.)

The absence of the type in a central role on the wide screen will end with the release of "The Memphis Belle" in mid-1990. Filmed on location in England by Enigma Productions, in cooperation with Warner Brothers, the film revolves around the last mission of the famous bomber in 1943. The studio hired five airworthy B-17s for the filming. Two came from the U.S. and were Bob Richardson's B-17F 42-29782 (N17W) and David Tallichet's 44-83546 (N3073G). Two came from France and were the IGN's 44-85643 (F-BEEA) and 44-8846 (F-AZDX) "Lucky Lady." The last Fortress came from England and was 44-85784 (G-BEDF) "Sally B". A sixth B-17, believed to be 44-83868 (of the Bomber Command Museum) was also used as a static example. In addition, numerous B-17 mock-ups were

constructed of cardboard and were, according to reports, stunningly realistic. The flyable B-17s were gathered at Duxford in July 1989 for the location filming. All the aircraft were repainted in, supposedly, water soluble paint, to represent early Eighth Air Force B-17Fs. N3703G, though a late-block B-17G, had been restored to exactly resemble an early B-17F with all turrets and other equipment working and was selected to represent the "Memphis Belle". Forty to fifty hours of flight time per aircraft were involved to complete the aerial scenes. The ex-Tallmantz B-25 camera ship, N1042B, was used as a camera platform. Additional filming was done at the ex-RAF field at Binbrook.

It was at Binbrook that F-BEEA was destroyed in a takeoff accident on 25 July, during the filming. Reports indicate that a possible cause was an overboost on the supercharger of the number three engine which caused uncontrollable swerving across the runway. The Fortress actually became airborne but the number four propeller hit a gravel pile causing that engine to fail also. The right wing tip then struck a tree and the plane spun around and broke in two. The ten people aboard escaped with minor injuries, but the bomber caught fire and was quickly consumed.

Aerial filmwork concluded in mid-August, and the film crews retired to studios in London to complete the film. Early reports had the film called "The Southern Belle" because rights could not be secured from Memphis. Apparently the the story line, not surprisingly given the history of such efforts, had been substantially changed from the actual events. Details were worked out though, and several original members of the crew of the original bomber were on hand during the filming as technical advisors. One can only hope, especially with the effort and expense committed to realistic hardware, that the reel story somewhat approximates the real story.

The B-17's major claim to fame on the small screen was "Twelve O'Clock High," a series derived from the film and produced for ABC Television between 1964 and 1966. Filmed by Twentieth Century-Fox, "Twelve O'Clock High" utilized all the available resources: a sound-stage mock-up of a B-17, use of the Air Force film library for action sequences (including liberal use of footage from the wartime documentary "The Memphis Belle"), external sets located at Chino, California, and a genuine B-17, compliments of the Ontario Air Museum (now Planes of Fame). The museum Fortress was an Air Force drone controller DB-17 which was the last active B-17 in the Air Force inventory. Retired in August 1959, the Fortress carried Air Force serial 44-83684 and a civil registration of N3713G. Ed Maloney had obtained the B-17 for his museum under a loan agreement in which the Air Force retained ultimate control. During the early sixties Maloney had set up shop at Ontario Airport and kept his large but somewhat ratty collection on the east ramp. The B-17, however, was usually parked at Chino.

The external sets built at Chino Airport made use of the left over buildings from the field's Cal-Aero wartime days. The current airport administrative area was the headquarter set for the series. Additional quonset hut facades were set up, and camouflage netting was hung behind the set to hide the local roads and activity. Tents and other stage dressing added to the effect.

Other facilities on the airport were used, including the control tower and surrounding taxiways. The Air Museum's Fortress was only used for operational ground scenes; no aerial photography was required due to the film available from the Air Force. Embarking and arrival scenes were filmed, with N3713G becoming several B-17s with the quick application of fresh nose art. For the most part, however, N3713G was the C.O.'s B-17, the "Picadilly Lily."

In 1965 a B-17 fuselage section was brought into Chino. This was the wingless remnants of 44-83316 which had been in storage at Norton AFB. It was in fairly good condition but was used in numerous crash and burn sequences, and when the series was canceled in November 1966 the B-17 had been reduced to a charred hulk. Salvageable parts were later used to rebuild N6694C in South Dakota.

The series suffered from thin scripts and the original star, Robert Lansing, who played General Savage was "killed in action" half way through the series run. Paul Burke, playing Col. Joe Gallagher, was brought in as a more sympathetic character in an effort to boost the show's ratings. Nonetheless, the series was canceled in November 1966 but still makes the occasional return in obscure syndication.

Filming of the television series "Twelve O'Clock High" at Chino Airport. Fortress is N3713G, while series star Robert Lansing waits in jeep for scene to commence. Farmer

Hardware star of TV's "Twelve O'Clock High" B-17G N3713G, at Chino Airport in February 1966. Note abbreviated civil registration on tail posing as military serial. Turrets were installed in the airframe as opposed to mounting dummy turret shells to the fuselage exterior. Peltzer

Part Four:
The U.S. Survivors
·······
Complete Aircraft

Hade

40-3097 at Los Angeles Airport in 1947. The B-17D never found a home with the city and it was donated to the National Air Museum in 1949. Larkins

CHAPTER ONE: 40-3097

NATIONAL AIR AND SPACE MUSEUM
PAUL E. GARBER RESTORATION FACILITY
SILVER HILL, MARYLAND

■ ■ ■ ■ ■ ■

40-3097   B-17D to RB-17D

USAAC/USAAF

DATE	LOCATION	UNIT	CMD	REMARKS
28 APR 41	SEATTLE			ACCEPTED
MAY 41	MARCH	19 BOMB GROUP		
13 MAY 41	HAMILTON	19 BOMB GROUP		
14 MAY 41	HICKAM	11 BOMB GROUP		
10 OCT 41	CLARK	14 BOMB SQUADRON		
06 DEC 41	DEL MONTE	14 BOMB SQUADRON, 19 BG		DISPERSAL
17 DEC 41	BATCHELOR	14 BOMB SQUADRON, 19 BG		WITHDRAWAL
30 DEC 41	SINGOSARI	14 BOMB SQUADRON, 19 BG		WITHDRAWAL
25 FEB 42	AUSTRALIA			WITHDRAWAL
(42)	(assigned as personal transport, General Brett)			
(JUN 42)	(carried Cdr. Lyndon Johnson on tour of SW Pacific)			
25 AUG 42	LANGLEY			
07 NOV 44	KIRTLAND	237 BASE UNIT	CAF	
(07 NOV 44)	(fr: B-17D to: RB-17D)		—	
02 NOV 45	KINGMAN		RFC	

OTHER INFORMATION

DATE	REMARKS
06 APR 46	TRANSFERRED BY WAA TO CITY OF LOS ANGELES
MAR 49	DONATED TO NATIONAL AIR MUSEUM BY LOS ANGELES
MAR 49	PLACED IN STORAGE AT PARK RIDGE, IL
18 JAN 50	PLACED IN STORAGE PYOTE, TX
09 DEC 53	FLOWN TO ANDREWS AFB, MD
APR 61	DISASSEMBLED AND MOVED TO SILVER HILL, MD FOR INDEFINITE STORAGE

40-3097

Undoubtedly, one of the most famous of all surviving B-17s is B-17D 40-3097. Known to most as the "Swoose", this example is the only shark fin B-17 known to exist. It also was a survivor of the dark, early days of the war in the Pacific against Japan. Though repeatedly damaged as a result of enemy action, the "Swoose" was continually rebuilt with wreckage from less fortunate B-17s and flew numerous combat missions in meager attempts to stem the Japanese offensive in the Southwest Pacific. After newer, more potent B-17Es became available, 40-3097 was assigned as the personal transport of General George Brett, then deputy commander of Allied Forces in Australia. Later, after he had been assigned to duties in Central and South America, Brett continued to utilize the old veteran on his travels. The

The "Swoose" after its return from the Pacific in 1942. Location and date of photo are unknown. Fortress looks well worn, though some of the effect is caused by the poor camouflage paint job applied as the war started. NASM

"Swoose" was forgotten in victory, and went to Kingman to be scrapped, only to be saved by its wartime pilot who arranged for the city of Los Angeles to accept the aircraft as a war memorial. In 1949 it was donated to the National Air Museum, in whose custody 40-3097 has since remained. Though disassembled in long term storage, it is currently available for viewing at a NASM annex facility. There are, unfortunately, no active plans to restore this unique Fortress.

40-3097 was the 38th of 41 B-17Ds built by Boeing. It was accepted for service by the Army Air Corps on 25 April 1941 in Seattle. Arrangements were underway for the 19th Bombardment Group, then deployed at March Field, California, to ferry twenty-one B-17C and Ds to Hickam Field, Hawaii, for assignment to the 11th Bombardment Group. The 19th Bombardment Group crews would check out their 11th Group counterparts before returning to California aboard ship. 40-3097 was attached to the group for ferrying to Hickam, and the flight was accomplished 13-14 May 1941.

The 11th Bomb Group was part of a build-up of American forces deployed in the Pacific to counter what were perceived to be hostile actions on the part of the Japanese military in the western Pacific. There were few B-17s in the Air Corps and most were concentrated in the 19th Bombardment Group at Albuquerque, New Mexico. Efforts, such as the May ferry flight, were underway to equip the 11th, 7th, and 5th Bombardment Groups with new B-17s as they came available, but a sense of urgency spread through the military commands to beef up the meager American forces in the Philippines as quickly as possible.

Thus in September 1941 the War Department decided to strip nine B-17s from the 11th and 5th Bomb Groups in Hawaii and send them to Clark Field. The nine aircraft were administratively assembled into the 14th Bombardment Squadron and assigned to the 19th Bombardment Group,

which was being prepared for a trans-Pacific ferry flight of its own the following month. The War Department then could count thirty-five B-17s to be at Clark Field by mid-October, the largest gathering of four-engined heavy bombers ever assembled, and a serious counter to threatening Japanese actions against Southeast Asia and the Southwest Pacific. The War Department further planned to deploy the 7th Bombardment Group, partially equipped with the new B-17E, to the Philippines in early December.

40-3097 and eight other B-17Ds were detached from the bomb groups at Hickam and ferried to Clark Field via Midway Island, Wake Island, Port Moresby, and Darwin. Under the command of Major Emmett "Rosie" O'Donnell, the squadron pioneered the route to be followed by the 19th Bombardment Group and successive waves of aircraft to follow to the Southwest Pacific in the ensuing years. Arriving at Clark in early October, the 14th Bombardment Squadron joined a motley collection of largely obsolete P-35s and a few new P-40s spread across a number of auxiliary airfields to form the basis of the American airpower in the Philippines.

The twenty-six B-17s of the 19th Group left Hamilton Field, near San Francisco, beginning 16 October 1941 under the command of Lt. Colonel Eugene Eubank. The last elements of the group arrived at Clark on 04 November, completing the deployment of Fortresses to be available when the war started five weeks later.

The 19th Bombardment Group was reorganized to include the 14th Bombardment Squadron among its four operational squadrons and headquarters unit. The group began training and conducted patrols of the waters surrounding the island of Luzon. Clark, located some fifty miles north of Manila on Luzon, was the only base thought capable of handling the B-17, and was a turf surfaced field with soft perimeter areas which forced only a limited dispersal of the heavy aircraft. The only other field suitable to handle the B-17 was at Del Monte on the island of Mindanao. Roughly six hundred miles south of Clark Field, Del Monte was located on a pineapple plantation where development of facilities began in late November.

American military forces in the Pacific were placed on alert in mid-November. A heightened state of alert began on 27 November, though messages from the War Department were somewhat ambiguous about what actions could be taken against Japanese threats. On 06 December it was decided to deploy two of the 19th Group's squadrons to Del Monte, including the 14th Bombardment Squadron and 40-3097. Clark Field was left with nineteen Fortresses, three of which were not operational due to repair work underway. Most 19th Group Fortresses retained their natural aluminum finish despite frantic efforts with the sole paint gun on the field.

Thus was the stage set for the Japanese attack upon Clark Field and the Philippine Islands, which occurred on 08 December and a full eight hours after the raid on Pearl Harbor. Endless debates have surrounded the actions of the Army commander, General Douglas MacArthur and his air commander, General George Brereton, as well as numerous factors which caused seventeen B-17s to be parked across Clark Field when the Japanese swept over shortly after lunchtime. (Two B-17s remained on patrol.) It is beyond the scope of this material to enter the debate; suffice to say the Fortresses had departed Clark Field that morning as a measure of protection after numerous rumors and reports of attacks had been received, and spent several hours milling over Luzon. The airborne B-17s had returned for fuel and bombs in preparation for planned offensive action when the Japanese hit the airfield with high-altitude bombers, followed by low level attacks by fighter aircraft.

All seventeen B-17s were badly damaged or destroyed. Several would be patched together and would fly again. For the most part, however, the air force installation at Clark was effectively reduced to a landing strip; all facilities for servicing and supporting aircraft were destroyed. It would fall to the undamaged B-17s (40-3097 among them) and the meager facilities at Del Monte to carry on the war.

The following weeks would see a desperate holding action performed by the Bomb Group and the other Allied units fighting the Japanese onslaught. The B-17s would be sent singly or in pairs from Del Monte on long, fatiguing, staging flights to Clark for fuel, before proceeding to attack the numerous Japanese targets available to the north. Besides

the toll on men, the long flights were especially wearing on the aircraft as parts and facilities to provide maintenance were unavailable. Heroic mechanics and flight crews struggled to piece together aircraft from the wrecks which returned from the feeble missions, shot full of holes, crews drained, having dropped a few bombs more often than not through overcasts and having no apparent effect on the massive offensive the Japanese were mounting.

After the Japanese invasion of Luzon, the remaining B-17s were pressed into evacuating personnel and essential supplies from the face of the advancing enemy. The Japanese established air bases on Luzon while the Bataan defenders were entrenching themselves, and Del Monte came under attack from Japanese aircraft.

40-3097 and the remaining B-17s were withdrawn to Australia's Batchelor Field, near Darwin, on 17 December and soon it and other survivors would stage through Del Monte for their raids on Japanese forces on Luzon. 40-3097 suffered as all the other aircraft. Initially commanded by Lt. Hank Godman, he and his crew took the B-17D north on seemingly futile missions again and again. Their B-17 had been feebly camouflaged and soon came to resemble a patchwork of parts of so many airplanes bolted and rebolted together to keep it flying. Other B-17s of the twenty or so to survive the first day of the war were lost with painful regularity, either in action or through operational accidents and crash landings of other aircraft returning from action. Expected replacements were a long time coming, and did not begin to trickle in until mid-January of 1942.

When reinforcements finally began arriving, they were part of the long-awaited 7th Bombardment Group and were a mixed bag of B-17Ds and the new B-17Es. Most were ferried via a new route which proceeded through South America, Africa, the Near East and across to South East Asia and into Australia. The new aircraft, plus the few survivors from the Philippines, were moved northwest to Singosari Field in Java, where they continued to mount attacks against the advancing Japanese forces. The deployment lasted only two months as the enemy closed in around Java also, and by late February 40-3097 and the other B-17s were again evacuating forces to Australia.

The pilot of 40-3097 at that time was Captain Weldon Smith who, upon watching yet another salvaged tail section replace the shot up one on his aircraft, dubbed his B-17D the "Swoose" after a popular song of the era—"Alexander the Swoose"—half swan, half goose. Soon he had painted the creature near the main entrance door on the right waist, below which he added "It Flies" perhaps as a hint of encouragement to the growing number of doubters. Shortly thereafter, the "Swoose" was withdrawn from combat in favor of the new B-17Es now arriving for duty. Though there were still an insufficient number of aircraft available, the condition of 40-3097 plus the inferior defensive armament made it necessary to place the Fortress in a non-combat role. The "Swoose" was assigned to General George Brett, then Deputy Commander of Allied Forces in Australia and ranking American commander, as his personal transport, and Capt. Frank Kurtz became his pilot. 40-3097 was dispatched on flights throughout Australia and remaining Allied territory, carrying Brett and other military commanders and visiting dignitaries.

On one occasion, in June 1942, the "Swoose" carried future president Lyndon Johnson, then a Congressman and active Navy Lt. Commander, on a fact finding mission through New Guinea and Australia. On one flight Kurtz and his crew, while relying on faulty magnetic compasses, became disoriented and had to put the B-17D down on a remote ranch to seek directions. Johnson and the fifteen other dignitaries tumbled out of the Fortress to seek accommodations and ground transportation to their next destination. The following day Kurtz caught up with Johnson and they all went their merry way.

Lt. General Brett was reassigned to the Caribbean Defense Command, partially as a result of friction between himself and General MacArthur, and the "Swoose" carried him home to Washington D.C. in the summer of 1942. En route, Kurtz and 40-3097 reportedly set a number of speed records, surprising in the fact that anyone was thinking of such things at the time.

After the obligatory War Bond Tour, the "Swoose" continued serving as General Brett's personal transport through 1944, winging its way through South and Central America. But by November 1944, having been redesignated as a RB-17D (obsolete for primary mission), the aircraft was assigned to the 237th Base Unit of the Continental Air Force at Kirtland Field in New Mexico. Its utilization at Kirtland is unknown, but apparently remained there through the balance of its operational life.

"The Swoose" got lost in the post-war rush to demobilize. Probably one of the few remaining early series B-17s, and with a distinctive combat history of its own, 40-3097 nonetheless was relegated to Kingman for disposal. The "Swoose" was just another forgotten aluminum veteran to be consigned to the scrap heap.

One who didn't forget was Colonel Frank Kurtz. Knowing his old charge was at Kingman, he urged the city of Los Angeles to obtain it for use as a War Memorial. The city agreed, and the necessary arrangements were completed to transfer the aircraft from the War Assets Administration to Los Angeles. Kurtz and much of the crew that flew with him during 1942 came to Kingman in April 1946 to fly the bomber to its new home. Also along on the flight were the mayor of Los Angeles and Kurtz's wife. Upon arrival at Los Angeles Municipal Airport, a rain-soddened crowd of 3000 people welcomed the aircraft and witnessed its formal acceptance by the city.

Los Angeles, despite the city's best intentions, never found a suitable display site for 40-3097. It sat at the airport for three years awaiting further plans, which emerged when the city graciously, and with a sense of relief, donated the bomber to the National Air Museum in Washington. Kurtz was called upon once again to coax his faithful friend back into the air on another final flight to its new home. In April 1949 he and National Air Museum curator Paul Garber flew the "Swoose" into storage at a National Air Museum facility at Park Ridge, Illinois. It remained there until January 1950 when it was flown to Pyote, Texas for additional storage with other aircraft from the National Air Museum's collection. On 09 December 1953 it made its final flight from Texas to Andrews AFB in Maryland, arriving on 12 December. It was placed in outdoor storage there until April 1961 when it was disassembled and moved overland to the NASM's Silver Hill facility in Maryland. It remained in outdoor storage and through the sixties a crescendo of criticism was heaped upon the National Air and Space Museum, not only for the condition of the "Swoose", but also for the similarly stored B-29 "Enola Gay" plus dozens of other rare and historically significant aircraft. By the mid-1970s 40-3097 and other disassembled exhibits were finally stored

40-3097 leaving Los Angeles in April 1949 with Frank Kurtz and Paul Garber at the controls. The historic aircraft was destined for a storage facility at Park Ridge, Illinois. Larkins

indoors on specially constructed dollies which enabled movement and close storage with a minimum chance of damage. The annex area is available for tours, and the dusty, musty, covered with preservative, disassembled B-17D can be viewed as it awaits unscheduled restoration.

Given the historical importance of the B-17 to the story of American airpower, and in particular that this aircraft is the only known early-series Fortress with a special history of its own, it is unfortunate that the "Swoose" has never been restored and displayed. Every few years it seems there is an effort in the aviation community to push the NASM toward action. The countless hours of work required, plus a lack of funding and display space have thus far kept the project from proceeding. Late word has the "Swoose" finally in the five year restoration plan but much hinges on the construction of an annex facility at Dulles Airport for the NASM. It would seem plausible that the "Swoose" could be made available for a restoration effort similar to that performed on "Shoo Shoo Shoo Baby" in Delaware. Even further, it would seem appropriate that the Boeing Company might step forward with an offer to restore the Fortress as a gracious nod of recognition to the airplane which firmly established the Boeing Company, and for which it remains well known.

The "Swoose" in storage at Andrews AFB during the late fifties. Aircraft remained there until 1961 when disassembled and moved to the Silver Hill facility where it remained in outdoor storage for several more years. Besecker

In storage at Andrews AFB. Note the B-17G blown nose, which is now mounted on the B-17F (42-3374) on display at Offutt AFB. Note also the non-standard dark gray undersurface. Besecker

41-2595   B-17E to XC-108A

USAAC/USAAF

DATE	LOCATION	UNIT	CMD	REMARKS
14 FEB 42	SEATTLE			ACCEPTED
28 FEB 42	MCDILL	97 BOMB GROUP		
29 MAR 42	SARASOTA	97 BOMB GROUP		
19 APR 42	MCDILL	97 BOMB GROUP		
07 JUL 42	OGDEN	97 BOMB GROUP		
11 SEP 42	WALLA WALLA	97 BOMB GROUP		
01 OCT 42	RAPID CITY	97 BOMB GROUP		
19 FEB 43	AINWORTH FLD 383 BG			
23 FEB 43	TINKER FLD			
23 MAR 43	WRIGHT FLD			
(17 AUG 43)	(To Project 90507, C-108 project)			
02 MAR 44	FAIRFIELD		ASC	AVAILABLE
(04 MAR 44)	(Availability cancelled due engine difficulties)			
(11 MAR 44)	(Aircraft departed U.S.)		ATC	
—	(XC-108 deployed to Chabua, India)		ATC	
(18 OCT 44)	(Aircraft returned to U.S.)		ATC	
OCT 44	DOW	1379 BASE UNIT	ATC	
08 DEC 45	DOW	147 BASE UNIT	CAF	
(26 DEC 45)	(Salvage authorized)			

41-2595

Certainly one of the rarest surviving B-17s, and the second oldest American survivor, is B-17E 41-2595, whose major claim to fame is that it was one of four Fortresses which were converted to a C-108 configuration. 41-2595 was lost to history from 1945 until 1985, when the disassembled airframe was located and recovered. Its fate is still somewhat uncertain, as it is in very poor condition and will require years of work and much money to create a complete aircraft.

41-2595 was built by Boeing as the 202nd B-17E and was accepted by the Army Air Force on 14 February 1942. Through the balance of 1942 the B-17 was used in operational training with the 97th Bomb Group and was variously based at Sarasota, Florida; McDill Field, Florida; Ogden, Utah; Walla Walla, Washington; and Rapid City, South Dakota. On 23 February 1943, 41-2595 was assigned to the 383rd Bomb Group and was based at Ainworth Field, Nebraska. Shortly afterwards, however, the airplane went to Tinker Field in Oklahoma, and on 23 March 1943 41-2595 was transferred to Wright Field in Ohio. The airplane was apparently used as a staff transport of some sort through the spring and early summer of 1943, making occasional trips to Biggs Field in Texas.

As noted in Part II, the C-108 program was established to test the feasibility of adapting existing B-17s to a cargo-carrying role. Four B-17s were converted, the Fairfield Air Service Command at Patterson Field, Ohio, handling the program and apparently performing several of the conversions themselves at their shops. 41-2595 was the second B-17 selected for the C-108 program and the conversion work was performed at Patterson Field.

**Another view of the aircraft in 1945, along with part of
the ATC crew which manned the XC-108A.** Taylor

41-2595 at McChord Field in 1944 shortly after the modifications were completed. This view shows to good advantage the large cargo door similar to that added to many civil examples in the post-war years.
Army Air Force via Bowers Collection

Rare photo of 41-2595 at Goose Bay in late 1945. Rudder and elevators are marked in red. Taylor

The Fairfield Air Service Command supplemented the Air Materiel Command modification center system as headed by nearby Wright Field. Fairfield shops fitted torpedo racks in B-26s, installed additional guns and armor on B-25s, converted B-17s to photographic F-9s, modified B-24s with additional turrets and equipment for sea-search duty, and other work as assigned. Both the C-108 and C-109 (B-24 program parallel to the C-108 modification of the B-17) were directed by the Fairfield Air Service Command.

41-2595 was brought into the C-108 program on 17 August 1943, becoming the XC-108A in a conversion completed by March 1944. The primary modifications all centered on making the Fortress into a standard transport type capable of carrying troops, large cargo, or injured personnel in a evacuation capacity. Armor and armament was stripped from the bomber. The interior arrangement was reworked, with the radio operator and navigator moving into the cockpit behind the pilots where the top turret had once been positioned. The nose compartment was rebuilt to provide for cargo, litter, or troop transport, access being gained by either the crawlway under the cockpit or a solid, hinged nose piece which replaced the built-up frame and glass assembly of a standard B-17E. The bomb-bay doors were sealed and the bulkhead between the bomb-bay and what had been the radio-compartment was opened up. The bulkhead between the radio compartment and the waist area was removed. Provisions for litters, cargo, or troop-transport were installed in both the former bomb-bay and the aft fuselage. A large, upward-hinging cargo door was installed in the left waist position to ease loading and unloading operations.

After initial testing was completed at Wright Field, the XC-108A was slated for an operational test in India ferrying men and equipment over the Hump into China. Though deemed ready for service in early March 1944, 41-2595 would develop continual engine problems which apparently plagued it through its entire test period. Whether this was primarily due to the state of the engines on the airframe, or the different operating conditions required by the airplane's new mission is open to question, but things started off poorly when initial engine difficulties required a week delay in the aircraft's departure as required engine maintenance was performed.

In late March the airplane left for India, its planned ferry route taking it through the Caribbean to South America, across to Africa and northeastward to India. Carrying a four man ferry crew and two passengers, the plane loaded up in Miami for the hop to Puerto Rico but again developed engine difficulties. As the plane was in a test series, maintenance had to be coordinated through Wright Field which only slowed repairs. After stopping in Puerto Rico, the flight continued to Belam, Brazil. Four hours out of Belem, and over the jungles of northeastern South America, engine number three caught fire. The engine was shut down, but efforts to ex-

tinguish the fire were unsuccessful and it continued to smolder. The pilot gave permission to anyone who wanted to bail out, but the foreboding jungle no doubt gave everyone second thoughts about that option, and all decided to stay with the C-108 as long as possible. The pilot nursed the plane to Belem and a successful landing, with the crew chief and a passenger jumping from the plane with fire extinguishers as it rolled to a stop on the runway. Repairs took another week before the crew made the trans-Atlantic hop to the Ascension Islands, followed by a leg to Accra in present day Ghana. More engine difficulties ensued there, causing extensive delays and resulted in the ferry flight stretching to almost eight weeks.

After finally arriving, the XC-108A was operationally based at Chabua in India, though details of it actual use are not available. One would suspect, however, that given the difficulties of the ferry flight and the altitudes involved in transporting material into China, the XC-108A was not successful.

In any event, 41-2595 returned to the U.S. in October 1944 via the North Atlantic ferry route, arriving at Dow Field near Bangor, Maine on 18 October 1944. The aircraft was assigned to the 1379th Base Unit was put to use as a transport. Flight operations were conducted to Greenland and Newfoundland, as well as throughout the northeastern U.S. The military record card indicates 41-2595 was later assigned to the 147th Base Unit and the Continental Air Force, but apparently its duties remained the same. Its last operational flight was conducted in mid-December 1945 and was subsequently authorized for salvage at Dow Field, possibly after a gear failure and belly landing, and thought to have been broken up for scrap.

However, the story of 41-2595 does not end here. It would appear that the owner of a auto junk yard near Dow Field made a successful bid on 41-2595 for salvaging, as well as a B-25, a C-47, an O-47 Owl and who knows what else. He hauled his booty away to his junkyard and let his kids have at the old airplanes. The B-25 was cut up, drawn and quartered like a side of beef. The C-47 and O-47 suffered a similar fate. However, the B-17 was found too big and strong, and only suffered great gashes and initial efforts at disassembly. The nose was cut off forward of the cockpit and the tail section was cut into four pieces. The wings were damaged from the rear spar aft, and other parts suffered at the effort at scrapping. The remains were then left to be swallowed up by an advancing forest of undergrowth and a receding memory.

The aircraft remained pretty well untouched until 1968. In that year a fellow restoring a B-25 in Massachusetts heard of the possibility of a B-25 airframe rotting in Maine. He and a crew of several men came looking for salvageable parts and found the XC-108 instead. The group was somewhat dismayed by the lack of a B-25, but decided to disassemble the B-17 and remove it instead. Without securing permission from anyone, they went ahead and demated the wings from the fuselage and then broke the fuselage into component parts. The engines, propellers, and landing gear were detached. As they began loading the material aboard the trucks, it was quickly determined that there was more airplane than available room. In the end, all that was taken were the engines, cowlings, landing gear, and propellers. The group disappeared into the sunset, but the components resurfaced in 1986 when an offer was made to the National Warplane Museum at Geneseo, New York, for the material in exchange for a few rides on the museum's B-17, 44-83563*. The museum donated the rides, but the supposed donor disappeared again into the sunset, and hasn't been seen since.

The second discovery of the XC-108A remains was made by Steve Alex of Bangor, Maine. In 1985 Alex purchased them from the two sons of the original owner, who had since passed away. Alex knew that Mike Kellner, a thirty year old vintage aircraft buff from Crystal Lake, Illinois, was intent on getting ahold of a B-17 for restoration, and promptly resold the Fortress to him for $7,250.

Kellner faced the monumental task of gathering the various pieces of the historic plane from the overgrown woods, transporting them from Maine to his home in Illinois, and somehow amassing the financial and logistical means to reconstruct the bomber. On the first two items he has been successful. The entire airplane has been moved to Galt Airport in Illinois, with all but the fuselage stored in enclosed trailers. The problems of restoring the bomber is obviously a much tougher nut to crack. Beyond the obviously poor condition of the airframe and the lack of readily available parts and manuals for the B-17E, Kellner has to establish some financial backing and find some people with the technical expertise to pull the airplane together.

Kellner has come under some criticism from several fronts. Many established museums and collectors with the means to tackle the project would like to get ahold of the plane, and feel that Kellner will not be able to properly restore it. Also, Kellner has stated he intends to bring the plane back to a standard B-17E configuration, removing the unique modifications which set it apart from other Fortresses. Kellner sees this as the only practical option to insure he can obtain popular support from airshow and museum crowds, many who wouldn't know what a C-108 was or understand the historical significance of the type. However, as the trend in aircraft restorations move toward more and more realistic representations of historically valuable aircraft, it would be unfortunate to attempt to reconvert the XC-108 back to a B-17E just to create a greater demand for the plane on the airshow circuit.

Nonetheless, Kellner is paying the bills, and he anticipates a fifteen year program to restore the plane back to flying condition. He is seeking any assistance offered, from parts and

technical manuals to people, perhaps retired Air Force mechanics, who may have worked on these planes and would like to dive headlong into a volunteer project of immense proportions. Financial assistance is also needed, and Kellner is considering a number of possibilities to help raise funds. He hopes to start the project soon, and one can hope that as the XC-108A comes back together Kellner will rethink his decision and maintain the airplane in its historic and unique configuration.

Nose section as found by Michael Kellner in Maine during the recovery trip in September 1985. The whole area was overgrown with vegetation and extracting the material proved difficult. Kellner

Loaded for the trip to Illinois, 41-2595 shows the remnants of its military markings. The extent of the restoration project is painfully evident. Kellner

The major remaining component of 41-2595 is the forward fuselage, still remarkably intact considering its history. Kellner

Chapter Three: 41-24485

Memphis, Tennessee

■■■■■■

41-24485   B-17F-10-BO to TB-17F

USAAF

DATE	LOCATION	UNIT	CMD	REMARKS
15 JUL 42	SEATTLE			ACCEPTED
19 JUL 42		MODIFICATION CENTER		
31 AUG 42	BANGOR	ATC		
(25 SEP 42)	(departed U.S.)			
26 OCT 42	BASSINGBOURN	91 BOMB GROUP	8AF	
(07 NOV 42)	(first mission: Brest, France)			
(17 MAY 43)	(last mission: Wilhelmshaven, Germany)			
(25 JUN 43)	(return to U.S. for war bond tour)			
23 DEC 43	MCDILL	483 BOMB GROUP	3AF	
21 OCT 44	COLUMBIA	329 BASE UNIT	3AF	
18 NOV 44	MCDILL	326 BASE UNIT	3AF	
MAY 45	DREW	327 BASE UNIT	3AF	
(04 MAY 45)	(fr: B-17F to: TB-17F)		—	
(08 JUN 45)	(declared excess)		—	
02 JUL 45	ALTUS			STORAGE
08 AUG 45	ALTUS		RFC	

OTHER INFORMATION

DATE	REMARKS
46	TRANSFERED FROM RFC TO MEMPHIS
MAR 46	AIRCRAFT FLOWN FROM ALTUS TO MEMPHIS FOR PERMANENT DISPLAY

41-24485

Probably the most famous of all the surviving B-17s is the "Memphis Belle". Heralded during the war as the first B-17 to complete twenty-five missions in Europe with the same flight crew, the "Belle" returned to the U.S. to a war bond tour and the release of a documentary on the aircraft and crew. The post-war path followed by this famous B-17F was not quite as smooth, as it barely escaped the scrapyard and suffered at the hands of vandals and an apathetic public while on display in Memphis. The past few years have been kinder, and a completely restored "Memphis Belle" is now on display at a new museum in Memphis.

41-24485 rolled from the Boeing production line in Seattle on 15 July 1942. It was immediately flown to a modification center, probably at the United Airlines facility at Cheyenne, arriving on 19 July. It emerged in late August, and was flown to Gowen Field, Idaho. There, the aircraft's new crew met the aircraft. Led by Lt. Robert Morgan, the crew took the B-17 to Bangor, Maine, in preparation for the trans-Atlantic flight to England for combat duty.

At Bangor, Morgan selected the name for the new bomber. Apparently, Morgan and crew then flew the B-17 from Bangor to Memphis in early September 1942, as part of a series of shakedown flights, so the aircraft's namesake, Miss Margaret Polk of Memphis (the subject of Morgan's affections), could personally christen the aircraft. The "Memphis Belle" subsequently returned to Maine, and

41-24485 at Washington National Airport in 1943, believed early on the war bond tour which followed its return from Europe.
NASM

departed for England on 25 September.

Upon arrival, 41-24485 was assigned to the 324th Bombardment Squadron of the 91st Bombardment Group, based at Bassingbourn, near London. It had pin-up nose art applied by Corporal Tony Starcer, who also painted nose art for "Shoo Shoo Shoo Baby" and other famous B-17s. The "Memphis Belle" was dispatched on its first mission on 07 November 1942 against submarine pens at Brest, France. The "Belle" continued to fly missions through the winter and into the spring, and gained the distinction of carrying its crew safely through what was a dangerous period of American bomber operations against Germany. The only injury suffered by the crew were inflicted on the tail gunner by attacking fighters, and the crewman recovered quickly.

The 91st Bomb Group was selected to be the focus of a documentary to be produced by the Army Air Forces 1st Motion Picture Unit, commanded by Major Paul Mantz in Hollywood. Director William Wyler and his film crew flew with the group for thirteen missions, five of them aboard the "Memphis Belle". As the "Belle" neared the end of its tour, Wyler focused in on the saga of this particular Fortress, and the documentary eventually would become the story of the aircraft as an example of the experiences shared by the airmen of the Eighth Air Force. (The motion picture was not released until April 1944, after the "Belle" had returned to the U.S. and its crew dispersed to other units.)

41-24485 flew its last mission on 17 May 1943 against Wilhelmshaven, a port in Germany. Upon its return, the aircraft and crew were hailed as the first American bomber crew to survive twenty-five missions of vicious combat over Europe intact. Arrangements were made for the "Memphis Belle" and crew to return to the U.S. together for a war bond tour, and they departed in early June for home. Receiving a hero's welcome, the crew began a three month tour joined by Margaret Polk and the crew's mascot, a dog named "Stuka". The entourage put in appearances at such diverse places as Harlingen, Texas; Roswell, New Mexico; and Seattle, Washington.

Upon completion of the tour, Morgan delivered the B-17 to McDill Field in Florida for attachment to the 3rd Air Force's 483rd Bomb Group in training. It arrived on 23 December 1943. Morgan went on to train in B-29s and led the first raid by the new Twentieth Air Force against Tokyo. Other crewmembers of the "Belle" also joined new units and most saw combat again.

41-24485 never again fired a shot in anger, however. The former "Belle" plied out its days training new crews. While its combat documentary was being hailed by the public in the summer of 1944, the subject aircraft was plugging away in Florida. It went to Columbia, South Carolina in October

The "Memphis Belle" over wartime England. Note splotchy medium green paint applied to break up the lines of the aircraft in a further effort to camouflage. USAF via San Diego Aerospace Museum

1944 and assignment to the 329th Base Unit on the field. 41-24485 returned to McDill a month later, and remained for the balance of the war. In May 1945 it was assigned to Drew Field, Montana and, on 04 May, officially redesignated as a TB-17F. The new lease on life was short lived as a quick month later the aircraft was declared excess to requirement and dispatched to Altus, Oklahoma for storage. On 08 August 1945, two days after the "Enola Gay" had made its fateful trip over Hiroshima, it was assigned to the Reconstruction Finance Corporation for disposal.

The story of the "Memphis Belle" should have ended there. It was a forgotten aircraft, its wartime markings and corresponding heritage covered under a layer of anonymous Army olive drab. The only identity tying it to the past was a familiar serial number, but no one was around to care at Altus as hundreds of tired bombers poured in from around the world for eventual scrapping. It was only in early 1946, when a unnamed citizen of Memphis happened by the Altus boneyard, that the familiar serial was spotted. He checked with someone in Memphis who confirmed the identity of the famous bomber. Civic leaders of Memphis arranged to have the Fortress transferred from the RFC to their city as a war memorial. (While various sources keep insisting the Fortress was "sold" to Memphis for $300, this is doubtful. More probable is that the aircraft was transferred to Memphis in a manner similar to dozens of other communities who

received old warplanes for display; ownership remained in the hands of the federal government.)

A group from Memphis arrived in March 1946, led by a veteran B-17 pilot, to attempt to ferry the bomber to Memphis. They worked on the bomber for several days, and then took the B-17 back into the air for a test flight. The flight went so well that the crew decided not to take any chances and kept on going right to Memphis.

Soon the city had arranged to display the Fortress on a concrete pedestal located near the National Guard armory in Memphis. Displayed outdoors and with little public notice, the Fortress started an inevitable downhill slide, pushed along by vandals and the elements. Through the fifties and sixties the "Belle" slid, turning from war memorial to eyesore. Sporadic attempts at protection or restoration only resulted in terribly applied paint and/or inaccurate markings. Internal equipment not welded to the airframe had disappeared early on, and the broken bomber appeared on a terminal course.

There were those in Memphis, however, who refused to let the "Belle" go. Among them was businessman Frank Donofrio who, in 1972, formed the "Memphis Belle Committee". This evolved into the "Memphis Belle Memorial Association", established in 1975 by Donofrio and other concerned citizens of Memphis.

The task that lay before the group was immense. Without

resources, they had to protect the bomber from further damage, restore it to a semblance of its former condition, and provide a facility to finally protect it from destructive elements, people and otherwise. The B-17 had already been pulled from its location near the National Guard facility which was being moved. 41-24485 was towed to the Memphis International Airport where two different facilities, the National Guard installation and the Memphis Area Vocational-Technical School, performed work on the aircraft. The paint and engines were stripped. Control surfaces were removed, as was much of the remaining interior equipment. Removed parts were either placed in storage or rebuilt for eventual installation.

During the early eighties the restoration effort came under a great deal of criticism. Many felt the effort was being handled poorly and in an amateur fashion. Citing such things as a lack of corrosion control, poorly applied paint, and ignorance of accepted restoration procedures, critics urged that the U.S. Air Force Museum, which ultimately controlled the fate of the "Memphis Belle", intervene and remove the aircraft to their own facilities in Dayton or loan the aircraft to a group which had the skill to restore the bomber properly.

Viewing photos taken at the time, much of the criticism appears warranted. Paint was being applied inaccurately. Restoration efforts often only consisted of cleaning components or just painting them. Gathered equipment for eventual installation was of the wrong type. In short, the effort in no way matched the standards established by the Air Force Museum or demonstrated by the quality of restorations such as "Shoo Shoo Shoo Baby" in Delaware. It appeared that, until 1985 or so, the "Belle" would have been much better off at Wright-Patterson.

Pressure by the Air Force Museum and other critics paid off, however, as the aviation and historical community in Memphis realized it was close to losing the "Belle". Much need funding and assistance finally began to pour in, and the restoration effort was boosted by the shot in the arm. Missing equipment and donated items arrived, and the B-17 began to come together. Work was started on a unique dome structure, to house and protect the completed aircraft. Arrangements were made to have Tony Starcer, who had originally painted the artwork on the nose in 1942, recreate his effort on the freshly painted "Belle". His untimely death prevented that re-creation, but his nephew, Phil Starcer, was able to complete the application of the markings.

The entire effort culminated on 17 May 1987, when seven of the last thirteen flyable B-17s roared over the new home of the "Memphis Belle". The "Belle", resplendent in a new, accurate, combat paint scheme, was joined by seven of the original crew, including Bob Morgan, plus his one-time sweetheart, Margaret Polk. Finally after so many years of disintegration, 41-24485 has been given a home which will protect it and enable future generations to view this famous veteran of a war, the memory of which is quickly fading into the history books.

41-24485 on display in Memphis in 1968. Plexiglass crazed and paint faded, the B-17 nonetheless remained externally complete. Krieger

CHAPTER FOUR: 42-3374

OFFUTT AIR FORCE BASE, NEBRASKA

■■■■■

42-3374	B-17F-50-DL

USAAF

DATE	LOCATION	UNIT	CMD	REMARKS
26 MAY 43	LONG BEACH			ACCEPTED
27 MAY 43	DENVER	MODIFICATION CENTER		
16 JUL 43	DYERSBURG	373 SUB DEPOT	ASC	
(08 SEP 44)	(placed in Class 26)			
(20 NOV 45)	(reclaimed)			

OTHER INFORMATION

DATE	TRANSFER DETAILS
1945	TRANSFERRED TO MGM FOR USE IN FILM "FOOTPRINTS IN THE SKY" (NEVER PRODUCED)
1945	PLACED IN STORAGE AT MGM
1970	SAVED FROM SCRAPPING BY THE AIR MUSEUM. TRANSFERRED TO CHINO AIPORT
1982	TRANSFERRED TO BEALE AFB FOR DISPLAY
1989	TRANSFERRED TO OFFUTT AFB FOR DISPLAY

42-3374

One of three remaining B-17Fs in the U.S., 42-3374 was hidden in a storage lot at a major film studio for twenty-five years. It was saved from scrapping almost by accident, spent the next twelve years in disassembled storage at Chino Airport, before finally being reassembled for the Beale AFB Heritage Museum. It remained on display there until 1989, when the Air Force Museum suddenly reassigned it and had it moved to Offutt Air Force Base for use as a gate guardian.

42-3374 was built at Long Beach, California by the Douglas Aircraft Company. It rolled from the production line on 26 May 1943 and was accepted for service. 42-3374 was immediately flown to Denver, Colorado for modification at the Continental Airlines-run modification center. It emerged, ready for operational use, on 15 July 1943 and was flown to Dyersburg, Tennessee for assignment to the 373rd Sub Depot located there. As part of the Air Services Command and the Oklahoma City Depot, the purpose for the aircraft being based at Dyersburg is not known.

Subsequent utilization of 42-3374 at Dyersburg or other duty locations cannot be determined from available military records. What is known, however, is that 42-3374 was placed in Class 26 on 08 September 1944. Class 26 indicates the aircraft was available for assignment to non-flying roles, such as technical schools or training-related uses, or scrapped. The record card for 42-3374 ends with the notation that it was reclaimed as a RB-17F on 20 November 1945.

It would appear from other available sources that 42-3374 was transferred to the Metro-Goldwyn-Meyers film studio in 1945 for "Footprints in the Sky", a proposed film which never got beyond pre-production planning. An examination of 42-3374 today reveals that the skin on the lower part of the nose section had been removed, ostensibly for camera access into the nose and cockpit. Whether this was done in 1945 for the planned production, or later for another film, is not known. In any event, the B-17 was subsequently disassembled and placed in a studio storage lot.

MGM had amassed a substantial collection of aircraft in the course of producing various motion pictures. They slowly collected in disuse in a pair of lots in Culver City, California. The collection contained two complete B-24s, six SBD fuselages used occasionally as wind generators, a B-29, a Corsair, a P-38 and numerous other unique examples from cinematic history.

42-3374 at Chino Airport in 1981. The Fortress was never reassembled by the Air Museum staff and it was left to the Beale group to pull the aircraft back together. Author

They sat, largely forgotten, until the late 1960s when MGM decided to reorient its corporate direction away from films and toward hotels, and wanted the land where the airplanes were stored for other purposes.

Not considered worth auctioning, MGM moved forward with plans to scrap the material, but was willing to give any or all of it to anyone who could act quickly and get the airplanes and parts off MGM property. Unfortunately, arrangements to preserve the aircraft could not keep pace with arrangements to destroy the aircraft and many were scrapped.

Ed Maloney of the Air Museum was able to save 42-3374. The disassembled hulk was trucked off to Chino Airport and other Air Museum facilities in southern California. At one point the wings to 42-3374 were stored on a trailer behind Maloney's Buena Park "Planes of Fame" facility. The fuselage was on display at his Chino Facility on its belly. The aircraft was never reassembled by Maloney, and became the basis for a trade with the Air Force in 1981.

At that time, 42-3374 was made available to the new museum at Beale AFB, north of Sacramento in California. Arrangements were made to have the B-17 trucked, once again, to the Beale Museum where, over the span of a year, it was finally reassembled. Sitting on its own landing gear for the first time since 1945, it was obvious that in the various

moves across California 42-3374 had lost a number of components along the way. The final move to Beale had seen the inboard wing sections sliced laterally, totally destroying the internal structure of the wing. A coat of Army olive drab was applied by the museum staff to at least help the B-17 approximate a combat Fortress.

Somewhere in its obscure past 42-3374 was fitted with an early B-17 series nose piece, with the built-up nose glass structure as opposed to the blown clear nose piece of the "F" or "G" series Fortresses. Upon learning of the existence of the early nose, Robert Mikesh of the National Air and Space Museum beat a hasty path to Beale to talk trade. One major item lacking on the parts list for the NASM's B-17D 40-3097* the "Swoose" was a B-17D nose piece. 40-3097 had completed its Army Air Force service with a B-17G blown nose, so Mikesh arranged a trade of the two parts. Unfortunately, the perspex nose received by Beale off the "Swoose" was faded, yellowed, cracked, and ill-fitting. It generally detracts from the appearance of 42-3374, sending an already ratty looking airplane further downhill.

Another major problem with 42-3374 is the lower nose section. As noted earlier, the skin had been removed from the lower section of the nose for planned camera access. Whoever pieced the lower section back together did an extremely poor job and the results reek of amateur efforts.

Later, someone tried to verify the identification of the Fortress by using paint remover to try and reveal the original data block on the nose. It would appear that too much was used and the resultant goo promises that the data block as it once existed beneath the paint has been obliterated.

Still, the museum staff at Beale was trying to bring the Fortress up to an acceptable static display level. A working ball turret was installed and attached to a makeshift electrical system. Some components were removed and sent out for external restoration, and the plan was for the B-17 to become an excellent static display and externally complete. Their other exhibits, ranging from a B-29 nose section, to prime examples of the B-25 and A-26, are all well kept and accurate. The museum facility itself is one of the best the Air Force Museum Program has created, thanks to a large and hard working volunteer staff. However, in May 1989 the B-17 was disassembled and trucked to Offutt Air Force Base to become a gate guardian. Apparently, at the behest of SAC's commanding general, it was ordered that an available B-17 be brought to SAC's headquarters for use. That Offutt already had a B-17 on display at the SAC museum did not seem to matter, and, at this writing, 42-3374 is disassembled and awaiting further plans. If those materialize, the B-17F will join a B-52 at the main entrance to Offutt AFB.

42-3374 at Beale AFB with the ill-fitting B-17G blown nose. The damaged paint beneath the third nose window was an aborted attempt to verify the aircraft's military serial. Author

Detail of the lower nose section. Note the terribly patched skin, once opened up for camera access. Author

The disassembled B-17F at Offutt AFB in August 1989. Hade

Chapter Five: 42-29782

Museum of Flight
Seattle, Washington

■■■■■■

42-29782   B-17F-70-BO to N6015V to N17W

USAAC/USAAF

DATE	LOCATION	UNIT	CMD	REMARKS
13 FEB 43	SEATTLE			ACCEPTED
17 FEB 43	CHEYENNE	MODIFICATION CENTER		
04 MAR 43	BLYTHE		–	
16 MAY 43	MCCLELLEN		–	
15 JUN 43	MOSES LAKE		–	
(24 JAN 44)	(departed U.S.)			
(10 MAR 44)	(returned U.S.)			
04 MAY 44	DREW		–	
05 NOV 45	ALTUS		RFC	

CIVIL

DATE	TRANSFER DETAILS
10 SEP 46	FR: WAR ASSETS ADMINISTRATION TO: CITY OF STUTTGART, AR, FOR USE AS WAR MEMORIAL
?	TO: GERALD C. FRANCIS (OBTAINED AIRCRAFT AT REQUEST OF THE CITY OF STUTTGART)
23 APR 53	TO: MAX AND JOHN BIEGERT, BEN WIDTFELDT; LINCOLN, NB
(15 JUN 53)	(LETTER FROM GENERAL SERVICES ADMINISTRATION, US GOVERNMENT, TO CIVIL AERONAUTICS AUTHORITY, REQUESTING THAT CAA NOT ISSUE REGISTRATION TO 42-29782 DUE TITLE DISPUTE)
(06 MAY 54)	(GSA RELEASES INTEREST IN AIRCRAFT FOR $20,000)
26 OCT 61	TO: A.B. SELLARS, SAFFORD, AZ
17 APR 63	TO: AIRCRAFT SPECIALTIES, PHOENIX, AZ
18 FEB 81	TO: GLOBE AIR, INC., MESA, AZ
11 JUN 85	TO: PORTAGE BAY, INC., SEATTLE, WA

42-29782

If there were a grand old lady among the surviving Fortresses, 42-29782 would be it. A staple among the civil Fortress fleet since the early fifties, N17W has steadily plied the skies primarily as an air tanker, but also made the occasional motion picture appearance. N17W is one of three surviving "F" series B-17s, and the only flying example. It is now in semi-retirement and displayed at the impressive new Museum of Flight located where 42-29782 first saw the light of day: Boeing Field in Seattle.

42-29782 was accepted by the Army Air Force on 13 February 1943. It was subsequently flown to the United Airlines modification center located at the Cheyenne Municipal Airport in Wyoming, arriving on 17 February. It emerged ready for service two weeks later and was initially assigned to a training unit at Blythe Field in the California desert.

N17W in its first incarnation as a sprayer in 1959. Note the two F-84 tip tanks on the external bomb shackles and the spray bars beneath the wings. Aircraft was based at Phoenix, Arizona. Gann

N17W as a tanker. Owner Max Biegert had leased the B-17 to Abe Sellards who installed the retardant tank in May 1960. The spray bars came off later and Sellards bought the B-17 in October 1961. Gann

The tanker regained spray bars in 1965 for a project. The retardant tank was removed. Note the B-25 and A-26 tankers in the background at the Phoenix Airport.

C. Jansson via Peltzer Collection

For one scene in "1000 Plane Raid" N17W was set up for a simulated belly landing. Two trenches were dug to accept the main landing gear and the Fortress was rolled down into them. Note the undamaged propellers and the "battle damage."

T. Piedmonte via Besecker

Though not confirmed from the military records available, it appears that 42-29782 spent its operational utilization in stateside training units. From Blythe it went to McClellen Field in Sacramento, California on 16 May 1943, possibly for an overhaul at the Sacramento Air Depot. A month later it was assigned to Moses Lake, Washington and another training unit.

The aircraft record card notes an accident which occurred at Moses Lake on 20 September 1943. The right main wheel came off the landing gear during a landing or take-off, and the right wing settled to the runway. Damage to the number three and four propellers, and presumably their respective engines, resulted.

The aircraft may have deployed overseas during the first three months of 1944, though this is not clear from the record card. Some sources have indicated it served with the Eighth Air Force in Britain during the period but this is doubtful. It was back in the country by late spring 1944 and the Army Air Force was re-equipping units with the new B-17G beginning in early 1944. That an old B-17F would be deployed to Europe for combat is difficult to envision.

In May 1944 42-29782 was assigned to Drew Field, Montana, and remained based there until the Fortress was withdrawn from service in November 1945 and flown to the RFC lot at Altus, Oklahoma for disposal.

42-29782, as were several other weary B-17s at Altus, was made available by the Reconstruction Finance Corporation to municipalities desiring war memorials. This particular B-17F was transferred to the city of Stuttgart, Arkansas, for display purposes on 10 September 1946. As in similar agreements negotiated throughout the country by the RFC, ownership of the aircraft would remain with the federal government, a fact forgotten when the local governments later attempted to dispose of the aircraft themselves.

42-29782 was moved to Stuttgart, and photographs from the period show it was displayed in a small park in the city. At some point the legend "Great White Bird" was scrawled across each side of the bare aluminum skin of the nose. Turrets and other war time equipment had been removed, probably several years earlier when the aircraft had been assigned to wartime training units.

The B-17 remained on display for over five years, but the city of Stuttgart apparently tired of their war memorial and eventually sought to find a way to dispose of it. A local individual named Gerald C. Francis offered to take the bomber off the city's hands, to which Stuttgart eagerly accepted. No legal transfer was effected; it would appear that Francis just moved the aircraft off city property and gained "ownership," or so everyone thought.

In April 1953 Francis sold the somewhat derelict B-17 to two brothers, Max and John Biegert, and their partner, Ben Widtfeldt, of Lincoln, Nebraska. Two months later the General Services Administration of the federal government sent a letter to the Civil Aeronautics Authority, precursor of today's Federal Aviation Administration, requesting that they refrain from issuing a civil registration number for 42-29782 as there was a title dispute involved. The Biegert brothers had disassembled 42-29782 and moved it to the local airport in Stuttgart to be rebuilt and ferried to Nebraska.

The ongoing dispute between the Biegerts and the government was resolved on 15 June 1953 when the government released their interest in 42-29782 for $20,000. The CAA had initially assigned 42-29782 a civil registration of N6015V on 25 November 1953, but on 21 April 1954 Max Biegert, in a letter to the CAA, requested the issuance of a registration number like "N17G" or "N17B" or something close to that sequence. N17W was the resultant registration. May 1954 registration records estimated total aircraft flight time to be about 500 hours, which is probably low given its extensive military use. Additional flight time figures presented here are based upon this initial figure as filed with the CAA.

The Biegerts set about to convert their newly won B-17 to an aerial sprayer. A total of seven tanks were installed on N17W. One 300 gallon tank was installed in the nose section, with two 425 gallon tanks installed in the bomb-bay. 3 tanks with a total capacity of 950 gallons were installed in the waist position, and two 450 gallon tip tanks off a Republic F-84 Thunderjet were hung from the external bomb shackles inboard of engines two and three. Total capacity was 3,100 gallons, and a load of 20,000 pounds was authorized by the CAA. The plumbing for all seven tanks must have produced a dramatic nightmare of pipes and pumps, which terminated in spray bars located near the trailing edge of the wings.

Between 1954 and 1961 the Biegert brothers employed N17W in a variety of projects, and also leased the Fortress to several civil operators who used it for application of pesticides across the country. One recorded use was to spray DDT across Lansing, Michigan in attempts to eradicate the gypsy moth. An overhaul in May 1957 resulted in the belly skin aft of the bomb-bay replaced, with total aircraft time at that point in excess of 900 hours.

Biegert leased N17W to Abe Sellards of Safford, Arizona beginning in 1960. In May of that year Sellards modified the aircraft further to allow its use as an air tanker, though it still retained the capability of being used as a sprayer with the spray bars attached to the wing. The FAA certified the aircraft to carry 2,000 gallons of retardant or spray material.

On 26 October 1961 N17W was sold to Sellards. Sellards, who helped form Aviation Specialties in 1963, removed the spray tanks and other equipment from the aircraft. It was employed as an air tanker and incorporated into the tanker fleet Aviation Specialties assembled. Registration was transferred to the new company on 17 April 1963.

Aviation Specialties, as noted elsewhere, operated a large

N17W made up for its role in "Tora Tora Tora" in early 1969 and en route to Hawaii. The fuselage insignia is oversized but the appearance is otherwise authentic. One of five Aircraft Specialties B-17s used in the film. Larkins

fleet of B-17s throughout the sixties and seventies. Based initially at Phoenix, the company later moved to Falcon Field in nearby Mesa. The company was reorganized as Globe Air in 1981 and quit business in 1985, which resulted in a large auction of their equipment gathered over twenty-some years.

N17W plied the path of the air tanker with the company, serving it faithfully until 1985. N17W accumulated in excess of 1000 hours of flight time during the period, and became a common sight near the major forest fires in the western U.S. as, initially, Tanker 84E, and later, Tanker 04.

N17W became a film star in January 1968 when it was hired as one of three B-17s to appear in the production of "1000 Plane Raid," a less-than-ambitious effort at recreating the Eighth Air Force of 1943. The Fortress arrived on location at the old P-38 interceptor base turned municipal airport at Santa Maria, California, on 14 January 1968. It was later joined by 44-83525* N83525 from Tallmantz Aviation and 44-83684* N3713G from the Air Museum. Over the following two weeks, the three B-17s and a Tallmantz B-25 camership were employed in a struggle to film a low-budget version of a dramatic attack on Germany. The results were predictable and the film was forgotten within months of its June 1969 release.

With four other Aircraft Specialties Fortresses, N17W regained Army olive drab for the cameras of Twentieth Century Fox in early 1969. Aircraft Specialties was hired to provide five Fortresses and all aircraft maintenance for the filming of "Tora Tora Tora" in Hawaii. The film effort resulted in a great fleet of Japanese aircraft replicas, specially created for the film, plus a variety of American P-40s, PBYs, and other types including the B-17s, to be gathered in Hawaii for

the production. The B-17s were painted in 1941 vintage Army Air Corps markings, and had turrets shells and guns remounted on the aircraft. The five Fortresses assembled in Oakland, California, in January 1969 for the trans-Pacific ferry flight. They were used to depict the arrival of portions of the 7th Bombardment Group B-17s at Hickam during the Japanese raid on Pearl Harbor.

After filming was completed, the five B-17s were flown back to Arizona, where N17W operated in a partial camouflage paint scheme through the 1969 fire season. By June 1969 N17W had accumulated 2508 hours of flight time.

N17W continued to be employed as an air tanker until 1985 when Aviation Specialties' succeeding company, Globe Air, called it quits and closed up shop. At that time, Globe Air operated four B-17s as tankers, plus a variety of other equipment. The assembled fleet, plus a mountain of spare parts, were either sold shortly before or during an auction held in October 1985 at the firm's base at Falcon Field. N17W was sold to a Seattle businessman, Robert Richardson, prior to the auction. The B-17 was officially registered to Richardson's company, Portage Bay, Incorporated.

Richardson is a member of the Museum of Flight, a group which has among its goals returning a B-17 to its birthplace. The Museum of Flight sprang from the Pacific Northwest Aviation Historical Foundation, which was founded in 1964. The Museum obtained the historic "Red Barn", Boeing's original factory, in 1975 and succeeded in moving it to the museum site at Boeing Field. The Museum has recently finished construction on its massive new facility which is capable of, among other things, handling a suspended B-17 from its interior structure.

The announced intent of Richardson and the Museum is that N17W will eventually be purchased by the museum. A concerted fund drive by the museum has been underway for several years to raise the money to buy the Fortress. It will be maintained in airworthy condition for at least a few years before going on permanent display in the museum.

In late 1988 the B-17F had its tanker paint scheme removed, replaced with Army Air Force markings over bare aluminum. A working Sperry top turret, cultivated from the remains of three found in a Georgia junk yard, was installed. A working ball turret has been put together and is about ready for installation.

In July 1989 it was flown to England for use in the filming of "The Memphis Belle". The long ferry flight went without a hitch until the final half hour when the Fort blew an engine. A replacement was obtained from the spares of "Sally B", which, coincidently, was one of the engines obtained from another U.S. air tanker, N5237V.

The only actual B-17F used in the film, the aircraft gained a myriad of markings over the six weeks it was utilized, both at Duxford and RAF Binbrook. N17W looks extremely authentic with its early Army Air Force paint, and the addition of turrets added a great deal to the appearance. (A ball turret shell was affixed to the belly as Richardson's working ball turret wasn't ready.) Fifty hours of flight time went into the film, which is reputed to have some superb B-17 film footage, replete with attacking Hispano Messhersmitts. The final markings to be carried have not been determined, but Richardson will be content to leave it in its final movie markings, painted as "Kathleen" for an indefinite period. The B-17 will now return to the museum flight line and makes it to the occasional air show. The best part, however, is that the airplane which made the Boeing Company famous has finally returned to its birthplace and a permanent home.

N17W back on the fire lines in Alaska during the summer of 1969. It retains much of its "Tora" paint with the addition of some high-visibility markings for its air tanker role. N. Taylor via Peltzer Collection

42-29782 in its last tanker scheme at the National Warplane Museum airshow at Geneseo in 1988. The Fortress was later given olive drab combat paint for its role in "The Memphis Belle" in 1989. Mitchell

CHAPTER SIX: 42-32076

UNITED STATES AIR FORCE MUSEUM
WRIGHT-PATTERSON AFB, OHIO

■■■■■■

42-32076   B-17G-35-BO to SE-BAP to OY-DFA to DANISH AF 672 to F-BGSH

USAAF

DATE	LOCATION	UNIT	CMD	REMARKS
19 JAN 44	SEATTLE		ATC	ACCEPTED
25 JAN 44	DENVER	MODIFICATION CENTER	ATC	
28 JAN 44	CHEYENNE	MODIFICATION CENTER	ATC	
06 FEB 44	GRAND ISLAND		ATC	
(02 MAR 44)	(departed U.S.)		– –	
MAR 44	BASSINGBOURN	91 BOMB GROUP	8AF	
(24 MAR 44)	(first mission: Frankfurt)		– –	
(29 MAY 44)	(last mission: Poznan)		– –	
(29 MAY 44)	(interned at Malmo, Sweden)		– –	
(04 DEC 44)	(given to Swedish government)		– –	

CIVIL AND OTHER

DATE	TRANSFER DETAILS
02 NOV 45	REGISTERED AS SE-BAP FOR FLIGHT TESTING
05 NOV 45	TO DANISH AIR LINES, REGISTERED AS OY-DFA
31 MAR 48	TO DANISH ARMY AIR CORPS, SERIAL 67-672
01 DEC 49	TO DANISH NAVY AIR CORPS
24 OCT 52	TO DANISH AIR FORCE
01 OCT 53	RETIRED FROM DANISH SERVICE
02 FEB 55	BABB CO., USA, AIRCRAFT BROKER
06 APR 55	INSTITUT GEOGRAPHIQUE NATIONAL AS F-BGSH
15 JUL 61	RETIRED FROM SERVICE AT CREIL, FRANCE
23 JAN 72	DONATED TO USAF MUSEUM
04 FEB 72	DISASSEMBLED, FLOWN FROM RHEIN MAIN TO W-PAFB, OH
JUL 78	TRANSFERRED FROM STORAGE TO DOVER AFB FOR RESTORATION
13 OCT 88	TO USAF MUSEUM FOR PERMANENT DISPLAY

42-32076

A challenging restoration undertaken by the 512th Military Airlift Wing has resulted in an outstanding example of a B-17 combat veteran. The ex-Eighth Air Force Fortress was interned in Sweden on its twenty-third combat mission, and continued in Swedish and Danish service after the war. It eventually became part of the fleet of Fortresses operated by the French Institut Geographique National and was active until 1961. It was close to the scrapman's torch when the French government donated 42-32076 to the USAF Museum in 1972. The restoration process, which began in 1978, was completed in October 1988 and the B-17G was flown to the Air Force Museum facility at Wright-Patterson AFB for permanent display.

42-32076 was an early-block B-17G delivered 24 January 1944. It was among the first B-17Gs built by Boeing to leave the production line without camouflage paint. The B-17G was sent to the Continental Airlines modification center at Denver the same day as delivery. It was immediately sent on to the United Airlines modification center at Cheyenne, however, arriving 06 February 1944. It was considered operational on 29 February and sent to a depot in preparation for assignment to the Eighth Air Force and a ferry flight across the North Atlantic. 42-32076 departed the U.S. on 02 March, destined for the replacement depot at Burtonwood, Warrington in England. Upon arrival, it was assigned to the 91st Bomb Group at Bassingbourn.

By 24 March 42-32076 had flown its first combat mission to Frankfurt. The aircraft was generally assigned to Lt. Paul McDuffee, who would fly thirteen missions in the aircraft before he completed his tour. His crew chief dubbed the Fortress "Shoo Shoo Baby", after the popular 1943 song. Initially only the name was applied, as their was some question about whether the aircraft would be camouflaged after

all. Once the decision was made that the bare metal B-17s would remain as such, pin-up nose art was added by Tony Starcer. After Mcduffee completed his tour the Fortress was turned over to his co-pilot, Lt. Robert Guenther, who reportedly added the third "Shoo" to the name. Guenther flew a number of missions in the bomber as aircraft commander, as did other 91st Group pilots.

On 29 May 1944 "Shoo Shoo Shoo Baby" was dispatched with the 91st Bomb Group to bomb a Focke-Wulf factory at Poznan, Poland, in Eastern Europe. The planned route required the assembled bombers to skirt the defenses of Berlin and fly a further two hundred miles to reach the target. Total distance planned for the mission exceeded fifteen hundred miles, trying the available range of the B-17.

Guenther, who commanded the aircraft on the mission, and his crew encountered difficulties early when an engine lost oil pressure as they crossed into Germany. The propeller on the engine would not feather, and with its drag the Fortress was forced from the defensive formation. They pressed on toward the target, however, and successfully dropped their bombs. During the return trip a second engine was damaged by flak and the propeller had to be feathered. Down to two engines, "Shoo Shoo Shoo Baby" was losing altitude and obviously would not make it back to England. A course was plotted for Sweden as the crew began jettisoning equipment to lighten the aircraft. Picked up for escort by a Swedish fighter, a third engine quit while on approach to the airfield at Malmo, Sweden. 42-32076 landed under the power of its last engine, following a B-24 with similar difficulties. Upon completing the abbreviated engine shutdown procedure, the crew was escorted from the aircraft by armed Swedish soldiers. The Fortress was parked in a storage area with the growing number of interned aircraft, and the crew was sent to a camp for Allied airmen.

Taxiing out for departure from Dover AFB, "Shoo Shoo Shoo Baby" at her finest. A. Florence via Grantham

At ceremonies on 13 October 1988 at Dover AFB, the original crew of "Shoo Shoo Shoo Baby" gather to commemorate the event.

A. Florence via Grantham

An exchange program was worked out in late 1944, and the crew and other interned Americans were flown from Sweden to England. Shortly afterwards, the U.S. government sold nine of the interned Fortresses to the Swedish government for $1.00. The Swedish government had the Swedish airline, SAAB, rebuild the nine B-17s into seven passenger airliners, and 42-32076 became SE-BAP for flight test purposes in November 1945. The modifications were extensive and saw the stripping of all military equipment from the airframes. An airline style interior was installed in the fuselage, and a lengthened, streamlined nose section replaced the conventional bomber nose. When completed, the seven B-17s had provisions to carry fourteen passengers and their baggage.

Five of the Fortresses remained in SAAB service, pioneering new routes for the airline. The other two B-17s, 42-32076 and B-17G-35-DL 42-107067, went to Danish Air Lines in November and December 1945. 42-32076 became OY-DFA in Danish service, and flew commercially until 31 March 1948 when the Royal Danish Army Air Corps took over and operated it with the serial of 67-672. It went to the Royal Danish Navy on 01 December 1949, and then the Royal Danish Air Force in October 1952. In Air Force service it was assigned to ESK-721 for a period, and was also used for transport, mapping, and communication duties with the three branches of the Danish military. It was withdrawn from use in October 1953 and placed in storage.

42-32076 was obtained by an American aircraft broker, the Babb Company of New York, on 02 February 1955. It was never issued an American registration and, indeed, it is doubtful the aircraft even moved from its Danish storage area. Three months later it was sold to the French Institut Geographique National (IGN), ferried by a Danish Air Force crew to Paris, and issued a French registration of F-BGSH.

The IGN operated a total of thirteen B-17s, acquired between 1947 and 1955, on world-wide photographic and geophysical survey missions. They still sponsor one flyable aircraft, B-17G-85-VE 44-8846 F-BGSP, and have sent another five of their number into museums for preservation.

F-BGSH was used by the IGN operationally until 15 July 1961 when it was retired from service at Creil, France. Soon it was engineless and stripped of useful equipment, and parked off in a corner of the airport to languish in the weeds. It suffered nose damage at one point, and it seemed but a short step to the scrapyard for the combat veteran.

Aviation author Steve Birdsall gains credit for saving the aircraft. While traipsing through France researching the fate of different aircraft he happened across the remains of "Shoo Shoo Shoo Baby". Aware of the combat heritage of the Fortress, he contacted the 91st Bomb Group Memorial Association to initiate official efforts to save the aircraft. The process came to fruition on 23 January 1972 when the French government donated the hulk to the USAF Museum.

During the following two weeks, Air Force crews from Rhein Main AFB in West Germany disassembled 42-32076 for transport overland to their air base and a planned flight to WrightPatterson AFB in Ohio for restoration.

The airframe was successfully moved to Germany. Loading operations onto a C-5A presented difficulties, however, as the B-17 center sections are too wide to be place vertically into the cargo hold of the giant aircraft. Not realizing the possibility the "Baby" might fly again, the wing section was sliced laterally to enable transport on the C-5. This would, naturally, have major ramifications in the later restoration process. Nonetheless, the parts were assembled into twenty-seven crates or shipping platforms, and loaded aboard the C-5. The flight to Ohio was accomplished on 04 February 1972.

Upon arrival, 42-32076 was placed into storage awaiting

facilities and funding to begin the restoration. The disassembled Fortress remained in this state until 1978 when the 512th Military Airlift Wing at Dover AFB, Delaware, agreed to take on the massive task. The parts were once again loaded onto a C-5 and transported to Delaware where the painstaking restoration soon began.

Considering the state of the received material, the resulting process of restoration was nothing short of a sweat-stained miracle. Beyond the in-itself difficult task of creating a complete aircraft out of parts disassembled years earlier half way around the world, the group also was intent on completing the B-17 with 100% original equipment. This necessitated removal of all of the many post-war modifications. Numerous windows had been cut into the fuselage. All vestiges of the original military interior were long gone, and other crew positions had long since been eliminated. Beyond restoration of the original interior, all types of military equipment had to be located, obtained, restored, and installed to reconstruct the many systems.

Early on, the decision was made to fly the "Baby" back to Wright-Patterson at the completion of the work. The laterally sliced wing center sections could not be reconstructed for flight which necessitated that a new components be located to make the aircraft airworthy. The center sections and engine nacelles out of a scrapped Fortress, 44-83542* N9324Z were obtained from Arizona and shipped to Dover. They were rebuilt and assembled into 42-32076 and reskinned outer wing panels were later attached. Hamilton-Standard overhauled the propellers and

prop governors, and four engines were donated by a private individual for overhaul and installation.

Much combat equipment had been donated through the years, and duplicated material enabled the group to trade around for needed items. Each flight-related system, such as the electrical and hydraulic systems, was assembled and tested for the eventual flight. Turrets went into the airframe as each original crew position was restored to its wartime condition.

As a result of the extensive sheet-metal work on the airframe, the Air Force Museum decided to camouflage the bomber, a concession of necessity. The late Tony Starcer, who did much of the artwork for the 91st Bomb Group during the war, volunteered to fly from his California home to Dover AFB to recreate his artwork on the nose of the restored bomber.

Project director Ray McCloskey, who worked consistently with a group of about six individuals over the span of nine years to complete the restoration, had anticipated that the Fortress would remain on display at Dover AFB for at least a year before it made its final flight to Wright-Patterson AFB and the Air Force Museum.

However, the Air Force Museum was eager to receive their prized Fortress and the schedule was moved up. The

Fresh from the Danish storage, here is 42-32076 in new French markings after arriving at Creil in 1955. The elongated nose and passenger windows, added by SAAB when it rebuilt the bomber, are seen to good advantage.
Air Force Museum via Bowers Collection

"Baby" returned to the air once again in August 1988, under the capable hand of Bill Hospers, owner of B-17G 44-8543* N3701G. A series of seven test flight were successful and the final ferry flight to Wright-Patterson AFB was scheduled for mid-October 1988.

Three short test hops were scheduled for 12 October, with Bill Hospers' son Robert at the controls, but they were delayed until the 13 October by crosswinds. Later that day, with a crowd of several hundred people looking on and representatives of the national media recording the event, Robert Hospers and copilot Quentin Smith took "Shoo Shoo Shoo Baby" off for its final flight to Wright-Patterson AFB. That event successfully culminated an international effort to return one of the few surviving combat veteran Fortresses to the Air Force Museum as a genuine representative of the air combat fought over Europe during World War II.

F-BGSH forlorn, rejected, and well on its way to the scrap heap while parked on the Creil airfield in the late sixties. Nose was damaged in a taxiing accident, while the engines were stripped for other IGN B-17s. MAP

F-BGSH on the IGN line at Creil in Septmeber 1964. Marson

Chapter Seven: 43-38635

Castle Air Museum
Castle AFB, California

■ ■ ■ ■ ■ ■

43-38635   B-17G-90-BO to TB-17G to EB-17G to ETB-17G to TB-17G to N3702G

USAAF/USAF

DATE	LOCATION	UNIT	CMD	REMARKS
29 AUG 44	SEATTLE		ATC	ACCEPTED
01 SEP 44	CHEYENNE		ATC	MOD CENTER
24 SEP 44	MINNEAPOLIS	1454 BASE UNIT	ATS	(?) STORAGE
30 MAR 47	CLINTON	4152 BASE UNIT	AMC	ALL WX CENTER
09 JUL 47	PATTERSON	4000 BASE UNIT	AMC	ALL WX CENTER
24 SEP 47	CLINTON	4152 BASE UNIT	AMC	ALL WX CENTER
(06 NOV 47)	(from: B-17G to: TB-17G)		— —	
24 NOV 47	PATTERSON	4000 BASE UNIT	AMC	ALL WX CENTER
14 JAN 48	CLINTON	4152 BASE UNIT	AMC	ALL WX CENTER
21 JAN 49	WRI-PAT	2750 BASE UNIT	AMC	ALL WX CENTER
02 FEB 49	GRIFFISS	2751 BASE GROUP	AMC	
(08 FEB 49)	(from: TB-17G to: EB-17G)		— —	
(13 APR 49)	(from: EB-17G to: ETB-17G)		— —	
13 APR 49)	GRIFFISS	3171 ELEC RESEARCH SQ	AMC	
11 JUL 51	GRIFFISS	530 BASE WING	ARD	
30 JUL 51	GRIFFISS	6531 LT SQ	ARD	
24 JUL 52	HANSCOM	6520 BASE WING	ARD	
20 AUG 52	HANSCOM	6520 TEST WING	ARD	
13 JUL 54	DAVIS-MONTHAN	3040 ACFT STOR SQ	AMC	
(56)	(from: ETB-17G to: TB-17G)		— —	
(AUG 58)	(reclamation authorized)		— —	

CIVIL

DATE	TRANSFER DETAILS
31 JUL 59	FR: CENTRAL AIRCRAFT DIVISION, ARIZONA AIRCRAFT STORAGE BRANCH, DAVIS-MONTHAN AFB TO: NATIONAL METALS COMPANY, PHOENIX, ARIZONA
14 NOV 59	TO: LOUIS KORDISH, LONG BEACH, CA
25 FEB 60	TO: C.J. FISCHER, CHATSWORTH, CA
21 SEP 60	TO: EDGAR NEELEY, (DBA FAST WAY AIR SERVICE), LONG BEACH, CA
25 APR 67	TO: TBM, INC., TULARE, CA
26 NOV 79	TO: USAF MUSEUM
(26 NOV 79)	(AICRAFT DELIVERED TO CASTLE AFB FROM CHICO, CA)
(18 APR 80)	(FAA registration cancelled)

43-38635

43-38635 is one of the few surviving Boeing-built Fortresses and served for a number of years in an electronics research capacity with the Air Force before conversion to an air tanker for use against forest fires. The aircraft now holds a place of honor at the Castle Air Force Base Museum near Merced, California.

This Fortress rolled from the Boeing production line in Seattle on 27 August 1944 and was accepted by the Army Air Force two days later. It was flown to the United Airlines modification center at Cheyenne, Wyoming, and was operationally available on 06 September 1944. It was then flown to Minneapolis via Patterson Field, Ohio, arriving on 24 September. There is some question about its use at Minneapolis, the aircraft record card indicating attachment to a Headquarters unit and placement in static reserve. In any event, the aircraft remained in the U.S. through the war, and was based at Minneapolis until 1947 when it was assigned

research role to be undertaken. The Fortress remained at the Center through 1949, based variously at Clinton and at the Headquarters of the Air Materiel Command, Wright-Patterson AFB.

On 02 February 1949, 43-38635 was assigned to the 2751st Base Group at Griffiss AFB in Rome, New York. It was redesignated as an EB-17G on 08 February, indicating assignment to a long-term test role, but was redesignated again on 13 April 1949, becoming an ETB-17G. On the same day, the B-17 was assigned to the 3171st Electronics Research Group at Griffiss, home of both the Rome Air Depot and the Rome Air Development Center. The Center was charged with the development of ground and airborne equipment and apparently the 3171st Electronics Research Group performed support roles for the Center. 43-38635 remained at Griffiss until 24 June 1952 when it was assigned to Hanscom AFB in Massachusetts and the 6520th Base Wing, which became the 6520th Test Wing on 20 August 1952. Presumably the Fortress performed similar electronic test

Freshly surplus 43-38635 at Long Beach in October 1959. Note the remnants of the All Weather Flying Center paint scheme. Peltzer

to the All Weather Flying Center based at Clinton County Army Airfield in Ohio.

The All Weather Flying Center was formed in September 1945 under the jurisdiction of the Air Technical Service Command based at Wright Field. It was established primarily to develop the means to operate aircraft under all conditions of weather and visibility. To achieve that goal, the All Weather Flying Division developed equipment, procedures, and techniques, many of which are still in use today. The Center was initially based at Clinton County Army Air Field but, with the closure of Clinton in November 1945, moved to Lockbourne Field, also in Ohio. Clinton was reopened the following year, however, and the Center moved back. By early 1947 the Center had a total of thirty five aircraft including one B-29, three B-17s, two B-25s, four A-26s, eight transports, and twelve fighter aircraft.

Among the B-17s assigned were 43-38635 and 44-8543*. 635 was redesignated as a TB-17G on 06 November 1947, there being no specific mission prefix available for the

work at Hanscom before it was placed in storage at Davis-Monthan AFB on 13 July 1954.

The Air Force authorized the disposal of 43-38635 in August 1958. It was sold by auction to National Metals Company of Phoenix, Arizona for $2,686, ownership transferring on 31 July 1959. It was issued the civil registration of N3702G. On 14 November of that year, National Metals sold the aircraft to Mr. Louis A. Kordish, of Long Beach, California. Three months later it again changed hands, being sold to Mr. C.J. Fisher of Chatsworth, California. Finally, on 21 September 1960, it was sold to Mr. Edgar Neeley, doing business as Fast Way Air Service at Long Beach Airport.

Fast Way converted the bomber to an air tanker by installing two 900 gallon tanks in the bomb-bay. N3702G was operated as Tanker 61 under contract to the Forest Service and the California Division of Forestry. It spent time based at Chino Airport in Southern California along with sister ship N3703G (44-83546*), also owned and operated by Fast Way.

On 25 April 1967, Fast Way sold both N3702G and N3703G to another tanker outfit, TBM Incorporated of Tulare, California. There was some difficulty proving title as TBM had to go back several owners to verify sales and clear up some paperwork discrepancies. Nonetheless, TBM would operate N3702G through the balance of its service life, Tanker 61 becoming a familiar sight throughout the western and southeastern U.S. in the annual battle against forest and range fires. By mid 1973, the airframe had amassed over 4200 hours of flight time, or roughly 1000 hours of use since it was bought surplus from the government. N3702G soldiered on until 1978 as many of the tired B-17 tankers became the subject of trades and sales in favor of fresher equipment.

N3702G went the Air Force Museum in an extensive three-way trade between TBM, the Museum, and Aero Union, a tanker outfit based at Chico, California. TBM traded their Fortress to Aero Union in exchange for two complete C-54 retardant systems. Aero Union, in turn, traded the Fortress to the Air Force Museum in exchange for a surplus C-54G, Air Force serial 45-556, parked at Davis-Monthan AFB. The Air Force Museum delegated the Fortress to the then-forming Castle Air Force Base Museum as the cornerstone for their developing static display.

TBM delivered N3702G to Aero Union at Chico. TBM had already stripped the retardant tanks and paint from the airframe, reinstalling the bomb-bay doors. Workers at Aero Union got busy and painted the old tanker in the colors of the 94th Bomb Group as commanded by General Frederick Castle, namesake of Castle AFB. An Air Force crew ferried the plane down to Castle, the bomber arriving on schedule through the hazy Central California skies on the afternoon of 26 November 1979.

Museum workers later reinstalled a full complement of gun turrets before placing 43-38635 in the anchor position on the museum display area. The lovingly polished bomber's future is assured, for its familiar form represents the heritage of the USAF as no other aircraft can.

One half of TBM Inc.'s B-17 tanker fleet at Chino Airport in 1970. Nine years later N3702G was traded to Aero Union for some C-54 tanker equipment. Matthews via Besecker

N3702G shortly before its transfer to the Air Force Museum at Chico in September 1979. J. Babcock via Gougon

Chapter Eight: 44-6393

March Field Museum
March AFB, California

■■■■■■

44-6393   B-17G-50-DL to CB-17G to VB-17G to CB-17G to VB-17G to CP-627 to CP-891

USAAC/USAAF

DATE	LOCATION	UNIT	CMD	REMARKS
22 JUL 44	LONG BEACH		ATC	ACCEPTED
27 JUL 44	KEARNEY		ATC	
08 AUG 44	GRENIER		ATC	
(08 AUG 44)	(departed U.S. to 15th AF, MTO)		– –	
10 MAY 45	BOLLING	1 BASE UNIT	CAF	
09 SEP 45	PATTERSON	4100 BASE UNIT	ATS	
(09 SEP 45)	(fr: B-17G to: CB-17G)		– –	
05 DEC 45	BOLLING	1 BASE UNIT	CAF	
05 MAR 46	OLMSTED	4112 BASE UNIT	ATS	
(various)	BOLLING	16 MAINT SUP GP	HQC	
		35 BASE UNIT	HQC	
15 SEP 48	CLARK	18 MAINT SUP GP	FEA	
25 OCT 48	NANKING	1134 SPEC ACT GP	HQC	
(14 FEB 49)	(fr: CB-17G to: VB-17G)		– –	
(variously assigned between CLARK AFB and NANKING)				
21 SEP 49	OLMSTED	MIDDLETOWN AIR DEPOT	AMC	
(22 SEP 49)	(fr: VB-17G to: CB-17G)		– –	
02 NOV 49	OTTAWA	1130 SPEC ACT GP	HQC	
(14 APR 50)	(fr: CB-17G to: VB-17G)		– –	
02 NOV 53	RANDOLPH	3510 FLT TRNG WG	ATC	
56	DAVIS-MONTHAN	3040 ACFT STRG SQ	AMC	
(JUN 56)	(dropped from USAF inventory)		– –	

CIVIL/POST USAF USE

DATE	TRANSFER DETAILS
JUN 56	TRANSFERRED FROM CAA, (USA) TO GOVERNMENT OF BOLIVIA AS ONE OF EIGHT AIRCRAFT
65?	REBUILT AND RE-REGISTERED AS CP-891
JAN 81	OBTAINED BY USAF MUSEUM FOR DISPLAY AT MARCH AFB

44-6393

March AFB, located in Riverside, California, is home of the 15th Air Force. Appropriately enough, the March Field Museum has a B-17 which may have been attached to the 15th Air Force in the Mediterranean Theatre during World War II. There's some question as to the actual identity of the aircraft on display, as all data plates were long ago removed during operations in South America, and the airframe is apparently a compilation of several damaged B-17s. Nonetheless, the aircraft file and Bolivian registration records would indicate that the Fortress at March is B-17G-50-DL 44-6393.

Presuming that the aircraft is 44-6393, then it is one of three Fortresses currently in the U.S. which may have seen combat during World War II. 44-6393 also enjoyed a full postwar usage as a staff transport with the USAF. The March AFB Fortress completed its operational life as a South American meat hauler. This B-17 was returned to the U.S. in 1980 by the U.S. Air Force Museum which made it available to the March Field Museum, then in the process of being established.

Accepted on 22 July 1944, the Douglas-built Fortress was flown to Kearney Field, Nebraska, and then to Grenier Field, New Hampshire, for preparation for a trans-Atlantic ferry flight. 44-6393 departed on 09 August 1944 for assignment with the 15th Air Force in Italy. Its unit assignment and/or combat record has not been established.

44-6393 was returned to the U.S. on 10 May 1945 and assigned to the 1st Base Unit with the Continental Air Force at Bolling Field in Washington D.C. The 1st Base Unit was assigned administrative support missions and 44-6393 was redesignated a CB-17G on 19 July 1945. Through the remainder of 1945 and continuing through 1947 the aircraft was variously assigned to the 1st Base Unit and the 35th Base Air Depot, both at Bolling, and the 4112th Base Unit at Olmsted Field, Pennsylvania. While at Bolling Field it was assigned to Lt. General Ira Eaker, then deputy commander of the Army Air Force, and carried the name "Starduster" on its nose.

On 10 March 1948 it was reassigned to the 16th Maintenance and Supply Group with Headquarters Command at Bolling. On 15 September 1948 the CB-17G was dispatched to the Far East Air Forces at Clark AFB and the 18th Maintenance and Supply Group. While deployed to the Far East it was redesignated a VB-17G on 29 December 1948 and saw assignment to the 1134th Special Activities Group, Headquarters Command in Nanking, China. 44-6393 remained based at Nanking, the capital of the Republic of China, until Communist forces took the city in April 1949 and the aircraft was withdrawn to Clark AFB.

Its Far East deployment ended on 21 September 1949 when it was returned to Olmsted AFB and downgraded to a CB-17G. 44-6393 remained with the Headquarters Command however, assigned to the 1130th Special Activities Group and diplomatic duty at the American Embassy in Ottawa, Canada on 02 November 1949.

On 14 April 1950 44-6393 once again became a VB-17G while in Ottawa, where it would remain through late 1953 when attached to the 3510th Flight Training Wing at Randolph AFB in Texas. 44-6393 would stay at Randolph as a

Operating as a CB-17G, 44-6393 was based at Bolling Field in Washington D.C. beginning in 1945. Here it is shown as assigned to General Ira Eaker, deputy commander of the Army Air Force, and carrying the name "Starduster." Note the flag above the cockpit. NASM

VB-17G through the balance of its USAF service. It was retired to Davis-Monthan AFB in early 1956 and dropped from the USAF inventory.

In June 1956 it and seven other B-17s were transferred to the government of Bolivia through the offices of the U.S. Civil Aeronautics Administration. The selected aircraft were ferried from storage at Davis-Monthan to nearby Tucson Municipal Airport where Hamilton Aircraft performed required maintenance. 44-6393 received two new engines and had some control surfaces recovered. They were ferried to Bolivia and received registrations between CP-620 and CP-627, with 44-6393 receiving CP-627. CP-627 eventually was operated by Lloyd Aereo Boliviano (LAB), the government airline, performing cargo operations on the rugged Bolivian routes into various Andean destinations and was one of 26 B-17s employed in Bolivian service.

Eventually, extensive modifications were performed to better adapt the Fortress to its mission. The interior was stripped and a large cargo door in the left waist position was installed. The Cheyenne tail gun position was carefully faired over and the cockpit area was rearranged with the installation of custom radio racks incorporated into the pilot's seat frames. The nose compartment was reworked, eliminating the windows and blown nose piece, which was replaced with a solid, hinged, access door.

CP-627 apparently suffered an accident sometime during the mid-sixties, not surprising in that at least seventeen of the 26 B-17s operated in Bolivia were destroyed in crashes. CP-627 was rebuilt with the remains of another Bolivian Fortress, CP-580 (B-17G-85-BO 43-38322) which had been damaged in an accident in 1965. Using the two airframes, a complete Fortress was built up and re-registered as CP-891.

CP-891 was retired by LAB in the late sixties and eventually was operated by Frigorificos Reyes to haul Bolivian beef from remote ranches in eastern Bolivia to La Paz. The animals were slaughtered at the ranches and dressed for transport. The beef was thrown into the cargo holds on CP-891 and flown off. (The stench and blood was still quite evident several years later after the Fortress had returned to the U.S.) CP-891 was one of the last B-17s operated in Bolivia.

In 1980 the USAF negotiated an agreement sending a C-118 (military version of the Douglas DC-6) to Bolivia in exchange for 44-6393. By that time, aircraft records indicated in excess of 13,000 logged flight hours.

A Bolivian crew ferried the B-17 north to Nogales, Arizona, arriving on 17 December 1980. The last leg to March AFB was completed on 10 January 1981.

The March Field Museum staff set out to reconfigure and repaint the bomber to approximate a combat example. The extensive modifications to the airframe precluded a complete external restoration. Initially, work crews tried to strip the multiple layers of paint, eventually resorting to sandblasting to complete the difficult job. The solid nose piece was removed and replaced with a blown glass nose, afterwhich volunteer Air Force paint crews then painted the B-17 in an olive drab 15th Air Force paint scheme. (At that time, there were no indications to the museum staff that the aircraft had actually been assigned to the 15th Air Force during World War II.) Final markings were applied as "2nd Patches," an actual 99th Bomb Group B-17G-80-BO. The serial number, inexplicably, was neither applied as 42-38201 (the original "2nd Patches") nor as 44-6393, as the Air Force Museum suggests that all aircraft under their jurisdiction carry correct serial numbers. Instead, the March Field aircraft was marked as B-17F-105-BO 42-30092. "2nd Patches" then took its place in the museum's display area.

In the years since arriving at March AFB a complete complement of power turrets shells or fiberglass replicas have been installed on the airframe. Unfortunately, the aircraft's general condition has otherwise deteriorated. The fabric covering on control surfaces is rotting and the airframe shows signs of neglect. Also, the lack of flexible gun positions and other windows detract from its appearance.

Obviously, efforts to restore the Fortress to its exact wartime configuration by the reinstallation of nose windows, waist positions, and tail guns would be prohibitively expensive for the limited resources of the museum. Plans in the works include the installation of a fiberglass replica of a standard tail gunner's compartment, and additional restorative work may eventually be performed. In the meantime, however, it would be appropriate for the museum to at least refinish 44-6393 in the markings as actually carried while it was attached to the 15th Air Force, including the application of a correct serial number.

44-6393 while attached to the U.S. Embassy at Ottawa, Canada in 1949. As a VB-17G, aircraft carries pre-war tail stripes in one of the few post-war attempts to bring the markings back. W. Balough via Menard

CP-891 shortly after arrival at March in 1981. Airframe eventually was sandblasted to remove the numerous coats of paint. Schultz

CHAPTER NINE: 44-8543

B.C. VINTAGE FLYING MACHINES
FORT WORTH, TEXAS

■■■■■■

44-8543 B-17G-70-VE to TB-17G to ETB-17G to JTB-17G to N3701G

USAAF/USAF

DATE	LOCATION	UNIT	CMD	REMARKS
17 OCT 44	BURBANK		ATC	ACCEPTED
(THRU 45)	(DATA MISSING)		– –	
(45)	(fr: B-17G to: TB-17G)		– –	
SEP 45	PATTERSON	4000 BASE UNIT	ATS	
30 NOV 46	MINNEAPOLIS		AMC	
29 MAR 48	WRIGHT-PAT	4000 BASE UNIT	AMC	
07 JUN 48	CLINTON	4152 BASE UNIT	AMC	ALL-WX CENTER
16 MAR 49	CLINTON	2760 BASE GROUP	AMC	ALL-WX CENTER
(16 MAR 49)	(fr: TB-17G to: ETB-17G)			
06 JUN 49	WRIGHT-PAT	2750 BASE WING	AMC	
17 APR 51	WRIGHT-PAT	2750 BASE WING	ARD	
11 NOV 52	WESTCHESTER	FTC*	ARD	BAILMENT
(56)	(fr: ETB-17G to: JTB-17G)		– –	
MAY 57	TETERBORO	FTC*	ARD	BAILMENT
MAR 59	DAVIS-MONTHAN		AMC	STORAGE
(MAY 59)	(reclamation authorized)		AMC	

(*Federal Telecommunications Corporation)

CIVIL

DATE	TRANSFER DETAILS
18 AUG 59	FR: 2704TH AIRCRAFT STORAGE AND DISPOSITION GROUP DAVIS-MONTHAN AFB TO: AMERICAN COMPRESSED STEEL CORP., CINCINATTI, OH
09 MAY 60	TO: AERO-AMERICAN CORP., CINCINATTI, OH
06 FEB 61	TO: ALBANY BUILDING CORP., FT. LAUDERDALE, FL
15 MAY 62	TO: JOHN B. GREGORY, FT. LAUDERDALE, FL
07 MAR 63	TO: DOTHAN LEASING AND RENTAL COMPANY, DOTHAN, AL
20 JAN 70	TO: DOTHAN AVIATION CORP., WHEELLESS AIRPORT, AL
04 OCT 79	TO: W.D. HOSPERS, FT. WORTH, TX
18 SEP 82	TO: B.C. VINTAGE FLYING MACHINES, N. RICHLAND HILLS, TX

44-8543

44-8543 has had a varied history. Though early military records are not available for the aircraft, it is possible the Fortress was used in combat during the last few months of the war. It was employed in two successful post-war test programs before coming to the civil market. As N3701G, the B-17 was utilized to transport fruit in Florida and then as a fire ant sprayer in Alabama. 44-8543 was eventually bought by Dr. William Hospers of Fort Worth, Texas, where today he and a core group of volunteers perform a running restoration on the B-17.

44-8543 was accepted for military use at Burbank on 17 October 1944. Due to the absence of early military records, its utilization between October 1944 and September 1945 has not been verified. Most of the Vega-built aircraft built in October 1944 went to Cheyenne, Wyoming, for modification, and it is possible that 44-8543 was similarly handled. Some sources have the B-17 assigned to the 486th Bomb Group in England, though details of combat assignments or missions flown are not available. It would not be inconsistent with aircraft from the -70 block of Vega built B-17s to see combat, as many of those Fortresses went to the 8th and 15th Air Forces in Europe for combat operations against the Third Reich. Also, there appear to be evidence of repaired combat damage on the skin of the belly of the bomber today. The source of that damage has yet to be confirmed.

The available military records on 44-8543 pick up in September 1945 where, as a TB-17G, the aircraft was assigned to base units at Patterson Field, Ohio with the Air Technical Services Command, which became the Air Materiel Command in 1946. It is probable that 44-8543 was assigned at an early date to the All Weather Flying Center, which was established under the Air Technical Service Command in September 1945 with units based at Clinton County Army Air Field, Ohio, and headquartered at Patterson Field. Clinton was closed in November 1945, and operational units of the All Weather Flying Center were moved to Lockbourne Field, also in Ohio. Lockbourne soon became too crowded and three months later the Center moved back to the reopened Clinton County Field, where it remained until February 1952.

44-8543 was based at Patterson until 30 November 1946 when assigned to Minneapolis, remaining with the Air Materiel Command. Its use at Minneapolis has not been determined, but it remained there until 07 June 1948 when it was back with the All Weather Flying Center at Clinton Field.

The Fortress was redesignated as an ETB-17G on 16 March 1949, suggesting assignment to a long-term test program and making it exempt from compliance with certain technical orders. Whether 44-8543 was assigned to a special program within the All Weather Flying Center or possibly loaned on a bailment contract to another user is not known.

Still as a ETB-17G, 44-8543 was assigned to the 2750th Base Wing at Wright-Patterson AFB and placed in the newly established Wright Air Development Center on 22 June 1951. The WADC was part of the new Air Research and Development Command and operationally assumed command of the All Weather Flying Center, which emerged from the reorganization as the Flight and All-Weather Test Division of the WADC.

44-8543 was at Wright-Patterson until 09 November 1952 when it became part of another test program under the auspices of the Air Materiel Command. In this program it was bailed under contract to the Federal Telecommunications Corporation and based at Westchester Airport, New York. Serving in a research role, 44-8543 was fitted with large wing-tip antennas and other electronic equipment. With the reassignment of the "E" prefix to an early warning radar role in 1956, the aircraft was redesignated as a JTB-17G, indicating the aircraft was in a temporary test role. It was based at Westchester until 1957 when moved to Teterboro Airport in New Jersey.

The Fortress remained with the FTC through the balance of its military utilization, and was flown from Teterboro to Davis-Monthan for retirement in March 1959. It was placed in storage and then made available for sale in May 1959.

44-8543 was purchased through sealed bid by the American Compressed Steel Corporation of Cincinnati, Ohio, for $5,026 on 18 August 1959. One of three Fortresses purchased by American Compressed Steel on that date, 44-8543 was issued the civil registration of N3701G. It, and the other two American Compressed Steel Fortresses (44-83563* and 44-83439), remained at Davis-Monthan for nearly a year. American Compressed Steel became the Aero-American Corporation in early-1960 and ownership of the aircraft changed.

A subsidiary organization called Aero-Associates, run by Aero-American executive vice-president Greg Board from Tucson's Ryan Field, sent a crew of mechanics to nearby Davis-Monthan in mid-1960 to prepare the three Fortresses for a ferry flight to Ryan. Greg Board moved all three B-17s that summer. His intent, and the business of Aero-America, was to find new civil owners for the airplanes.

All three B-17s remained parked at Ryan for another five months, when Board decided they would have more appeal on the civil market with cargo doors installed. Thus, he ferried the three from Ryan to Brownsville, Texas, where Intercontinental Engine Service installed the doors in the right waist position of all three aircraft. Board then returned them to Ryan Field.

On 06 February 1961, N3701G was purchased by the Albany Building Corporation of Fort Lauderdale, Florida. Some sources indicate it was purchased on speculation by

44-8543 while on loan to the Federal Telecommunications Commision in 1958. While with the FTC its initial designation was as an ETB-17G. After 1956 the B-17 was redesignated as a JTB-17G. Bowers Collection

44-8543 was assigned to the All-Weather Flying Center in 1946. Paint scheme included red nose and tail with yellow trim. Photo taken at Patterson Field in June 1946. Bowers

a ex-airline captain and that N3701G was put to work hauling vegetables from Andros Island, off the coast of Florida, to Fort Lauderdale. Hoppers were set up to load cucumbers and other produce through the radio compartment hatch and the now-handy cargo door. The B-17 would then dash to Fort Lauderdale for unloading, making several round trips a day.

On 15 May 1962 the B-17 was sold to John Gregory, also of Fort Lauderdale. Whether the ownership change was a paperwork shuffle or if the new owner employed it for other purposes is not known.

On 07 March 1963 N3701G was bought by Hugh Wheelless, who ran Dothan Aviation from Wheelless Airport near Dothan, Alabama. Wheelless added spray tanks and bars to the B-17 and operated it on contract the U.S. Department of Agricture and the states of Florida and Georgia in their continual battles against fire ants. Wheelless utilized several B-17s, including N5017N (44-85740*) and N4710C (44-85812) to spray the pesticide Mirex in the low

level attacks against the insects.

With new environmental awareness and other considerations prevailing, the spray attacks ended in 1976. The two surviving Fortresses at Dothan, N3701G and N5017N, began a slow, down-hill slide in disuse. Wheelless broke up his company in 1980, but 44-8543 was sold to Dr. William Hospers of Fort Worth, Texas on 04 October 1979.

Hospers had long wanted a Fortress. He began laying the groundwork for owning such an aircraft long before one came available for purchase. He long admired the B-17 but took a giant leap from admiration to ownership when he grabbed N3701G. Hospers found the old fire ant sprayer in reasonable condition at Dothan, but far from the restored, authentic bomber he wanted. Thus, over the past years he and a group of tireless volunteers have slowly de-civilianized 44-8543 and are bringing it closer to a combat configuration.

One of the few individually owned and operated B-17s, 44-8543 now wears the colors of the bomb group for which it may have actually flown during World War II: the 486th Bomb Group. Though N3701G was registered in Hospers' name originally, it is now officially owned by B.C. Vintage Flying Machines of Fort Worth. The "B.C." is Bill and Chuckie Hospers, who pay the bills and direct the operation of the old Fortress. The B-17 is now dubbed "Chuckie," and its crew, which includes their son Bob Hospers, treat their work on the B-17 as a labor of love, painstakingly rebuilding, polishing, and caressing the bomber back to original condition. Hospers estimates his hourly operating cost at $2000 which does not take into consideration the maintenance and restoration work which is performed when the bomber isn't flying. A dorsal turret shell has been installed back into the fuselage, though the interior mechanism is lacking. The Cheyenne tail gun unit has now been completely restored and reinstalled. The general condition of the Fortress is outstanding, and the aircraft is babied to the point that the original engines that came with the Fortress continue to pass all inspections and have yet to be overhauled. N3701G burns on average 200 gallons of fuel an hour with an additional 8 gallons of oil for the engines.

Chuckie Hospers was instrumental in organizing what has become known as the "B-17 Co-op" which has brought together the owners of most of the surviving B-17s and pooled resources in the search of parts. Contracts have been let with plexiglass manufacturers for orders of new blown noses. Hard to find items such as tires are being ordered in limited numbers for all those in need at one time to keep the costs down. Parts are traded back and forth in a spirit of cooperation to keep flyable aircraft airworthy.

44-8543 is based at Meacham Airport in Fort Worth and makes it to a large number of airshows each year. It is currently flying about fifty hours each year and in its original combat garb looks very much as lethal as it may have been nearly forty-five years ago.

N3701G shortly after purchase by Dothan Aviation in 1963. Spray bars installed under the wings were for spraying Mirex pesticide on fire ants. Peltzer Collection

44-8543 before turrets were reinstalled into the airframe. Krieger

44-83512	B-17G-85-DL to TB-17G			

USAAF/USAF

DATE	LOCATION	UNIT	CMD	REMARKS
23 MAR 45	LONG BEACH		ATC	ACCEPTED
25 MAR 45	TULSA	MODIFICATION CENTER	ATC	
18 MAY 45	PATTERSON		ATC	STORAGE
(19 JAN	(fr: B-17G to: TB-17G)		– –	
19 JAN 46	MCCHORD	53 RECON SQ	CAF	
30 MAY 46	MORRISON	53 RECON SQ	ATC	
08 JUN 47	KINDLEY	53 RECON SQ	ATC	
02 FEB 47	ROBINS	67 BASE UNIT	ATC	
12 DEC 47	ROBINS	4117 BASE UNIT	ATC	
09 JUL 48	PEPPERRELL	533 BASE UNIT	MTO	
01 OCT 48	PEPPERRELL	1225 BASE UNIT	MTO	
06 JUN 50	HILL	OGDEN AIR DEPOT	AMC	
11 SEP 50	LACKLAND	3700 IND WG	ATC	
(26 SEP 50)	(reclamation authorized)		– –	

44-83512

44-83512 entered short term storage shortly after being built, and emerged in 1946 to be attached to weather reconnaissance squadrons as a TB-17. It was initially based at McChord Field in Washington, and also spent time at Kindley Field in the Bermudas. After returning to the U.S. it served in a number of base units before being assigned to the Training Command and sent to Lackland AFB in Texas. It was authorized for disposal at Lackland and eventually became part of the Air Force History and Traditions Museum, which was the second officially sanctioned museum in the Air Force before the days of the USAF Museum Program. It has been suggested that this Fortress on display at Lackland had an actual combat record with the Eighth Air Force. As can be seen, the aircraft was not even built until hostilities in Europe had nearly ended, and did not emerge from the modification center at Tulsa, Oklahoma for an additional seven weeks.

44-83512 rolled from the Long Beach production lines of the Douglas Aircraft Company on 21 March 1945, and was accepted for service two days later. It was flown to the Douglas modification Center in Tulsa, Oklahoma, via Palm Springs and arrived on 25 March. It remained at Tulsa until 18 May and was flown from there to be placed in short-term storage at Patterson Field, Ohio.

44-83512 remained in storage until early 1946 when pulled for assignment to the Continental Air Force at McChord Field, Washington. Redesignated as a TB-17G, it was assigned to the 53rd Reconnaissance Squadron, which provided weather reconnaissance for the Army Air Force from McChord Field, and also from detachments at Grenier Field, New Hampshire, and Gander Lake, Newfoundland. 44-83512 remained with the unit but moved to Morrison Field, Florida, on 29 August 1946. On 08 June 1947 the Fortress was deployed to Kindley Field on Bermuda with the 53rd Reconnaissance Squadron, continuing to serve in a weather reconnaissance role.

By 09 November 1947 44-83512 had returned to the U.S. for assignment to the 67th Base Unit at Robins AFB, Georgia. It remained at Robins with that unit and, later, the 4117th Base Unit.

From Robins the TB-17G was attached to the Military Air Transport Service and based at Pepperrell Air Base near St.

Johns, Newfoundland. It was assigned to various units including the 533rd Base Unit and the 1225th Base Unit. Details of assignments with MATS are not known.

On 21 August 1950 44-83512 was reassigned to the Training Command and sent to Lackland AFB in San Antonio, Texas. Purpose for this assignment is unknown, as Lackland does not have any established facilities to handle aircraft; instead, it churned out officers and airmen destined for flight and technical schools at other air bases. However, several possibilities can be suggested. 44-83512 was assigned to the 3700th Independent Wing. It is possible that the aircraft was to be used as an instructional aid of some sort. Another possibility is that someone foresaw the development of a museum at Lackland and was slowly gathering aircraft. In any event, the Fortress was assigned to the base on 11 September 1950, and authorization for reclamation was given two weeks later. The B-17 was subsequently stricken from the Air Force inventory.

The Air Force History and Traditions Museum was established at Lackland AFB in 1956 as only the second officially sanctioned Air Force museum (behind the USAF Museum at Wright-Patterson AFB in Ohio). The collection has grown to include a variety of aircraft ranging from a P-47 Thunderbolt, a rare F-82 Twin Mustang, and a B-24 Liberator. 44-83512 officially went to the museum in 1957, and has been on display ever since.

44-83512 was eventually marked as a combat veteran, but still carried its correct serial number on its vertical stabilizer at Air Force insistence. It initially became "Princess Pat" and was representative of the 381st Bomb Group as it operated with the 1st Combat Wing in wartime England. It has been suggested in a few published sources that from the markings and stated history of the display aircraft that it actually saw combat during the war, which obviously is not correct.

In 1983 the aircraft was repainted as "Heaven Above" with appropriate nose art and other combat markings of the 388th Bomb Group of the 45th Combat Wing, Eighth Air Force. This B-17, in contrast to those at other Heritage Museums, has not had turrets or other combat equipment reinstalled. It also suffers from painted over windows, including the blown nose piece. In addition, years spent in the humid climate of southern Texas has created numerous corrosion problems which the museum staff plans to correct prior to performing any cosmetic return to a combat appearance. As one of the first Fortresses to be preserved on an Air Force base it has survived in reasonable condition and continues to suitably demonstrate the history and traditions of the Air Force to those who pass through Lackland AFB.

44-83512 at Lackland in August 1957. B-17 was painted with aluminized paint and placed on small stands. Stevens via Besecker

The ex TB-17G on display at Lackland in 1958. Tail insignia is unknown.
Dorr via Besecker

Latest markings carried by the B-17 as "Heaven's Above" of the 388th Bomb Group. Note the painted over windows and lack of turrets.
MAP

Chapter Eleven: 44-83514

ARIZONA WING-CONFEDERATE AIR FORCE
MESA, ARIZONA

■■■■■■

44-83514   B-17G-85-DL to DB-17G to DB-17P to N9323Z

USAAF/USAF

DATE	LOCATION	UNIT	CMD	REMARKS
24 MAR 45	LONG BEACH		ATC	ACCEPTED
MAR 45	?TULSA	MODIFICATION CENTER	ATC	
?MAY 45	?PATTERSON		ATC	STORAGE
(?MAY 45)	(?departed U.S.)		– –	
47	TACHIKAWA	13 ACFT REPAIR SQ	FEA	STORAGE
(?47)	(fr: B-17G to: RB-17G)		– –	
47	CLARK	38 RECON SQ	FEA	
MAR 49	TRAVIS	38 RECON SQ	– –	
MAY 50	OLMSTED	MIDDLETOWN AIR DEPOT	AMC	
(50)	(fr: RB-17G to: DB-17G)		– –	
50	EGLIN	3205 DRONE GP	APG	
(NOV 56)	(fr: DG-17G to: DB-17P)		– –	
56	PATRICK	3205 DRONE GP	APG	
DEC 57	PATRICK		APG	
DEC 58	EGLIN		APG	
JAN 59	DAVIS-MONTHAN		AMC	STORAGE
(MAY 59)	reclamation authorized)		– –	

CIVIL

DATE	TRANSFER DETAILS
31 JUL 59	FR: ARIZONA AIRCRAFT STORAGE BRANCH, USAF TO: ACME AIRCRAFT PARTS, INC., COMPTON, CA
17 NOV 60	TO: WESTERN AIR INDUSTRIES, ANDERSON, CA
06 JUN 62	TO: AERO UNION, ANDERSON, CA
17 JAN 78	TO: CONFEDERATE AIR FORCE, PHOENIX, AZ

44-83514

44-83514 is among the most authentically restored Fortresses flying. Obtained from an air tanker outfit, the fledgling Arizona Wing of the Confederate Air Force has poured tens of thousands of dollars and countless hours of labor to bring the B-17 back to the state it existed in when it rolled from the production line in 1945. Despite a recent mishap,

meticulous maintenance and tender loving care would seem to assure that this Fortress has years of flying yet before it.

The early operational history of 44-83514 is obscure. A portion of the aircraft's military records are missing and only a few hints of assignments have come to light through the years. What is known is that 44-83514 rolled from the Long Beach production line of Douglas on or about 24 March 1945. The aircraft may have been flown to the Douglas modification center at Tulsa shortly thereafter, though this has not been confirmed. It is quite likely that the aircraft was then sent into short term storage, probably at Patterson Field, Ohio, as were many other of the Douglas-built Fortresses in the same production block. Sketchy information available has the aircraft assigned in storage at Tachikawa AFB in Japan beginning about 1947. The Fortress may have been attached to the 5th Reconnaissance Group at Clark Field between 1948 and 1949 as an RB-17G.

The B-17 may have been sent from the Far East for operations at Travis AFB near San Francisco beginning in March 1949, and then sent through modification shops at Olmsted AFB, Pennsylvania for conversion to a DB-17G configuration. Subsequent assignment was probably to the 3250th Drone Group at Eglin AFB, Florida. The available military records pick up in 1956.

In 1956 44-83514 was modified to become a DB-17P at Olmsted AFB and attached to 3215th Drone Squadron at the Air Force Missile Test Center at Patrick AFB. 44-83514 remained at Patrick with that unit through the balance of it operational service, with the exception of two overhauls conducted at Robins Air Depot in 1957 and at the Oklahoma Air Depot, Tinker AFB, in mid-1958. The aircraft rotated back through Eglin briefly in late 1958 before retirement to Davis-Monthan AFB in mid-1959.

44-83514 remained in storage for only a few months. It was sold by auction to Acme Aircraft Parts of Compton, California, for $5289.99 on 31 July 1959. It received the civil registration of N9323Z at that time. Acme in turn sold it to Western Air Industries of Anderson, California for $8,000.00 on 17 November 1960. Both N9323Z and N9324Z (44-83542*) were sold to Western Air that day, destined to become air tankers.

Both Fortresses were ferried to Anderson for conversion. N9323Z was the first to be modified with the installation of two 1000 gallon retardant tanks in the bomb bay. At the time the conversion work was undertaken records indicate the aircraft had amassed 3309 hours of flight time. The Fortress became Tanker 17 and began a long and productive career.

Western Air Industries became Aero Union in 1962, and moved to Chico, California a short time later. Aero Union came to be one of the largest Fortress operators through the sixties and seventies, operating as many as six of the big Boeings along with a number of other veterans such as TBM Avengers and AF-2 Guardians. All the Aero Union Fortresses eventually had their Plexiglas nose pieces replaced by molded fiberglass nose cones, adding a distinctive look to the Forts and eliminating the need to locate a difficult to obtain part. N9323Z was fitted with the fiberglass nose in January 1965, at which point the aircraft log book stood at nearly 3900 hours.

N9323Z plodded along for another twelve years in the service of Aero Union, becoming their longest, continually

owned Fortress of the fleet. However, by 1977 critical part shortages and a reluctance on the part of various Forestry agencies to continue to utilize the old tankers led Aero Union to begin disposing their Fortress fleet. N9323Z was the second to be sold, behind N3509G (44-85778*). Knowing that Aero Union was looking for a buyer, tanker buffs Jim and Lora Babcock of Chico, California, convinced Aero Union management to bankroll an exhibition trip in N9323Z to Airsho77, the annual Confederate Air Force extravaganza which occurs every October in Harlingen, Texas. The pair almost single-handedly prepared the aircraft for the flight, removing the two retardant tanks and reinstalling bomb-bay doors dragged from behind some hangar. A discarded Plexiglas nose was located and installed, and a quasi-military paint scheme over the bright red tanker markings followed. Unit codes of the 95th Bomb Group were applied. 44-83514 regained its original military serial on the tail, and the name "Class of 44" on the nose. An assembled crew numbering in excess of a fourteen brought the plane to Harlingen in time for the air show. There, it joined "Texas Raiders" (44-83872*) for the weekend as the Confederate Air Force recreated World War II for the crowds. No apparent buyers appeared for N9323Z, so the crew brought the plane home to Chico. Several weeks later, however, a group of warbird enthusiasts, which had gestated into the Arizona Wing of the Confederate Air Force, purchased N9323Z. At the time of sale the Fortress had over 5,950 hours of flight time. N9323Z was brought to Falcon Field near Mesa, Arizona which, ironically, was also the home of the other large Fortress tanker operator, Aircraft Specialties. At Falcon, plans were initiated which would bring their new acquisition from a civilianized tanker back up to a nearly 100 percent authentic off-the-line B-17 Flying Fortress. N9323Z carried the 95th Bomb Group markings for several months after the purchase, but eventually the paint was stripped from the Fortress save the Aero Union applied belly paint aft of the bomb bay applied as protection from corrosive retardant chemicals. New markings as carried by the 457th Bomb Group Fortresses during World War II were applied. Nose art was, appropriately, a re-creation of the famous Betty Grable pinup. A state-wide contest to select a name for the Fortress had been held shortly after the aircraft was purchased, and "Sentimental Journey" won as befitting its new role.

A never-ending search for parts and combat equipment was begun, and soon a chin and ball turret had been located. Interior equipment was slowly obtained, restored, and installed in their original location. The airplane did not completely regains its external appearance, however, until a top turret was finally located and obtained from Art Lacey's 44-85790* in Oregon. All three turrets actually work, an oddity in this day of replica turrets installed on restored bombers. All crewman locations are now restored, down to the K-6 mounts for the waist guns.

N9323Z made a motion picture appearance in 1978, acting as set dressing at its birthplace—Long Beach Airport. It and a number of World War II-era aircraft, including several T-6s and a P-40, were used during the filming of "1941". No operational scenes were filmed with the Fortress, but its natural aluminum tail with the blue slash distinctively show up in the resulting scenes from the movie.

N9323Z began making annual pilgrimages to as many airshows as the Wing could afford. The Fortress has in excess of 7000 hours, and the CAF anticipates about 150 hours of flying per year for the foreseeable future. Maintenance and insurance costs are exorbitant, with engine overhauls costing over $24,000 per engine. Main tires are costing $1000 each. Costs are offset by fund-raising and some operational expenses are picked up by the air shows.

The effort suffered a severe setback in November 1988 when N9323Z skidded off the runway at Burbank, Califor-

nia while arriving for an airshow. The brakes had failed and the B-17 ran over a fence and a garbage dumpster beyond the overrun area at the end of the runway. The resultant damage was centered on the forward fuselage below the nose, ripped open by the dumpster, and to the left wing undersurface and flap. One propeller was damaged and the associated engine may also have been damaged. The B-17 was towed off and underwent repairs to enable it to be ferried back to Mesa, Arizona for much additional work.

The Fortress was flying again by spring 1989 but was damaged again in June 1989 when a sudden thunderstorm caught it on the ground in Albuquerque, New Mexico. All the control surfaces were damaged by hail, and once again the Fortress was grounded for additional work. However, that work was quickly completed and N9323Z completed its summer airshow tour successfully.

N9323Z shortly after purchase by the Arizona Wing of the Confederate Air Force in 1978. Carrying the markings of the 95th Bomb Group, the B-17 has the name "Sentimental Journey" applied but is lacking the famous Betty Grable pin-up nose art. Larkins

N9323Z shortly after conversion to tanker configuration by Aero Union. The B-17 in the rear is probably N9324Z which was purchased by Aero Union at the same time. Note that it still carries Air Force markings. Larkins

Another view of N9323Z in Aero Union's tanker garb. Larkins

CHAPTER TWELVE: 44-83525

WEEKS AIR MUSEUM
TAMIAMI AIRPORT, MIAMI, FLORIDA

■■ ■■ ■■

44-83525   B-17G-85-DL to DB-17G to N83525

USAAF/USAF

DATE	LOCATION	UNIT	CMD	REMARKS
29 MAR 45	LONG BEACH		ATC	ACCEPTED
APR 45	PATTERSON		ATC	STORAGE
(15 OCT 45)	(declared excess)		– –	
(07 NOV 45)	(returned to military use)		– –	
11 NOV 45	SO PLAINS, TX	4168 BASE UNIT	ATC	STORAGE
FEB 48	PYOTE, TX	2753 AC STRG SQ	AMC	STORAGE
MAR 50	OLMSTED, PA	MIDDLETOWN AIR DEPOT	AMC	
(21 JUN 50)	(fr: B-17G to: DB-17G)		– –	
19 JUL 50	EGLIN	3200 DRONE SQ	APG	
28 FEB 51	ENIWETOK	3200 PROOF TEST SQ	APG	
01 JUN 51	EGLIN	3200 DRONE GP	APG	
55	EGLIN	3205 DRONE GP	APG	
DEC 56	PATRICK	3205 DRONE GP	APG	
58	MATHER	3535 NAT WG	ATC	
58	PATRICK	MISSILE TEST CENTER	ARD	
58	EGLIN	ARMAMENT CENTER	ARD	
59	PATRICK	MISSILE TEST CENTER	ARD	
APR 59	DAVIS-MONTHAN	2704 ASDGP	AMC	
(AUG 60)	(declared excess)		– –	

CIVIL

DATE	TRANSFER DETAILS
(15 AUG 66)	(Lease agreement reached between USAF and Tallmantz Aviation for lease of 44-83525 for five years from date of delivery.)
(JAN 68)	(Tallmantz Aviation accepts 44-83525, ferries a/c to SNA, rebuilds for use in motion picture.)
(08 MAR 68)	(Initial application for registration filed with FAA.)
19 APR 72	FR: USAF MUSEUM TO: TALLMANTZ AVIATION, ORANGE COUNTY AIRPORT, CA
25 OCT 72	TO: I.N. BURCHINAL, PARIS, TX
11 APR 83	TO: WEEKS AIR MUSEUM, MIAMI, FL

44-83525

44-83525 was the last of the Air Force B-17s disposed from surplus stocks. It was used in several motion pictures and is now at Kermit Weeks' new museum in Miami, Florida, slated for a complete restoration.

525 was among the large group of late-model Douglas-produced B-17s which found post-war use in the Air Force. Accepted at Long Beach on 29 March 1945, 83525 was immediately placed in storage at Patterson Field in Ohio. It was declared excess to military requirements on 15 October 1945 but the Army Air Force had a change of heart and returned it to military use on 07 November 1945. The B-17 was then flown to South Plains, Texas, arriving on 08 November and again placed in storage. It was moved a second time, this time to Pyote Field, Texas, and assigned to the 2753rd Aircraft Storage Squadron on 28 June 1947.

525 remained in storage at Pyote until 31 March 1950 when it was flown to Olmsted AFB, Pennsylvania for modification to DB-17G status and assignment to the Air Proving Ground Command.

As a DB-17G, it arrived at Air Force Armament Center located at Eglin AFB, Florida, in July, 1950 and was assigned to the 3200th Drone Squadron. It was dispatched to Eniwetok Atoll in the South Pacific on 28 February 1951 for use in Operation Greenhouse, a series of four atomic test shots, the first of which was detonated on 07 April 1951. 44-83525 served as drone director for QB-17G drones used to collect samples and record test results.

Returning to Eglin in June 1951, it was reassigned to the 3205th Drone Group. It remained with this group, stationed primarily at Eglin but occasionally at the Missile Test Center at Patrick AFB in Florida until 1958. The aircraft also apparently spent a short time at Mather AFB in Sacramento, California, but was back at Patrick AFB and assigned to the APGC by late 1958.

In April 1959, 44-83525 was retired to Davis-Monthan AFB with many of the remaining DB-17's, and assigned to the 2704th Aircraft Storage and Disposal Group with an undetermined future.

As other DB-17s were farmed out to museums across the country, 44-83525 remained in storage. Eventually, the aircraft was moved to an area with public access and became part of an informal display with a few of the other rarities on the base, otherwise full of surplus B-29s, F-86s, B-50s, C-97s, and other Korean War vintage equipment, most of which would eventually be scrapped.

With the source of military surplus B-17s rapidly drying up, obtaining an example for commercial use, such as aerial spraying or motion picture production, became a matter of searching the civilian market for an aircraft becoming more and more sought after as their utility and value became apparent. Paul Mantz, the famed movie precision pilot, had once owned 78 B-17s after he had bought up a field of the surplus bombers in 1946, but he had scrapped all but one of them (B-17F-50-DL 42-3360 N67974). That example had been used a few films such as the MGM production "Command Decision" in 1948 but was sold in 1950 for lack of use.

(The B-17 work Mantz did for the movie "Twelve O'Clock High" in 1948, including his famous belly landing crash sequence, was all done with Air Force drones and drone controllers, the large number of which remained available probably led to his decision to sell his own B-17F).

Nonetheless, Mantz may have regretted his decision years later when a growing number of B-17 productions were commenced. Lacking a B-17 cut him out of involvement in a

44-83525 on informal display at Davis-Monthan AFB in the early sixties. Tallmantz Aviation returned the DB-17G to an airworthy condition for use in the film "1000 Plane Raid." Peltzer Collection

number of movies such as "The War Lover" (1961) or the TV production of "Twelve O'Clock High" (1964-1966). After Mantz merged his company, with that of rival Frank Tallman in 1961, forming Tallmantz Aviation, he redoubled his effort to find a B-17. Protracted negotiations with the Air Force resulted in Tallmantz's authorization to obtain the use of a B-17 in storage at Norton AFB in San Bernardino, California. That Fortress, B-17G-75-DL 44-83316*, was itself in an informal display setting along with a number of other Air Force aircraft, slated for dispersal to museums. (Tallmantz obtained for display a T-33, F-86D, F-86A, F-85 Goblin, F-107 and others from this Norton Collection for their International Flight and Space Museum at Orange County Airport, California.)

In 1964 Mantz dispatched a crew of mechanics to Norton AFB to determine the work necessary to fly the B-17. They found the B-17 in excellent shape and removed the control surfaces for recovering at the Orange County base of Tallmantz. Returning some weeks later to reinstall them, the Tallmantz people were dismayed to learn that the Air Force had removed and sold the wings of the Fortress, and had released the fuselage to 20th Century Fox for a studio mock-up under construction for the production of the TV series "Twelve O'Clock High."

The Air Force promised Tallmantz another B-17 but then Mantz was killed in an accident during the filming of "Flight of the Phoenix" in 1966. Frank Tallman was injured in a nonaviation accident and lost one of his legs. The ensuing chaos at Tallmantz Aviation and the maximum effort in gathering eighteen flyable B-25s for the film "Catch-22" prevented the company from claiming their promised B-17 until the middle of 1967.

The actual agreement between the Air Force and Tallmantz had been finalized shortly after Mantz's death. Dated 15 August 1966, it provided that the International Flight and Space Museum could lease 44-83525 for five years from delivery date at no cost beyond restoration and operating expenses. It also stipulated that Tallmantz could not use the B-17 in any profit-making venture beyond motion picture use and would make the B-17 available for public display and demonstration.

Some sources indicate that the B-17 carried the civil registration of N4250 while operated by Tallmantz. The FAA registration records for the aircraft, however, indicate that the only registration number assigned the Fortress was its modified military serial — N83525.

In July 1967 Tallmantz sent a crew of mechanics to Davis-Monthan AFB to inspect 83525, now dormant for eight years. They removed the control surfaces for recovering and inspected the aircraft, finding the B-17 in good condition though one engine would require replacement. The crew returned to Orange County with the control surfaces.

In the fall of 1967, Tallmantz agreed to provide their B-17 and a B-25 camera ship for the production of "1000 Plane Raid" to be shot on location at Santa Maria, California, in January 1968. Thus, with some urgency, a group of mechanics went back to Davis-Monthan in an earnest attempt to fly the B-17 back. Difficulties ensued, however, after an engine seized during ground runs. With a short deadline approaching, Frank Tallman sent Jim Appleby, an ex-Air Force and current Tallmantz B-25 pilot in an attempt to salvage the situation. Working with his hand-picked mechanics (and pilots), Wayne Burton and Bob Szimentiz, they replaced one engine, repaired another, and carefully checked the other two. Ground runs were difficult under the hot Arizona sun, as the uncowled R-1820-97s overheated quickly. Other systems were checked or repaired as required.

Finally, on Friday, 12 January 1968 (the B-17 was due in Santa Maria the following Monday), Appleby deemed the B-17 ready and that evening he ferried the reborn bomber to Orange County.

Tallmantz tried to ferry the bomber to its Orange County base in July 1967 but the effort was delayed until early 1968. Here, control surfaces have been removed for recovering at the Tallmantz shops. USAF via Criss

The Tallmantz crew swarmed over the Fortress the following weekend, repainting it to a studio-selected scheme and mounting turret shells to the exterior of the fuselage. Mechanical problems were corrected with both aircraft and pilots Appleby and Frank Pine (another B-25 camera ship pilot and General Manager of Tallmantz Aviation) ready for FAA certification Monday morning.

Once the paperwork was in order, Appleby flew the B-17 to Santa Maria with Pine following in B-25 cameraship N1203. Waiting at Santa Maria were B-17F 42-29782* N17W from Aircraft Specialties of Mesa, Arizona, and B-17G 44-83684* N3713G from the Air Museum at Ontario, California. Two weeks of filming ensued, producing a variety of photographic opportunities, remarkable only in that few showed up in the completed film, which was a disappointment even by Hollywood's skewed sense of realism.

44-83525 then returned to Orange County to await future film roles which, as it turned out, never materialized. After the financial disasters of the films "Tora Tora Tora",

Tallmantz mechanics work on two R1820s for eventual reinstallation. USAF via Criss

Mechanical work underway at Davis-Monthan in July 1967 to bring the B-17 back to airworthy condition. USAF via Criss

"Catch-22", and "The Battle of Britain", plus the growing anti-war sentiment of the period, few studio executives would consider another war epic. Tallmantz had invested in excess of $25,000 to restore the B-17 which now would, once again, sit in disuse.

525 was flown on rare occasion for demonstration purposes, making appearances at a Norton AFB open house, Mojave Airport, and a Los Angeles convention. A ferry flight associated from one of the displays resulted in a memorable occurrence.

Returning from the Los Angeles Airport, with Appleby at the controls, the number three engine turbocharger assembly, which ducts exhaust from the engine to the turbocharger itself, cracked and shifted inside the engine nacelle. The hot exhaust gas, acting as a blow torch, melted a large hole in the interior wing assembly, coming very near a fuel bladder. Appleby, noting the drop in manifold pressure on the engine, had fortunately reduced power but no other indications were available to betray the severity of his problem. The flight was short, however, and the B-17 landed safely. It was only after a post-flight inspection, and subsequent removal of lower wing panels, that the extent of the damage was realized. Repair components could only come from a scrapped B-17 wing as much of the interior structure would need replacement. Other projects demanded Tallmantz's attention, and the B-17 was indefinitely grounded.

Understandably, Tallman was quickly losing enthusiasm for operating a B-17 parking lot. He had gained title to the B-17 on 19 April 1972 through an elaborate trade with the Air Force Museum. He sent the Air Force two B-25s, a Snark missile, and an L-1. In return, he became the owner of the B-17.

Now he accepted an offer by Junior Burchinal, operator of the Flying Tiger Air Museum and a unique flight school for warbirds out of his duster strip near Paris, Texas. His collection included a B-25, P-51, FM-2, an A-26, an F9F, and a P38, most of which he made available for flight training. Tallman had worked with Burchinal before, using him as a B-25 commander during the filming of "Catch-22" in 1968. He had also made a number of aircraft trades with him.

Burchinal offered $30,000 for the B-17, which Tallman accepted. Thus, on 25 October 1972, Burchinal became the third owner of 83525. Then, for a few days in January 1973, one could hear the wailing pitch of the Wright R1820's as Tallmantz mechanics worked to put the bomber back into airworthy condition. Wing repairs, engine tests, and brake runs completed, the B-17 took to the air and turned to the east towards its new Texan home.

Burchinal didn't have too many takers on B-17 flight training, such as the demand was. Aside from the prospects of operating the four-engine bomber from a 2700 foot dirt-strip (though Burchinal was used to slapping B-25s and A-26s down on it), the costs of flying the thirsty aircraft approached $500 an hour.

Nonetheless, Burchinal put the plane to some use. He had planned to fly it back to California for a major role in the movie "MacArthur" but enroute engine difficulties changed those plans, 44-83525 arriving so late that only a short sequence was filmed at Indian Dunes (north of Los Angeles and a set for the TV series "Baa Baa Black Sheep") for use in "MacArthur."

The B-17 was repainted again and marked as "Suzy-Q," though the studio paint jobs began giving the aircraft a ratty appearance. Burchinal subsequently moved the airplane to Florida, and then Ely, Arizona as plans for various museums were initiated and fell through. Burchinal had intended to strip the paint and polish out the skin again, plus perform some other restorative work, when federal drug agents began taking a particular interest in his general operation.

Burchinal was eventually convicted of charges relating to his sale of various aircraft to drug smugglers. While in prison, he sold 44-83525 to Kermit Weeks. The sale was finalized on 11 April 1983.

The Weeks Air Museum in Florida is fast becoming known as a prime museum with restorations of the highest quality. Weeks has a large collection growing larger. He acquired 44-83525 and also owns parts of three more B-17s, 44-83316*, 44-83542*, and 44-83722*, now in storage in California.

Weeks planned on moving the B-17 from Texas to Florida in May 1985. After checking the aircraft over thoroughly and overhauling engine accessories (mags, pumps, fuel lines, etc.), plus performing several hours of engine checks, Weeks departed Burchinal's strip for the Municipal Airport at Paris for a fuel load. Immediately after take off, the number two engine failed and Weeks was unable to feather the propeller. The short flight ended safely, but Weeks decided at that point to completely overhaul all the engines and props before flying the B-17 again. The engines were pulled and the B-17 sat until May 1987 when Weeks returned with his four fresh engines.

After reinstalling the engines, additional ground runs were performed with all four engines apparently running well. A successful test flight was accomplished but difficulties ensued on a second flight when the number four engine experienced a sudden drop of oil pressure and a rise in engine temperature. Landing quickly, it was determined that the engine had metal in the oil sumps and that engine would require another replacement. After that work was completed, and finally satisfied that he had four healthy engines, Weeks flew the airplane to Miami.

Kermit Weeks is now planning a complete overhaul of all the systems. Instead of a piecemeal approach, he intends a thorough and detailed restoration. He is collecting parts and adding to his already large supply though, until full attention and resources can be allocated, 44-83525 will remain in outside storage. He expects it to be painted in standard Army Air Force O.D. paint when finished, and then assume its proper position as "Queen of the Skies" on Weeks's flight line.

N83525 in combat colors at the Santa Maria Airport in January 1968. Turrets are shells externally attached to the fuselage. Note unusual camouflage scheme carried for "1000 Plane Raid." T. Piedmonte via Besecker

"Balls of Fire" at Tallmantz Aviation at Orange County Airport in 1969. Aircraft rarely flew between 1968 and 1972 when Jr. Burchinal purchased it. Peltzer

CHAPTER THIRTEEN: 44-83546

MILITARY AIRCRAFT RESTORATION CORPORATION
ON DISPLAY AT
MARCH AFB, CALIFORNIA

■■■■■■

44-83546   B-17G-85-DL to CB-17G to VB-17G to N3703G

USAAF/USAF

DATE	LOCATION	UNIT	CMD	REMARKS
03 APR 45	LONG BEACH			ACCEPTED
06 APR 45	TOPEKA	MODIFICATION CENTER	ATC	
17 APR 45	SOUTH PLAINS		ATC	STORAGE
21 JUN 45	PATTERSON		ATC	STORAGE
31 JUL 45	SAN FRANCISCO		ATC	
(31 JUL 45)	(fr: B-17G to: CB-17G)			
17 NOV 45	MATHER		ATC	
19 DEC 45	BOLLING	1 BASE UNIT		
(DEC 45)	(assigned Air Forces Europe)		AFE	
DEC 45	WEISBADEN	501 STRAT RECON GP	AFE	
03 SEP 48	OLMSTED			
19 SEP 48	ERBENHIEM	7160 BASE UNIT	AFE	
(16 OCT 48)	(fr: CB-17G to: VB-17G)			
02 NOV 48	ANDREWS		SAC	
12 NOV 48	OFFUT	3902 BASE UNIT	SAC	
08 NOV 50	HANEDA		FEA	
13 OCT 54	DAVIS-MONTHAN 3040 ACFT STOR SQ		AMC	
(APR 59)	(reclamation authorized)			

CIVIL

DATE	TRANSFER DETAILS
31 JUL 59	FR: USAF AIRZONA AIRCRAFT STORAGE BRANCH, DAVIS-MONTHAN TO: NATIONAL METALS COMPANY, PHOENIX, AZ
11 SEP 59	TO: FAST-WAY AIR, INC., LONG BEACH, CA
25 APR 67	TO: TBM INC., TULARE, CA
24 MAY 86	TO: MILITARY AIRCRAFT RESTORATION CORP., LONG BEACH, CA

44-83546

44-83546 was converted to a CB-17G configuration shortly after it was delivered to the Army Air Force. It served as such while assigned to Air Forces Europe and later, as a VB-17G, was assigned to the Far East Air Force during the Korean War. After being sold as surplus equipment it was used as an air tanker for nearly twenty-five years. In 1986 ownership passed to David C. Tallichet's Military Aircraft Restoration Corporation and 4483546 is currently on display with the March AFB collection at Riverside, California.

44-83546 was accepted by the Army Air Force at Long Beach on 03 April 1945. It was sent to Topeka, Kansas, for required modifications and then sent into short-term storage at South Plains, Texas. On 21 June 1945 it was moved to Patterson Field, Ohio for further storage, though it was withdrawn on 31 July for converstion to a CB-17G.

Shortly thereafter it was assigned to the Air Transport Command at San Francisco, where it remained until November 1945 when it was apparently overhauled at Mather Field near Sacramento. In December of that year it was assigned to the 1st Base Unit at Bolling Field in Washington, D.C. and then to Air Forces Europe and the 501st Strategic Reconaissance Group at Weisbaden, Germany. It remained in Europe for several years and was assigned as the personal aircraft for General Idwall Edwards, then commander of Air Forces Europe. It was redesignated as a VB-17G on 16 October 1948. Shortly afterwards it was retuned to the U.S. for assignment to the Strategic Air Command, first at Andrews AFB and then at Offut AFB while attached to the 3902nd Base Unit.

In early November 1950, with the Korean War five months old, 44-83546 was assigned to the Far East Air Force and flown to Haneda, Japan. It remained based in Japan through the balance of its operational usage, with the exception of one overhaul conducted at the Middletown Air Depot at Olmsted AFB in June 1952.

While based at Haneda, photographic evidence suggests that it was assigned, at one point, to Major General Glenn Barcus as a personal transport. At the war's conclusion in 1954, 44-83546 was reassigned to the Air Materiel Command and flown to DavisMonthan AFB to be placed in storage with the 3040th Aircraft Storage Squadron. It remained in storage until April 1959 when it, as most other remaining Air Force B-17s, was released for disposal.

It was sold via auction to the National Metals Company of Phoenix, Arizona for $2,686.86, cheap even by 1959 standards, and ownership transferred on 31 July 1959. National Metals sold the aircraft to Fastway Air, Incorporated, of Long Beach, California only six weeks later. Fastways installed two 900 gallon tanks in the bomb bay during July

N3703G in late 1959 at Long Beach Airport. Civil paint scheme was apparently applied by Fastways Air at Long Beach, its first civil operator. B-17 was not converted to a tanker until July 1960. Gann

Early tanker use of N3703G at Chino in July 1960. One of the first two B-17s to be converted for use as a tanker (the other being N17W), it retains the civil paint scheme but had the crudely applied tanker number added. Gann

44-83546 in the summer of 1962 at Chino. Civil paint scheme was largely stripped but carried a bright orange tail. Note the added windows in the radio compartment and the air stair style main entrance door—both evidence of its earlier use as a VB-17. Larkins

Another tanker scheme worn by N3703G. Photographed at Porterville in 1974, the aircraft has a reddish-orange tail and white upper surfaces. Fortress operated by TBM Inc. beginning in 1967.
Ditty via Besecker

1960 as one of the first B-17s tanked for fire fighting. Maintenance records indicate that the airframe had 5328 hours of flight time logged to that point.

Operating as Tanker 78, N3703G would join sister ship N3702G (43-38635*) as Fastways tanker fleet, the pair operating in the annual battle against forest and range fires in the western U.S.

The two tankers were sold to TBM, Inc. of Tulare, California, on 25 April 1967. TBM would continue to operate them as tankers through the late seventies when stablemate N3702G was traded to the Air Force Museum.

As the B-17 air tankers were withdrawn from use due to age and lack of parts, N3703G was sold to the Military Aircraft Restoration Corporation (MARC) of Long Beach, California, which is owned and operated by David Tallichet. Tallichet has amassed a huge warbird collection through the years, going to the ends of the earth to recover rebuildable wrecks. Most of his collection is scattered throughout the country, with a large portion of the flyable aircraft on display at the March Field Museum in Riverside, California. Many of his rebuildable aircraft were in storage hangars at Daggett Airport in the California desert near Barstow, unfortunately the scene of a destructive fire in 1986 in which many rare aircraft were destroyed. The company is now based at the Chino Airport where much of MARC's restoration work is performed.

Tallichet, who owns a chain of specialty restaurants across the nation, was a wartime B-17 co-pilot with the 100th Bomb Group in Britain, but first dabbled with civil B-17s as he ob-

tained 44-83663* on loan from the USAF Museum for use in his now-defunct "Yesterday's Air Force" flying museum. Recounted elsewhere, 44-83663 was not owned by Tallichet and ultimately ended back with the Air Force Museum. The purchase of N3703G firmly placed a Fortress into Tallichet's collection.

Tallichet brought the B-17 back to military configuration with the reinstallation of power turrets and a 94th Bomb Group combat color scheme. Marked as B-17F-110-BO 42-30604, his company manufactured and installed an early-style tail gunner compartment, replacing the stubbier "Cheyenne" tail gun modification. Also added was an early-style Sperry dorsal turret recovered from a South Pacific wreck in the early seventies. With the B-17F-type tail guns, early-style turrets, and the absence of a chin turret, 44-83546 looks much the part of a 1943 8th Air Force B-17F. What is significant is that much of the equipment works. The bomb-bay is operable, including the bomb shackles. The Norden bombsight is not only operable but works in conjunction with the autopilot. The B-17 is under a constant state of restoration to return it to complete authenticity.

In 1989 N3703G was hired for use in the filming of "The Memphis Belle" in England. Further cosmetic restoration was performed, down to reskinning the nose of the B-17 to remove the chin turret patch and rework the windows into a true "F" style arrangement. As the B-17 was the only one of the five hired to have an operable ball turret, it was selected to be used as the starring "Memphis Belle". In July 1989 it was ferried over to England and received a 1942 era combat paint scheme. Filming took place at Duxford and RAF Binbrook, which had recently closed. Nearly fifty hours of flying was performed by the crew for the film, an ex-Tallmantz Aviation B-25 being used as the camera ship. In August 1989 N3703G returned to the U.S. and joined the warbird airshow tour, already in progress. The paint scheme looks very authentic on the aircraft, helped along by the weathering and other touches added by the film makers. All that's needed to fully restore the appearance to a true B-17F configuration would be the addition of the longer style B-17F blown nose piece.

Back in 1981 Tallichet worked out an agreement with the March Field museum to display a number of MARC's collection on the museum's flight line. Most military bases have strong reservations about allowing civilian aircraft on their facilities but, in this case, not only do both parties benefit but the general public is also able to see more aircraft incorporated into the display. N3703G, when not dispatched on airshow duty or receiving maintenance at MARC's Chino base, continues to share the March flight line with B-17G 44-6393*, which allows museums visitors the treat of seeing two of the historic Fortresses parked side by side.

Operating as a VB-17G, 44-83546 during the Korean War. Merritt via Menard

N3703G in tanker colors as operated by TBM Inc. in April 1973. Gougon

On the ramp at March AFB as part of the March Field Museum display though owned by the Military Aircraft Restoration Corporation. Author

MARC manufactured an early-style tail "stinger" unit which he used to replace the "Cheyenne" type tail gunner compartment as originally carried by the B-17G. The new unit was somewhat longer than it should have been, and was later modified. Author

STRATEGIC AIR COMMAND MUSEUM
OFFUTT AFB, NEBRASKA

■■■■■■

44-83559	B-17G-85-DL to DB-17G to DB-17P			

USAAF/USAF

DATE	LOCATION	UNIT	CMD	REMARKS
05 APR 45	LONG BEACH		ATC	ACCEPTED
12 APR 45	PATTERSON		ATC	STORAGE
(15 OCT 45)	(declared excess)		– –	
(07 NOV 45)	(returned to military use)		– –	
09 NOV 45	SOUTH PLAINS	4168 BASE UNIT	ATC	STORAGE
15 JUN 47	PYOTE	4141 BASE UNIT	AMC	STORAGE
17 FEB 50	PYOTE	2753 ACFT STORAGE SQ	AMC	STORAGE
07 MAR 50	OLMSTED	MIDDLETOWN AIR DEPOT	AMC	
(21 JUN 50)	(fr: B-17G to: DB-17G)		– –	
22 JUN 50	EGLIN	3200 DRONE GP	APG	
28 FEB 51	KWAJELEIN	3200 DRONE GP	APG	
31 MAY 51	EGLIN	3200 DRONE GP	APG	
13 OCT 52	HOLLOMAN	3205 DRONE GP	APG	
20 OCT 52	EGLIN	3205 DRONE GP	APG	
30 NOV 52	EGLIN	3203 MISSILE SUP GP	APG	
18 DEC 52	EGLIN	3205 DRONE GP	APG	
03 JUL 53	SCOTT	3310 TECHNICAL TNG WG	APG	
26 JUL 53	EGLIN	3205 DRONE GP	APG	
10 SEP 53	HOLLOMAN	3205 DRONE GP	APG	
(56)	(fr: DB-17G to: DB-17P)		– –	
AUG 58	PATRICK	3205 DRONE GP	APG	
(MAY 59)	(retired to Strategic Air Command Museum)			

44-83559

44-83559 spent its operational life as a drone director and participated in a least one series of nuclear tests undertaken in the South Pacific during the early 1950s. In May 1959 the aircraft was withdrawn from duty and flown to Offutt AFB to become part of the Strategic Air Command Museum.

44-83559 was accepted by the Army Air Force on 05 April 1945 at Long Beach. It was immediately flown to Patterson Field in Ohio for storage, as were most of the late Douglas-built Fortresses, and declared excess on 15 October 1945. 559 was returned to military use on 07 November 1945

and flown to South Plains, Texas and long-term storage. It was moved to Pyote Field, Texas on 15 June 1947, remaining in storage until 07 March 1950 when it was flown to Olmsted AFB for conversion to a DB-17G drone director. It was redesignated as such on 21 June 1950.

It was assigned to Eglin AFB and the 3200th Proof Test Wing and its 3200th Drone Group. On 28 February 1951 44-83559 was deployed to Kwajalein Atoll in the South Pacific for use as a drone controller of QB-17 drones utilized in the Greenhouse Series of nuclear tests. In these latter series, the devices were detonated at Eniwetok Atoll with flight operations based at Kwajalein.

The DB-17 returned to Eglin in late May 1951 and remained until 13 October 1952 when it was assigned to the 3205th Drone Group, Detachment 1, at Holloman AFB in New Mexico. While based at Holloman, 44-83559 was also attached to the 6580th Missile Test Wing. On 20 October 1952 it returned to Eglin and attached to the 3205th Drone Group again, and later, the 3203rd Missile Support Group.

On 03 July 1953 559 was assigned to the 3310th Technical Training Wing at Scott AFB, Illinois, returning once again to the 3205th Drone Group and Eglin AFB on 10 September 1953. It moved back to Holloman on 10 September 1953, remaining there for five years with the successor unit of Detachment One, the 3225th Drone Squadron. 44-83559 was redesignated as a DB-17P in 1956 and transferred to

Patrick AFB in Florida, where it was withdrawn from service in May 1959.

The Air Force relegated 44-83559 to the Strategic Air Command Museum at SAC Headquarters at Offutt AFB, Nebraska. The Fortress was flown to the museum in May 1959 and has been on continuous display ever since. It is currently finished with camouflage colors and painted in the colors of "King Bee", an Eighth Air Force B-17F-65-DL from the 100th Bomb Group. The original "King Bee" had been commanded by a former director of the Strategic Air Command Museum, and 44-83559 has been refinished down to the application of "King Bee"'s serial number, 42-3474, somewhat in exception to the Air Force policy on application of accurate serial numbers.

Ex DB-17G on the ramp at Offutt AFB in June 1967.
Gerdes via Besecker

44-83559 at the SAC Museum. The "0" in the serial number denotes that the aircraft was procured in 1944 and not 1954 as would otherwise be indicated.
Gerdes via Besecker

Same aircraft a decade later in July 1978. Only changes evident through the years is an apparent coat of aluminized paint and the reapplication of very standard markings. Krieger

44-83559 in May 1960, shortly after its arrival at the SAC Museum and still retaining the last markings carried in Air Force service. H. Levy via Bowers Collection

CHAPTER FIFTEEN: 44-83563

NATIONAL WARPLANE MUSEUM
GENESEO, NEW YORK

■■■■■

44-83563   B-17G-85-DL to CB-17G to VB-17G to N9563Z

USAAF/USAF

DATE	LOCATION	UNIT	CMD	REMARKS
07 APR 45	LONG BEACH	ATC ACCEPTED		
10 APR 45	PATTERSON		ATC	STORAGE
(25 MAY 45)	(fr: B-17G to: CB-17G)		— —	
(25 MAY 45)	(departed U.S. for Luzon)		— —	
(30 APR 47)	(assigned to FEAF/PACS)		— —	
30 APR 47	TACHIKAWA		FEA	
(03 AUG 48)	(fr: CB-17G to: VB-17G)		— —	
13 DEC 48	KISARAZU	13 ACFT REPAIR SQ	FEA	
17 JUN 49	TACHIKAWA		FEA	
22 DEC 49	CLARK	24 MAI GP	FEA	
27 DEC 49	TACHIKAWA		FEA	
(03 AUG 50)	(assigned to FE Air Materiel Com)		FEA	
25 AUG 50	YOKOTA	3 BOMB WING (L)	FEA	
30 NOV 50	YOKOTA	6161 BASE WING	FEA	
(19 FEB 52)	OLMSTED	MIDDLETOWN AIR DEPOT	AMC	
30 APR 52	HANEDA	6003 BASE FLIGHT SQ	FEA	
JUN 55	DAVIS-MONTHAN	3040 ACFT STORAGE SQ	AMC	STORAGE
(APR 59)	(reclaimation authorized)		— —	

CIVIL

DATE	TRANSFER DETAILS
18 AUG 59	FR: USAF ACFT DISPOSITION GROUP, DAVIS-MONTHAN TO: AMERICAN COMPRESSED STEEL CORP, CINCINNATI,OH
09 MAY 60	TO: AERO-AMERICAN CORP, CINCINNATI, OH
11 OCT 61	TO: COLUMBIA PICTURES, INC., NEW YORK, NY
02 FEB 63	TO: AVIATION SPECIALTIES, MESA, AZ
23 FEB 66	TO: AIRCRAFT SPECIALTIES, MESA, AZ
18 FEB 81	TO: GLOBE AIR, INC., MESA, AZ
10 JAN 86	TO: NATIONAL WARPLANE MUSEUM OF GENESEO, NY

44-83563

One B-17 with a particularly interesting history is 44-83563. After serving as a Air Force VIP transport for ten years, the Fortress found use in three motion pictures, served for years as an air tanker, and now is on display at the National Warplane Museum in Geneseo, New York.

44-83563 was accepted by the USAAF on 07 April 1945 at Long Beach and placed in immediate storage at Patterson Field, Ohio. However, unlike most of the late block Douglas B-17s, 83563 was assigned a mission quickly and pulled from storage a month later. It was redesignated as a CB-17G and dispatched to the Far East for use as a staff transport. Its initial assignment was apparently to the Philippine Islands.

On 30 April 1947, 44-83563 was formally assigned to the Far East Air Force's Pacific Air Services Command and based at Tachikawa, Japan. On 03 August 1948 it was redesignated as a VB-17G and spent the balance of its military use transporting and administrative staff throughout the Far East. Photographic evidence indicates that it transported General Dwight D. Eisenhower at least one time while assigned to the Pacific Air Service Command. It was briefly assigned to the 39th Troop Carrier Squadron, and then transferred to the Far East Air Materiel Command.

Beginning in 1949 the Fortress was assigned to the 13th Aircraft Repair Squadron, first at Kisarazu AFB, and then back at Tachikawa. On 03 August 1950, some six weeks after the North Korean Army swept into South Korea, it was assigned to the Far East Air Materiel Command and based at Yakota, Japan with the 3rd Bomb Wing (Light), equipped with Douglas B-26 Invaders being used against North Korean targets.

On 30 November 1950 it was transferred to the 6161st Air Base Wing, also at Yakota. After returning the United States in February 1952 for an overhaul at the Middletown Air Depot at Olmsted AFB, Pennsylvania, 44-83563 returned to Japan and was assigned to the 6003rd Base Flight Squadron of the 6000th Base Service Group at Haneda. One of five VB-17s with the unit, 44-83563 was assigned the task of transporting civil and military dignitaries throughout the Far East. The unit also operated General MacArthur's VC-121A, 48-0613, which went to General Matthew Ridgeway when he assumed command of United Nation forces in Korea in 1952.

44-83563 remained at Haneda until June 1955 when withdrawn from service and flown to Davis-Monthan AFB for storage. The ferry flight was made by way of Travis AFB in California, Wright-Patterson AFB in Ohio, and Washington National Airport, dropping off passengers along the way before making the final flight to Arizona.

44-83563 joined the growing number of B-17s in storage at Davis-Monthan and remained there for three years. The

Air Force authorized disposal of it and many of the surplus Air Force B-17s in the spring of 1958. Placed up for auction, it was sold to the American Compressed Steel Corporation of Cincinnati, Ohio, on 18 August 1959 for $3,156.00. The FAA issued the registration number of N9563Z to the Fortress. American Compressed Steel bought two other Fortresses that day, B-17G-G-70-VE 44-8543* which was issued the civil registration of N3701G, and B-17G-80-DL 44-83439, which became N131P.

American Compressed Steel Corporation became Aero-American in 1960. The company was in the business of reworking surplus military aircraft for civilian and foreign customers. There is much to suggest that among Aero-American's customers was the Central Intelligence Agency, for the CIA had developed through the early sixties a network of companies which could further its covert goals. Aero-American and a subsidiary, Aero-Associates, plus Intermountain Aviation of nearby Marana Airpark, were implicated in several attempts to secretly ferry Douglas A-26 Invaders to foreign governments at the bidding of the CIA. In any.event, Aero-American's purchase of the three B-17s had no such dramatic intent. They apparently bought them on speculation that they could find someone who would want the old planes.

Greg Board, a colorful Royal Australian Air Force combat pilot turned mercenary, was the driving force behind Aero-American. Based at Ryan Field, located twenty miles west of Tucson, Board had assembled a crack crew of mechanics and pilots to turn surplus junk into working aircraft. In the summer of 1960 Board turned his crew loose on the Fortresses at Davis-Monthan Working quickly, they went through the three B-17s, including 44-83563, and brought them back to flying condition, whereupon Board ferried them the short distance to Ryan Field.

The three B-17s sat at Ryan until December 1960 when Board flew them to Brownsville, Texas, to have large cargo

Rare photo of 44-83563 while based in Japan as a VB-17G in 1955. A short time later the aircraft was flown back to the United States for retirement at Davis-Monthan. Louria

44-83563 in movie colors for "The War Lover" in 1961. Tail serial changed several times during the filming to reflect different aircraft. Note absence of right waist gun position, replaced by the cargo door. MAP

Post-movie production tour. 44-83563 gained glossy paint and new markings. Photo taken at Washington National Airport in November 1962. Mikesh

Another view of N9563Z on its "War Lover" promotional tour. Mikesh

Out to pasture and awaiting a new owner at Tucson Airport in February 1963. Peltzer Collection

doors installed in each of the fuselages by Intercontinental Engine Service. Board felt the value and utility of the aircraft would increase substantially with the doors.

Apparently Board's assumption was correct as shortly afterwards N3701G was sold to the Albany Building Corporation, of Fort Lauderdale. It was used to haul vegetables from Andros Island, off the coast of Florida, to Fort Lauderdale for several years, before embarking on a more distinguishing utilization as an air tanker. N131P was purchased by Paramount Aquariums, Inc. of Vero Beach, Florida, where it was converted for use as a tropical fish transport. Meanwhile, pilot John Crewdson, of Film Aviation Service Limited, a British firm specializing in providing aircraft and crews for film productions, had been hired by Columbia Pictures to provide three B-17s for the film production of John Hersey's novel "The War Lover", to be shot at Bovingdon Airfield in Britain.

Crewdson had attempted to obtain the three Israeli Air Force B-17s, 44-83811, 44-83753, and 44-83851 but, much to his dismay, found they had been broken up for scrap, though he was able to purchase the intact fuselage of 44-83811 for studio shots, plus a number of spare parts. Crewdson then came to Arizona to seek out Greg Board and immediately purchased N9563Z on behalf of Columbia Pictures. Board and Crewdson then flew to Dallas-Love Field to inspect the Navy PB-1s rotting there. This was, as noted in other sections, the remains of a group of thirteen surplus PB-1Ws purchased by American Compressed Steel for possible conversion to B-17 executive transports. Plans had not

materialized, however, and the PB-1s had been turning derelict since 1957.

Board and Crewdson selected two PB-1Ws, Bu77243 (USAAF 44-83883 N5229V) and Bu77240 (USAAF 44-83877 N5232V) for rebuilding and eventual sale to Columbia Pictures. Board's mechanics immediately started working on the aircraft, and three weeks later Board and Crewdson ferried the the two bombers to Ryan Field.

At Ryan, preparations for the trans-Atlantic formation ferry flight to Britain were well underway. Radios and navigation equipment were installed in N9563Z, the lead aircraft on the flight. Turrets and other military equipment, located and procured from various surplus yards across the country, were installed, tested, and removed to the fuselage of 63Z, the large cargo door now proving its worth. Spare parts and tools enough to support three B-17s on a flight half-way around the world were loaded aboard the three bombers. Each of the B-17s was inspected and reinspected to insure a trouble-free flight. Flight crews were checked in the B-17s, all preparations steering toward a contracted delivery date, to Bovingdon Airfield, of 09 October 1961.

The copilot of the lead aircraft, N9563Z, was aviation writer Martin Caidin, who wrote a book, "Everything But The Flak" from his experiences on the ferry flight. Telling a colorful story of what was probably the last formation flight of Fortresses across the Atlantic, Caidin embellished the tale in his own unique way to create a larger-than-life epic. Nonetheless, the book provides as much detail as anyone could possibly want on the delivery flight.

Purchased by Aviation Specialties in early 1963, N9563Z was converted for use as an air tanker. Shown here in 1965 or 1966 at Mesa, Arizona. B. Baker

On the ramp at Oakland Airport enroute to Hawaii for the filming of "Tora Tora Tora" in January 1969. Turrets have not yet been attached. MAP

New tanker paint scheme on N9563Z. Photo taken at Mesa, Arizona in April 1967. Peltzer

Near the end of its use as a tanker is N9563Z at Santa Rosa Airport in July 1983. Larkins

The three B-17s left Ryan Field on September 23, 1961, the silver N9563Z leading with the two dark blue ex-Navy PB-1s in trail. They arrived in England on schedule on 09 October. In between, Caidin recorded their suffering through numerous engine failures, fires, horrendous weather, near mid-air collisions, international incidents as they tussled with Russians and Cubans at Gander, imprisonment in Portugal for gun running, countless drunken bashes, and all the other things that normally happen on such ferry flights. A pretty busy couple weeks for most people, but Crewdson followed it by coordinating and performing much of the flying for the film.

"The War Lover" was actually a cut above most of the genre, at least with respect to the hardware involved. Crewdson and his company did a spectacular job in recreating the combat Fortresses, and the flying scenes, particularly Crewdson's solo buzz job at Bovingdon Airfield, were memorable. At the conclusion of the filming in early January 1962, a decision was made to scrap N5229V and N5232V. Apparently their condition after the filming, plus

excessive import duties and taxes, were the death knell to the two B-17s and they were broken up.

N9563Z suffered a better fate. It was flown back across the Atlantic where it was used by Columbia for a promotional tour to publicize "The War Lover". Retaining the turrets but repainted with a glossy combat paint scheme, it had the name of the motion picture painted on the underside of the wings and would fly over cities and drop leaflets to the eager masses below.

It was later used by Columbia as a camera ship to film air-to-ground scenes for the motion picture "Dr. Strangelove", simulating the view from a B-52 making a low level trans-Arctic attack on the Soviet Union.

On 23 February 1963 N9563Z was sold to Aviation Specialties of Phoenix, Arizona. They converted it to an air tanker with the installation of tanks in the bomb-bay. Ownership of the Fortress was later transferred to Aircraft Specialties, a holding company derived from the original company, and operations were shifted to nearby Mesa, Arizona.

In 1967, Aircraft Specialties agreed to provide five B-17s for use in the motion picture "Tora Tora Tora" to be shot in Hawaii. N9563Z would join N620L (44-85840), N621L (44-85774), N17W (42-29782*), and N3193G (44-85829*) at NAS Ford Island on Oahu, to be painted once again in AAF olive drab for the cameras. Aircraft Specialties also provided all aircraft maintenance for the the large number of aircraft gathered by Twentieth Century Fox for the film.

At the conclusion of the filming N9563Z returned to the more mundane tasks of helping fight the annual battle against forest and range fires in the western U.S. Wearing tanker number 89, 63Z became a familiar sight in Arizona and California.

In 1981 Aircraft Specialties was reorganized as Globe Air, Incorporated, and the company operated as many as five B-17 tankers plus a number of TBMs, DC-4s, DC-6s, DC-7s, and a variety of other types in wide-ranging operations which covered all aspects of aerial application. However, in 1985 the principle owners decided to liquidate their business and put the whole operation on the auction block.

The Globe Air auction, held in October 1985, not only made available the wide cross-section of vintage aircraft operated by Globe, but also their vast storehouse of spare parts and discarded equipment. Three of Globe's four Flying Fortresses were dispersed in prior sales and during the auction itself.

The National Warplane Museum of Geneseo, New York, submitted the winning bid of $250,000 for N9563Z. The Museum had been organized in 1983 and is still one of the few vintage aircraft collections in the northeastern part of the country. The collection had grown to include a P-40 and a PBY, plus a half dozen other types, but took a major step forward with the acquisition of the B-17. Financed through $500 pledges from members, as well as a cooperative local bank, the museum has brought the Fortress back to combat appearance. The tanker paint scheme, as well as an additional seven layers of paint, were stripped from the airframe while it was still at Falcon Field. It flew in bare-metal with basic markings for several years, but in 1987 was finished as "Fuddy Duddy," a 447th Bomb Group aircraft from the Eighth Air Force. The colorful paint scheme sports yellow cowls and tail surfaces, and provided a rallying point for a reunion of the original "Fuddy Duddy" crew which was held at the museum in September 1987.

Construction is underway on a large hangar for the Fortress and other aircraft from the collection, necessary given the harsh winters of upstate New York. The firm footing and sound planning of the National Warplane Museum would suggest that 44-83563 will remain operational for years to come, and provide the centerpiece for yet another impressive display of vintage aircraft.

Waiting for a call, N9563Z on fire duty at Prescott, Arizona in June 1977. Retardant tanks are shown to good advantage. Author

Chapter Sixteen: 44-83575

BEAVER COUNTY AIRPORT, PENNSYLVANIA

■ ■ ■ ■ ■ ■

44-83575   B-17G-85-DL to TB-17H to SB-17G to N93012

USAAF/USAF

DATE	LOCATION	UNIT	CMD	REMARKS
07 APR 45	LONG BEACH		ATC	ACCEPTED
09 APR 45	TULSA		ATC	MOD CENTER
07 MAY 45	CHEYENNE		ATC	MOD CENTER
23 MAY 45	HUNTER FIELD		ATC	
(11 JUN 45)	(departed U.S.)		– –	
	(possible South American deployment)			
(30 APR 47)	(assigned 6th AF, Caribbean Air Command)			
01 JAN 48	BORINQUN	1 RESCUE SQUADRON	CAC	
(01 JAN 48)	(fr: B-17G to: TB-17H)		– –	
01 JUL 48	RAMEY	1 RESCUE SQUADRON	CAC	
(01 JUL 48)	(fr: TB-17G to: SB-17G)		– –	
22 MAY 49	HOWARD	1 RESCUE SQUADRON	CAC	
(27 SEP 49)	(assigned Military Transport Organization?)			
12 OCT 49	RAMEY	1 RESCUE SQUADRON	MTO	
29 DEC 49	ALBROOK	1 RESCUE SQUADRON	MTO	
16 OCT 50	RAMEY	1 RESCUE SQUADRON	MTO	
24 APR 51	ALBROOK	1 RESCUE SQUADRON	MTO	
14 JUN 51	KINDLEY	1 RESCUE SQUADRON	MTO	
09 FEB 52	KIRTLAND	4901 SUPPORT WING	ARD	
(15 FEB 52)	(assigned Air Reseach and Development Cmd)			
(52)	(aircraft ferried to Nevada Test Site)			

CIVIL

DATE	TRANSFER DETAILS
*14 MAY 65	FR: ATOMIC ENERGY COMMISSION COMMERCIAL CONTRACT OFFICE REYNOLDS ELECTRICAL ENGINEERING COMPANY (PROJECT MANAGEMENT BRANCH), U.S. AEC NEVADA OPERATIONS OFFICE
	TO: VALLEY SCRAP METAL, PHOENIX, AZ
*05 MAY 65	TO: AIRCRAFT SPECIALTIES, MESA, AZ
18 FEB 81	TO: GLOBE AIR, INC, MESA, AZ
10 JAN 86	TO: COLLINGS CHILDREN'S TRUST FUND, WENTWORTH, NH

*dates as recorded in FAA registration records apparently in error.

44-83575

Another Fortress with a diverse and unusual history is 44-83575. Beginning active service as an air-sea rescue TB-17H, this Fortress went on to serve as a static target for a nuclear test at the Nevada Test Site, to be rebuilt by an air tanker operator who painstakingly restored the Fortress into a usable tanker. After the B-17 tankers were retired, a new civil owner restored 44-83575 to combat configuration and turned it into a premier flying example of the type. Unfortunately the summer of 1987 saw 44-83575 nearly destroyed in an airshow accident, but all signs point to yet another resurrection of this phoenix from the ashes.

44-83575 rolled from the Long Beach production lines of Douglas on 07 April 1945, being accepted the same day by the Army Air Force. It was flown to the Douglas modification center at Tulsa, Oklahoma, arriving on 09 April. It left Tulsa on 06 May bound for Cheyenne, Wyoming and additional modifications, being deemed ready for service on 18 May 1945.

The aircraft was ferried overseas, leaving the U.S. on 11 June 1945. Deployment information is not available, but the aircraft apparently passed through Natal, Brazil. It is possible that the Fortress had been redesignated as a B-17H and deployed to the Caribbean or South America.

In any event, it is known that the aircraft was assigned to the Caribbean Air Command and the 6th Air Force by 30 April 1947, attached to the 1st Rescue Squadron at Borinquin Air Station in Puerto Rico. By that time it had been redesignated as a TB-17H, indicating modification and use as an Air-Sea Rescue Fortress with a lifeboat slung under its belly.

44-83575 would remain with the 1st Rescue Squadron but would see various assignments to Ramey AFB in Puerto Rico, plus Albrook AFB and Howard AFB in the Panama Canal Zone. On 01 July 1948 it was redesignated as an SB-17G to conform with the modified designation system as established by the new USAF.

On 14 June 1951 it was reassigned to Kindley Field on Bermuda, continuing to serve as an SB-17G. However, its fate took a turn when, on 09 February 1952, it was assigned to the Special Weapons Center at Kirtland AFB, New Mexico. It is probable the B-17 never actually was based at Kirtland, but the aircraft now became part of the Air Force Special Weapons Command. Shortly afterwards it and another Kindley SB-17G, 44-83722*, plus an additional 5 B-17s, were flown to Yucca Flats near Mercury, Nevada and part of the Nevada Test Site. The Nevada Test Site was administered by the Atomic Energy Commission and, beginning in 1951, became the domestic location for nuclear detonations. The B-17s were brought into the site to become targets and research instruments to test the effect of an atomic blast. They were parked at varying distances from ground

Rebuilding efforts underway on the test site by the Aviation Specialties crew under the direction of John King.
Reynolds Electrical via Leon

New fabric and aluminum patches have been installed to return 44-83575 to an airworthy condition.
Reynolds Electrical via Leon

Military serial painted out, N93012 is readied. Note that the Air Sea Rescue and Military Air Transport Service markings are still quite evident. Reynolds Electrical via Leon

Safely parked at Falcon Field, N93012 would sit for another twelve years before joining the tanker fleet. Peltzer

Under a very slow rebuilding process, it would appear 44-83575 lost parts as quickly as it gained them. MAP

Finally working as an active air tanker, N93012 in August 1985 at Redding, California. It was the tanker's last season with Globe Air. Peltzer

zero to determine changes in blast effects at different ranges.

44-83575 was used in the first series of tests conducted in 1952 as part of Operation Snapper. The study was entitled "Vulnerability of Parked Aircraft to Atomic Bombs" and sought to establish the survivability of different aircraft configurations and locations to nuclear weapons. 44-85735 was subjected to three nuclear detonations. In the first, the aircraft was parked approximately 10,000 feet from a one kiloton explosion. 44-83575 survived intact. In the second test, the aircraft was parked the same distance from a thirty-one kiloton device, and suffered damage which would have required over 4000 hours to repair. For the last test, the aircraft was situated 8,000 feet from a nineteen kiloton explosion, and it was determined the aircraft would have required 5274 man hours to repair the damage, which was considered uneconomical. Skin damage from the shock wave was the primary result, though the aircraft also became intensely

radioactive. After evaluating damage to the seven B-17s and the 21 other aircraft used as targets, the report concluded that the conventional landing gear configuration and broad wing area made designs similar to the B-17 most vulnerable to nuclear explosions.

At the completion of the program it and the other test vehicles were towed or pulled to a spot on the edge of Yucca Lake to sit and radiate. They were largely forgotten, though as the material "cooled off," parts began to disappear to souvenir hunters. When it was determined that the B-17, as well as all the surrounding scrap, was safely decontaminated, it was offered for sale in a salvage bid in 1964.

44-83575, as part of the 800 ton scrap bid (which also contained the remains of 44-83722) was sold to Valley Scrap Metal of Phoenix, Arizona in April 1965. (The FAA paperwork on the aircraft indicated the sale date as 14 May 1965; the date discrepancy was probably the result of Aircraft

Specialties trying to secure FAA permission for the impending ferry flight and the rush to complete paperwork.) The net cost to Valley Scrap was $269 for the Fortress.

Aircraft Specialties of Mesa, Arizona then purchased the two Fortress airframes from Valley Scrap with the intent of flying 44-83575 off the lake. The other Fortress, 44-83722, had suffered too much damage to repair, but it was apparent to Aircraft Specialties, if no one else, that 575 wasn't that far from being flyable. They purchased it as scrap, however, paying 1.5 cents per pound. Valley Scrap had agreed to have the material off the Site within six weeks of the contract date, so the sales agreement with Aircraft Specialties contained the same stipulation.

First task which lay before Abe Sellards and Richard Packard, two owners of Aircraft Specialties, was arranging permission for initial mechanical work to be performed right at the Test Site. Few people believed it was possible to make the aircraft airworthy in such a short time, given its condition and the lack of many parts. Nonetheless, permission was secured and John King, chief of maintenance at Aircraft Specialties, arrived with a work crew and a truckload of parts.

King found the aircraft basically intact. However, as noted before, there was much skin damage from the atomic blast effect. The control surfaces were damaged and stripped of fabric. Most of the control cables had been removed and all the instruments in the cockpit were gone. Everything was covered or filled with desert sand. King and his crew, which varied between three and six men at any one time, disassembled and cleaned all the mechanical components. Over 4000 feet of control cable was restrung through the fuselage, and the gaping holes on the instrument panel were filled with instruments. Sheet metal fabricators worked next the the bomber, stripping off warped skin and custom fitting new aluminum panels in their place. Mechanics brought the engines back to life, and systems checks were run. The old Air Force serial was painted out, replaced by the new FAA registration of N93012.

In the latter stages of the project John King dubbed the old bomber the "Lady Yucca," and the name was soon applied to the nose. (Also applied was a pin-up figure "liberated" from an appropriate magazine.) The aircraft, still wearing the remnants of its air-sea rescue MATS paint scheme but showing the evidence of much reskinning, was considered ready for its ferry flight to Falcon Field, in Mesa, Arizona on 14 May 1965.

That morning, with Aircraft Specialties president Abe Sellards and John King at the controls, 44-83575 departed Yucca Flats on its first flight in fourteen years. Arriving at Falcon Field, N93012 still faced major rebuilding to put the aircraft into top mechanical condition for its new assignment as an air tanker.

That rebuilding effort finished the job started at Yucca Flats, but took nearly ten additional years. Much of that time the aircraft remained parked in outdoor storage, with additional parts removed for use in the rest of the B-17 fleet. Four zero-time engines eventually replaced the old engines that came with the plane. A great deal of additional skin repair was required and the electrical and other systems were overhauled. Any remaining non-essential military equipment was removed to save weight. Two retardant tanks plus the associated plumbing were installed in the bomb bay. Aircraft Specialties already operated three Fortresses (N3193G, N9563Z, and N17W) plus numerous other sprayers and air tankers. N93012, as Tanker 99, joined the tanker fleet in 1977, and during the following years was widely used in the southwestern U.S. It was variously based during fire work at Winslow, Arizona, as well as several California air tanker base.

Tanker 99 would remain active with Aircraft Specialties and its successor, Globe Air, until 1985 when the principal owners of Globe decided the liquidate their assets and close their business. In the process of disposing of their fleet, much of which was sold at an auction conducted in October 1985, N93012 was sold to aircraft collector Bob Collings of Stow, Massachusetts. Collings had air tanker veteran Ed Boyles and restorer Tom Reilly ferry N93012 to Reilly's Vintage Aircraft restoration facility located in Kissimmee, Florida. They departed Mesa on 28 January 1987 and arrived the next day. The B-17 went into the shops on 01 April 1987 and emerged a new airplane at the end of July. Reilly had worked his way through the old tanker giving it a general overhaul. The propellers were rebuilt, the fuel tanks and lines replaced, new glass was installed, and new tires and brakes went onto the axles. Reilly custom manufactured a new interior, and replaced the bulkheads stripped from the airframe twenty years earlier. Military equipment was added as available, including the addition of a chin turret. N93012 was repainted as "Nine-O-Nine," depicting a famous 91st Bomb Group Fortress of the Eighth Air Force.

The original "Nine-O-Nine" was B-17G-30-BO 42-31909 and was particularly distinguished because it had completed 140 missions with the 91st Bomb Group between 02 March 1944 and 25 April 1945 without a crew fatality or injury. That record also included a 100% completion rate (no missions aborted) and eighteen missions to Berlin. At the completion of the war the Fortress was a patchwork of repairs, mismatched paint, and showed the wear of hard use in the skies over Europe. It returned to the U.S. and was scrapped at Kingman.

Further restoration efforts were planned for the replicated "Nine-O-Nine," including the addition of the dorsal and ball turrets, but N93012 was ready for flying and it joined the airshow circuit in the summer of 1987.

On 23 August 1987, during an air show at Beaver County Airport, 25 miles north of Pittsburgh, Pennsylvania, N93012 was involved in a landing accident which resulted in substantial damage to the aircraft and twelve injuries to crewmembers on board. According to the National Transportation Safety Board, the Fortress landed long on the 4000 foot runway and could not stop before rolling off the end of the pavement and down a hundred foot embankment. The Fortress also rolled across two telephone poles at the bottom of the ravine. The resultant damage would have been considered irreparable twenty years ago, but efforts began immediately to repair the aircraft. Three of the the four engine nacelles were badly bent, and the landing gear mounting structure in the number two nacelle was all but destroyed. The lower wing surfaces and tail suffered severe damage, as did the lower part of the nose.

The B-17 was partially disassembled and hauled from the site. It went into a hangar at the airport and repairs were started. Through the efforts of volunteers from the local area, under the direction of Scott Royce of the Confederate Air Force, the B-17 has slowly come back together. The horizontal stabilizer was replaced. The wings were removed and disassembled. Desert sand from years past was found and removed. One wing panel was repaired by US Air, the airline, as it operates a maintenance base on the field. US Air also did some work on the landing gear assemblies. A new #3 engine nacelle was obtained from the "Shoo Shoo Shoo Baby" restoration effort in Delaware, and another nacelle was completely disassembled and rebuilt. All four engines were zero-timed and freshly overhauled props were added. Systems not overhauled the first time around have now been completed, and the bomb bay doors are now operable. Replica dorsal and ball turrets have been installed, and new glass was installed where needed. It was hoped that the effort would be completed by the 1989 air show season, but that schedule was not met. It is now expected that the aircraft will be flying by the end of 1990.

N93012 in its new colors an Geneseo, New York in the summer of 1986. Kanary

The damaged B-17 being lifted from the site at Beaver County Airport. Kanary

The results of a long landing and a strong crosswind, at Beaver County Airport on 23 August 1987. Kanary

Work on the fuselage nearing completion. It is planned that the aircraft will fly again in 1990. Kanary

A Phoenix rising again, 44-83575 being rebuilt in 1988. Kanary

"Nine-O-Nine" as it appeared shortly before the crash. Krieger

Chapter Seventeen: 44-83624

Dover Air Force Base, Delaware

■■■■■■

44-83624	B-17G-95-DL to MB-17G to TB-17G to DB-17G to DB-17P			

USAAF/USAF

DATE	LOCATION	UNIT	CMD	REMARKS
26 APR 45	LONG BEACH		ATC	ACCEPTED
30 APR 45	PATTERSON	4100 BASE UNIT	ATS	STORAGE
(15 OCT 45)	(declared excess)		— —	
(07 NOV 45)	(returned to military use)		— —	
07 NOV 45	SOUTH PLAINS	4168 BASE UNIT	ATC	STORAGE
20 JUL 47	PYOTE	4141 BASE UNIT	AMC	STORAGE
26 OCT 47	OLMSTED	4112 BASE UNIT	AMC	
(21 JAN 48)	(fr: B-17G to: MB-17G)		— —	
16 FEB 48	EGLIN	1 EXP GUIDED MIS GP	APG	
(04 JAN 49)	(fr: MB-17G to: TB-17G)		— —	
24 MAR 49	EGLIN	3200 PROOF TEST GP	APG	
		3200 DRONE SQ	APG	
		3200 TEST WG	APG	
(various)		3201 AIR BASE GP	APG	
		3203 MIS SUPPORT GP	APG	
		3203 DRONE GP	APG	
		3205 DRONE GP	APG	
		550 GUIDED MIS GP	APG	
11 OCT 54		3560 PTN GP	APG	
56	OLMSTED	MIDDLETOWN AIR DEPOT	AMC	
(56)	(fr: TB-17G to: DB-17G)		— —	
56	EGLIN	3205 DRONE GP	APG	
(56)	(fr: DB-17G to: DB-17P)		— —	
(JUN 57)	(transfer to USAF Museum)			
(16 JUN 89)	(transfer to Dover AFB Historical Center)			

44-83624

This particular Fortress was the long-standing display aircraft at the Air Force Museum in Dayton, Ohio until the freshly restored "Shoo Shoo Baby" arrived in October 1988. It was removed from the museum area and, after several months of storage, disassembled and moved to Dover AFB for restoration and display at the Dover AFB Historical Center.

44-83624 was accepted as a B-17G-90-DL at Long Beach on 26 April 1945 and, like most other Douglas-produced B-17s in late blocks, was immediately flown to storage at Patterson Field, Ohio, and declared excess in October 1945. A month later 624 was returned to military use but was flown to South Plains, Texas for further storage with the 4168th Base Unit. On 20 July 1947, 624 was once again moved, this time to Pyote Field, Texas, for further storage with the 4112nd Base Unit.

On 26 July 1947, 624 was removed from storage and sent to the Middletown Air Depot at Olmsted AFB, Pennsylvania, for modification as missile carrier for test purposes. Redesignated MB-17G on 21 January 1948, 44-83624 was assigned to the Air Proving Ground Command at the Armament Center, Eglin AFB, Florida.

As an MB-17G, 44-83624 was probably involved in testing American versions of the German V-1, designated JB-2, one of which was carried under each wing. The 1st Experimental Guided Missile Group, to which 44-83624 was assigned on 16 February 1948, had participated in Joint Task Force 7 at Eniwetok Atoll during Operation Sandstone in 1947. MB-17s were also used to carry small drone aircraft used as aerial gunnery targets in tests at the Armament Center.

The "M" prefix having been reapplied as a medical evacuation designator in 1948 resulted in 624 being redesignated as a TB-17G on 04 January 1949. This was somewhat unusual in that the aircraft apparently continued to be utilized at the Armament Center in various test and drone squadrons. Most B-17s used as such were designated DB-17s in 1948 to denote drone controller aircraft. However, it is apparent that this particular aircraft had not been specifically modified to a drone controller configuration; thus the TB-17 designation. (The TB-17, while technically a "training" adaptation of the B-17, came to be used as a "catch-all" designation for B-17s assigned a special-use but without an appropriate prefix.)

44-83624 was attached to the 550th Guided Missile Group on 04 January 1950, and followed the successive units as a system of drone squadrons were developed. The Fortress went with the 3200th Proof Test Wing when that unit was broken off from the 550th Guided Missile Group, and was variously attached to it and the 3201st Air Base Support Group. It remained with the unit when the 3200th Proof Test Wing became the 3200th Drone Group with its three squadrons. It was also variously attached to several other Eglin units such as the 3560th Proof Test Wing and 3205th Drone Group through the years.

In 1955 the TB-17 apparently spent time assigned to the San Bernadino Air Depot at Norton AFB, California, and the Ogden Air Depot at Hill AFB, Utah, though the specific purpose for the assignments are unclear. In any event, the aircraft came to the Middletown Air Depot at Olmsted AFB for modification to drone controller status and redesignated as a DB-17G. 624 then went back to Eglin AFB and the

3205th Drone Group to join its numerous DB-17G brethren. Additional modifications to DB-17P configuration were undertaken at Eglin in 1956.

In June 1957 the aircraft was retired from service and transferred to the USAF Museum at Wright-Patterson AFB in Dayton, Ohio. It was placed on outdoor display with its DB-17P markings intact until 1960 when power turrets were reinstalled and it was given olive drab combat colors. Marked to represent a B-17G of the 381st Bomb Group, it still carries the correct "483624" (as required by Air Force regulations) serial on the tail.

The B-17 was moved from the original museum location to a new, larger facility in October 1971. It, like all the other museum aircraft, made the seven mile trip overland via freeways and surface streets. Larger aircraft, like the museum's XB-70 and B-29, required that outer wing panels or other sub-assemblies be removed, but the Fortress made the journey intact.

Fortunately, there was room at the new facility for the B-17 to be displayed indoors, anchoring the World War II area of the museum much as it had the American air effort in Europe. It remained on display for the subsequent eighteen years in much the same condition.

As noted earlier, the Air Force Museum staff was eager to get "Shoo Shoo Baby" on display. Shortly after the combat veteran arrived, 44-83624 was moved from the exhibit area and replaced. 44-83624 was need in restoration also. Some parts, such as the top turret, had been removed and used on "Baby," while the rest of the airframe was basically the same as it was when it arrived at them museum in 1957.

The Dover AFB Historical Center had requested the aircraft, and the Air Force Museum agreed to assign 44-83624 to the new Heritage Program museum. The B-17 was disassembled and prepared for transport aboard a C-5. Once again, the inboard wing sections were found too wide to fit into the C-5 cargo hold, so the aft 22 inches of each were carefully removed at skin lines, and the internal structue of the wing disassembled for transport. The B-17 was moved on 16 June 1989 to Dover AFB. It has since been partially reassembled and will undergo a cosmetic restoration. For the time being the Fortress will remain with the same paint and markings. By early 1990 it should join the small but growing aircraft collection at Dover AFB.

44-83624 at the old Air Force Museum facility on outdoor display. Aircraft retains DB-17G markings it wore when retired to the museum in June 1957. Krieger

Another view of 44-83624 at the museum in 1960. Besecker

CHAPTER EIGHTEEN: 44-83663

HILL AFB, UTAH

■■■■■■

44-83663	B-17G-90-DL to TB-17G to BRAZILIAN AIR FORCE 5400 to N47780			

USAAF/USAF

DATE	LOCATION	UNIT	CMD	REMARKS
01 MAY 45	LONG BEACH		ATC	ACCEPTED
03 MAY 45	SOUTH PLAINS		ATC	STORAGE
04 JUN 45	PATTERSON		ATC	STORAGE
16 OCT 45	GARDEN CITY	4132 BASE UNIT	AMC	STORAGE
09 DEC 46	PYOTE	4141 BASE UNIT	AMC	STORAGE
(08 NOV 50)	(reclamation authorized)		— —	
(21 NOV 50)	(reclamation canceled)		—	
(26 MAR 51)	(assigned to Brazilian Military Command)			
18 APR 51	RIO DE JANEIRO		BMC	
(09 NOV 51)	(fr: B-17G to: TB-17G)		— —	
(12 JUN 53)	(transfer to Brazilian Air Force)			

BRAZILIAN AIR FORCE (as serial #5400)

APR 51	RIO DE JANEIRO	CTQ*		SAR/TRAINING
JUN 51	RECIFE	CTQ*		
OCT 51	RECIFE	1ST/6TH GRUPO DE AVIACAO		
(05 OCT 68)	(transfer to USAF Museum)			
05 OCT 68	WRI-PAT			USAFM

*Centro de Treinamento de Quadrimotores (Four-engined Aircraft Training Center)

USAFM

1968-1973	(aircraft in storage at Wright-Patterson AFB)
(06 JUN 73)	(aircraft loaned, via renewable 1 year periods, to Yesterday's Air Force for non-flying display at Chino Airport, California. Ferry registration N47780)
(1973-1985)	(YAF ferried N47780 to Chino, where it remained for five years, then ferried to Topeka, Kansas, where it remained for several years, then to St. Petersburg, Florida. USAFM cancelled loan agreement in 1983 and repossesed 44-83663.)
(1986)	HILL AFB, UT — MUSEUM

44-83663

44-83663 was placed in storage shortly after being built where it remained until 1951 when transferred to the Forca Aerea Brasileira (Brazilian Air Force) for use in Search and Rescue work. It was returned as a gift to the USAF Museum in 1968, and stored for five years. 44-83663 was loaned to David Tallichet's Yesterday's Air Force in 1973 as a non-flying display, and spent the following decade moving about the country in search of an adequate display site. It ended up in Florida in somewhat less than ideal condition in 1983, when the Air Force decided to take the aircraft back. Initial attempts were made to fly the bomber, but it was eventually dismantled and ferried to Hill AFB, Utah, aboard a C-5 Galaxy. It will be displayed at the Heritage Museum located at the base.

44-83663 was built at Long Beach and was accepted for service on 01 May 1945. It was immediately flown to South Plains, Texas, and placed into short term storage. It was removed and flown to Patterson Field, Ohio, a month later where it remained until 16 October 1945. At that time 44-83663 was dispatched to yet another storage facility, this one located in Garden City, Kansas. The aircraft remained there for a little over a year before being flown to Pyote, Texas, and long term storage with the 4141st Base Unit.

The Fortress would remain at Pyote through 1950 when, on 08 November, the Air Force decided it had no further use for the aircraft and authorized its reclamation. Presumably, efforts were underway to transfer the aircraft to the Forca Aerea Brasileira (FAB) under the auspices of the Military Assistance Program and the Rio Pact. In any event, the paperwork was reshuffled and the Air Force canceled its reclamation authorization on 21 November 1950 and, instead, transferred the Fortress to Rio de Janeiro on 18 April 1951.

Officially under the command of the USAF until 12 June 1953, 44-83663 and five other B-17s were apparently operationally transferred to the FAB in April or May 1951 for assignment to the Centro de Trainamento de Quadrimotores (CTQ), the four-engined aircraft training center located at Rio de Janeiro. The CTQ moved to the Recife Air Base in June 1951. The USAF redesignated 44-83663 as a TB-17G on 09 November 1951, and it can be presumed that it and the other B-17s were being flown by Brazilian aircrews with the technical assistance of USAF crews. The B-17s were the first large aircraft operated by the Forces Aerea Brasileira and an operational squadron of aircraft for use in Search and Rescue and Photo Reconnaissance duties was being prepared with the assistance of the U.S. military.

In October 1953 the CTQ was renamed the 6th Grupo de Aviacao and became operational at that time. An additional seven B-17s were transferred from the USAF to the FAB in late 1954-early 1955 and the entire Fortress inventory was serialed between 5400 and 5411 (one Fortress, 44-85579, had crashed in July 1952 and thus did not receive a serial number.)

Of the twelve B-17s, seven were allocated for SAR roles, and the other five were used for reconnaissance. 44-83663, as 5400, made the first trans-Atlantic flight for the FAB on 01 September 1953, flying from Natal, Brazil to Dakar, Senegal. FAB B-17s also made numerous trans-Atlantic flights in support of Brazilian Army troops stationed at Suez with the United Nations peacekeeping force deployed between 1957 and 1960.

A total of four B-17s were lost between 1951 and 1968,

when the Fortresses were withdrawn from service and replaced by Lockheed RC-130Hs. At that time, only four B-17s remained active, the remainder having been retired earlier to support the operational aircraft. Three of the four last B-17s were marked for preservation, 5400 being returned to the United States for display at the USAF Museum. 44-83663 was flown north by a Brazilian crew and arrived at Wright-Patterson on 05 October 1968.

The Air Force Museum, which already had a B-17 on display (44-83624*) placed 44-83663 in storage pending a decision on its future. In the days before the establishment of the USAF Museum Program, there were few places the Fortress could go. The Fortress remained in storage for five years until 1973, when an agreement was reached between the USAFM and Yesterday's Air Force. The agreement stipulated that 44-83663 would be loaned to the YAF as a non-flying display for their Chino, California museum. A renewable one-year term was approved, with facilities made available to YAF mechanics to place the B-17 in airworthy condition for the ferry flight to Chino.

Yesterday's Air Force was the museum end of David Tallichet's Military Aircraft Restoration Corporation. Tallichet held a large number of vintage aircraft as a result of world wide searches which included combing the forgotten battlefields of the South Pacific and the far reaches of the Canadian wilderness. Much of the collection, consisting primarily of recovered wrecks and derelicts, was in storage at Chino along with Ed Maloney's collection. Tallichet, who operates a series of specialty restaurants across the country, still maintains restoration facilities at Chino Airport.

Tallichet sent mechanics to Wright-Patterson to prepare the Fortress for its ferry flight. Tallichet had been a B-17 co-pilot during World War II, but he called upon Jim Appleby, who had flown Tallmantz's B-17 (44-83525*) and who had amassed a large amount of B-17 experience in the Air Force, to fly the bomber from Dayton to Chino with Tallichet as co-pilot. The flight was successful and the Fortress arrived to take up residence in late 1973. The FAA had issued a registration number of N47780 for the ferry flight.

As Tallichet had no formal museum at Chino, the B-17 sat on the ramp for nearly five years. It carried USAAF markings in the form of insignia and tail serial, though the remnants of the removed FAB markings could be seen clearly on the skin. It carried a full complement of gun turrets, courtesy of the Air Force Museum, and appeared to be in pretty good condition as it joined Planes of Fame's Fortress N3713G (44-83684*) at Chino.

In early 1977, an agreement had been worked out with the Combat Air Museum of Topeka, Kansas to become the first of what was to supposed to be a growing number of YAF "wings" spreading across the country to display the collection. Under the terms of the agreement, the Combat Air Museum would provide a hangar for display of the aircraft,

Rare photo of FAB 5400 in Brazilian service. B-17 44-83663 was utilized in the reconnaissance role until retirement in 1968. Note dual ADF antennas above the cockpit. Date and location of photo unknown.
via Wetsch

44-83663 at Chino with Yesterday's Air Force in 1975. Remnants of Brazilian markings in evidence. Aircraft appears well worn.
Ditty via Besecker

pay any expenses and associated costs of ferrying and operating the aircraft, and perform a set amount of restoration on them. Under those terms, a substantial amount of Tallichet's airworthy collection was moved to Topeka. In the summer of 1977 44-83663 would join the group at Topeka after a ferry flight from Chino.

That ferry flight was conducted with a radioless B-17 which hadn't flown in five years and less than ideal weather conditions. Crewed by Tallichet, Combat Air Museum curator Gene Smith, and flight engineer Brian Wandel, the B-17 flew IFR (I Follow Roads) via numerous detours and suffered the vicissitudes of cantankerous engines but arrived safe and sound in Topeka.

Combat Air Museum's affiliation with Tallichet and the YAF was short lived. Combat Air Museum terminated the agreement in December 1978, citing lack of funds and general support from Tallichet. Combat Air Museum swung out on its own, and has managed to evolve into a growing museum still located in Topeka.

44-83663 languished at Topeka until the fall of 1980 when it was flown to another YAF facility at the St. Petersburg-Clearwater Airport in Florida. Site of a proposed YAF museum, the Fortress was repainted in olive-drab combat colors and marked as a spurious Eighth Air Force Fortress. The Florida YAF museum failed to materialize, Tallichet apparently losing interest in putting together a facility to display his collection. The assembled material in Florida began to suffer the elements, and the Fortress continued its downhill slide.

In 1983 the Air Force Museum informed Tallichet that it would be canceling the loan agreement and would take the Fortress for display at the Cleveland National Air Museum. A crew was dispatched from the Air Force Museum to prepare the Fortress for its ferry flight. Initially, the Fortress would have to be moved a mile or so from the old museum site to a hangar where maintenance work would be performed. In moving the B-17, a main landing gear sank into soft soil, forcing the aircraft to swing around the gear, which damaged the left wing and the tail wheel. After repairs were completed, ground runs indicated engine difficulties and further inspections revealed spar corrosion in the wings. The Air Force Museum, which by this time had decided the Fortress would instead go to the Heritage Museum at Hill AFB in Ogden, Utah, made the decision not to fly the aircraft further and disassembled it for transport aboard an Air Force C-5A to Utah. In a curious note, the work crew as able to slide the wing center sections into the C-5 fuselage with a bare three inches to spare, a feat not accomplished by the crew which transported "Shoo Shoo Shoo Baby" from France. That journey resulted in laterally sliced, and internally destroyed, wings.

Arriving in November 1986, 44-83663 has since been reassembled and painted in the markings of the 493rd Bomb Group, Eighth Air Force, as based in England during World War II. Nose markings are of "Short Bier", which apparently was never actually applied to a USAAF B-17, though it was used on a 493rd Group B-24 (lost in France) before the unit transitioned to B-17s in the summer of 1944. The crew of "Short Bier" never got around to painting the moniker on their B-17.

The Fortress is to become the centerpiece of a new $4 million museum complex which will house a number of large aircraft including 44-83663 and offer permanent pro-

tection from the climate. As it happens, Hill AFB was named for Major Ployer P. Hill, the Army test pilot who was killed in the crash of the Fortress prototype, Boeing Model 299, in October 1935. The B-17 thus not only represents the heritage of the Air Force at the Hill Museum, but also provides a particular connection to the history of the air base.

Reassembling the B-17 at Hill AFB in 1986, a volunteer crew unites engine number two with its nacelle. Lindquist

44-83663 was transported from Florida via C-5A. Through careful loading, the wing center sections traveled intact. Lindquist

Two of the FAB B-17s grounded to become spare parts sources to keep the remaining four B-17s flying. #5406 was withdrawn from service in 1966, while #5411 was used until 1968, shortly before 44-83663 was withdrawn. Neither of these aircraft survive. NASM

CHAPTER NINETEEN: 44-83684

PLANES OF FAME
CHINO AIRPORT
CHINO, CALIFORNIA

■■■■■■

44-83684   B-17G-90-DL to DB-17G to N3713G

USAAF/USAF

DATE	LOCATION	UNIT	CMD	REMARKS
07 MAY 45	LONG BEACH		ATC	ACCEPTED
11 MAY 45	PATTERSON		ATC	STORAGE
(15 OCT 45)	(declared excess)		– –	
03 NOV 45	SOUTH PLAINS	4168 BASE UNIT	ATC	STORAGE
(07 NOV 45)	(returned to military service)		– –	
07 JUL 47	PYOTE	4141 BASE UNIT	AMC	STORAGE
17 FEB 50	PYOTE	2753 ACFT STORAGE SQ	AMC	STORAGE
31 MAR 50	OLMSTED	MIDDLETOWN AIR DEPOT	AMC	
(21 JUN 50)	(fr: B-17G to: DB-17G)		– –	
18 JUL 50	EGLIN	3200 DRONE SQ	APG	
30 NOV 50	EGLIN	3200 DRONE GP	APG	
28 FEB 51	EGILIN	3200 PROOF TEST GP	APG	
01 APR 51	ENIWETOK	3200 PROOF TEST WG	APG	
31 MAY 51	EGLIN	3200 PROOF TEST WG	APG	
20 SEP 51	HOLLOMAN	3200 PROOF TEST WG	APG	
15 NOV 51	HOLLOMAN	3200 DRONE GP	APG	
02 DEC 51	HOLLOMAN	3205 DRONE GP	APG	
(NOV 56)	(fr: DB-17G to: DB-17P)		– –	
06 AUG 59	DAVIS-MONTHAN	– –	AMC	STORAGE
(SEP 59)	(to: The Air Museum, Claremont, CA)			

CIVIL

DATE	TRANSFER DETAILS
24 SEP 59	FR: 2704 AIRCRAFT STORAGE AND DISPOSITION GROUP, DAVIS MONTHAN AFB, TUCSON, AZ
	TO: THE AIR MUSEUM, CLAREMONT, CA
(10 JUL 81)	(FAA registration certificate revoked for not filing appropriate paperwork)

44-83684

44-83684 served as a drone director during its active Air Force years between 1950 and 1959. After being withdrawn from service, it was placed on permanent loan with The Air Museum (later Planes of Fame) located first at Claremont, California, which later moved to Ontario and again to Chino. With the Air Museum, 44-83684 became a TV star for use in the television production of "Twelve O'Clock High," filmed partially at Chino Airport between 1964 and 1966. (See Part 3, Section 3.) Retaining its TV name of "Picadilly Lily", 44-83684 has now been grounded by the Air Force but continues to greet visitors to the Planes of Fame facility at Chino Airport.

44-83684 was one of the many late Douglas-produced B-17s which went straight from the factory into storage. Accepted on 07 May 1945, it was flown from Long Beach to Patterson Field, Ohio, arriving on 11 May and placed into short term storage. Deemed excess to military use on 15 October 1945 (as were most other B-17s in storage), initial steps were taken to transfer it to the Reconstruction Finance Corporation. The Army Air Force decided to retain some of its Fortresses however, and 44-83684 was reinstated to the inventory and flown to South Plains, Texas, for long-term storage.

It remained at South Plains until July 1947 when it and other stored Fortresses were moved to Pyote Field, also in Texas, and placed in storage initially with the 4141st Base Unit, and then the 2753rd Aircraft Storage Squadron. 44-83684 remained at Pyote through March 1950 when withdrawn and assigned to the Air Materiel Command for conversion to a DB-17G drone director. It was flown to Olmsted AFB in Pennsylvania and its Middletown Air Depot where the conversion was undertaken. It was redesignated as a DB-17G on 21 June 1950 and assigned to the Air Proving Ground Command.

On 18 July 1950 44-83684 arrived at Eglin AFB, Florida, and attached to the 3200th Drone Group, which was part of the 3200th Proof Test Wing. On 28 February 1951 the wing was deployed to Eniwetok Atoll in the South Pacific for use during the Greenhouse Series of nuclear tests involv-

ing the new hydrogen bomb. 44-83684 and the rest of the unit provided drone and drone controllers for the test series. 44-83684 returned to Eglin in May 1951, where it remained until assigned to Holloman AFB and Detachment One of the 3200th Drone Group on 20 September 1951.

In December 1951 the structure of the Drone Groups were changed and many of the drone controllers and drones were assigned to the 3205th Drone Group, which eventually would come to have most of the DB-17 and QB-17 aircraft in the Air Force inventory. Detachment One at Holloman later became the 3225th Drone Squadron, one of four squadrons of the Group which were variously deployed at Eglin AFB, Holloman AFB, NAS Pt. Mugu, and Patrick AFB.

44-83684 would spend the balance of its Air Force utilization at Holloman AFB and the 3225th Drone Squadron, aside from occasional overhauls conducted at Olmsted AFB. 44-83684 underwent additional modifications in 1956 and was redesignated as a DB-17P.

44-83684 would, in fact, continue to soldier along until the very end of the line, becoming the last operational Air Force B-17. It was utilized on the last DB-17/QB-17 mission conducted on 06 August 1959 from Holloman AFB when 44-83684 controlled QB-17G 44-83717 as a target for a Falcon air-to-air missile fired from an F-101 Voodoo jet fighter. It was the last of 600 similar missions conducted from Holloman. A few days later ceremonies were conducted at the base as this last Fortress was mustered out of the service and sent off to the Davis-Monthan boneyard for an unknown future.

As it happened, 44-82684 would spend only a short time at Davis-Monthan. It was arranged that the aircraft would be placed on permanent loan with Ed Maloney's Air Museum located in Claremont, California, some thirty miles east of Los Angeles. The arrangement was consummated on 24 September 1959 when the newly registered N3713G became a privately operated museum piece. Maloney put his new Fortress to work quickly as 44-83684 appeared in an episode of TV's "Dick Powell Theatre" in a show about the famed 100th Bomb Group.

Ed Maloney was a peculiar sort of visionary. Starting with a Japanese "Baka" flying bomb in 1946, Maloney collected

44-83684 as a DB-17G at Wright-Patterson AFB in August 1956.
W. Balogh via Menard

Same aircraft at retirement ceremonies at Holloman AFB in August 1959. DB-17 was used on last DB-17/ QB-17 mission and was the last of the Air Force B-17s in active use. Crew is preparing to fly aircraft on final flight to Davis-Monthan.
USAF via Criss

44-83684 at Davis-Monthan. Note unusual configuration of tail serial. USAF via Criss

Another view of 44-83684 at Davis-Monthan in 1959.
USAF via Criss

Ed Maloney obtained 44-83684 in a long-term loan agreement in September 1959. Here is the Fortress at Chino shortly after arrival.
Peltzer

otherwise unwanted junk through the years. That the junk included a P-47 Thunderbolt, F4U Corsair, Bearcat, and other surplus military airplanes set him apart from other collectors. By the late fifties Maloney had organized his collection into the Air Museum of Claremont. In 1959 he arranged to obtain 44-83684, and in 1963 he had moved his collection to the nearby Ontario Airport for display. Most of his aircraft were ratty on the verge of derelict, as were most of the civil surplus military aircraft around at that time. This was long before the aviation community attached any value to the warbirds, and Maloney found little support for his operation. The aircraft were relatively easy to obtain, coming from the Air Force in loans, by trades, or by purchase of civil equipment. The difficulties ensued, however, when trying to finance any restorative or protective work on his collection.

By 1969 he opened a joint facility in tourist-rich Orange County with an automobile collector. Dubbed "Cars of the Stars/Planes of Fame", the facility set no dramatic tourist records but gave Maloney a place for part of his non-flying collection. Some of the less ratty grounded exhibits were set up in dioramas and accompanying photos or signs rounded out the museum. The shoestring budget of the operation prevented it from reaching its potential, and by 1973 the facility was closed and Maloney's collection was spread again across Southern California airports, with the majority of it located at Chino Airport.

Chino is well known now as a warbird's mecca, with a number of high-quality warbird restoration shops and museums located on the field. Back in the early sixties, it was a sleepy, ex-military flight training airport with a variety of deadbeat military surplus junkers about. Its major distinction was that of being used for outdoor exteriors during filming of the television series "Twelve O'Clock High" between 1964 and 1966. The old airport administration buildings, built during the war, were dressed up to become the home

of the 918th Bomb Group. The airfield and ramp area were used also, and Twentieth Century-Fox, producers of the TV series, contracted with the the Air Museum to provide N3713G as window dressing for operational scenes.

Donning blackish-grey top surfaces and grey undersurfaces and a set of 91st Bomb Group markings (to blend with combat footage available from Air Force sources for the black and white series), N3713G became the "Picadilly Lily" for General Frank Savage and later, Colonel Joe Gallagher. It was used for taxiing sequences, embarking and debarking scenes, and other operational set dressing.

As noted elsewhere, the series suffered many drawbacks, but at its best it offered some good wartime B-17 footage for those mid-sixties folks who balked at watching the "Beverly Hillbillies." With the cancellation of the series in late 1966, the set and N3713G slowly slid downhill in disuse.

N3713G enjoyed a quick resurrection, however, in late 1967 when the producers of the film "1000 Plane Raid" hired Maloney to provide one of three B-17s to be brought in to Santa Maria Airport on the California coast for yet another reel remake of the Eighth Air Force in action. Maloney and his museum crew scrambled to bring the Fortress up to something resembling airworthiness, only to be confounded by an engine failure on a test flight shortly before the B-17 was to depart to Santa Maria on Saturday, 13 January 1968. A gofer was dispatched to nearby Orange County Airport, where Tallmantz Aviation was furiously trying to button together its recently obtained B-17 (44-83525* N83525) for the same film. Returning with a borrowed cylinder, the Air Museum crew set about to rebuild their ailing engine on the ramp at Ontario Airport. Completing their task overnight, the Fortress set out for Santa Maria the next afternoon with pilots Maloney and Don Lykins at the controls.

Arriving, they found B-17F 42-29782* (N17W) from Aircraft Specialties of Mesa, Arizona already on the field. N83525 would arrive the following afternoon, several hours late, after a quick ferry flight from Orange County. All three would be repainted in movie combat colors to blend with the planned use of black and white Air Force footage and sequences from the film "12 O'Clock High" tinted for the color production. N3713G became AD-F with the name "Bucking Bronco" applied to the nose.

Filming commenced a few days later, the production company also utilizing as a camera ship one of the two B-25s operated by Tallmantz Aviation. Numerous taxiing scenes, a crash sequence, and takeoff and landing sequences were filmed over the next two weeks, as were a series of air-to-air sessions involving two of the B-17s and the B-25. A reportedly memorable buzzing sequence was filmed with Lykins and Maloney at the controls of N3713G, and photographs indeed reveal scant feet between the Fortress's ball turret and the ramp. At the end of the production the assembled air force dispersed to their home fields. As noted elsewhere, "1000 Plane Raid" was somewhat less than successful after its release in 1969.

N3713G returned to take up residence at Chino Airport. It made it to a number of airshows in the following two years but eventually came back to a permanent roost at Chino. Beginning around 1970, N3713G wore the colors of the 452nd Bomb Group, with standard AAF olive drab upper surfaces and grey undersurfaces. No squadron codes were applied. A chin turret was refitted to the nose, and a genuine ball turret was installed. In 1977, the "square L" of the 452nd

was replaced by the "square K" of the 447th Bomb Group. Once again, no squadron codes were carried. Finally, in 1982, N3713G reverted to straight olive drab colors with no group markings applied.

The Air Museum's collection was a mess by the late sixties, but over the next decade a resurgence of interest in the warbirds enabled the museum to finally find a financial footing and put the renamed "Planes of Fame" operation into a better position. By late in the seventies the museum was regularly churning out well restored rarities from its shop, and was able to put on a number of successful airshows at the airport. In the early eighties Planes of Fame was constructing new hangars and other facilities to house their rare aircraft, and the museum finally achieved a measure of respect among those who were distraught at the condition of the collection as it had disintegrated in earlier years.

The times were not quite as kind to N3713G. With all four Wright R1820-97s run out, and with the Air Museum without funds to overhaul them or maintain the other systems on the Fortress, the Air Force Museum grounded the B-17 in 1971.

Today, 44-83684 (as it is still marked) remains a signpost for Planes of Fame as the Fortress majestically greets visitors to the facility. Every few years it receives yet another layer of paint to cover the excessive bird droppings and smog-eaten residue of its last olive drab coat. A group of B-17 veterans do their best to keep the Fortress open on weekends for visitors to tour its interior. While it's sad to note that it's unlikely the B-17 will fly again, other Fortresses have suffered far worse fates than this one, and it is probable that the "Picadilly Lily" will continue to hold a spot at Chino Airport for years to come.

44-83684 in "12 O'Clock High" colors at Chino in the early sixties. 91st Bomb Group markings were used to help match footage from the wartime documentary "The Memphis Belle." Larkins

N3713G made up as "Bucking Bronco" for "1000 Plane Raid" in January 1968 at Santa Maria Airport.
Piedmonte via Besecker

Filming in progress at Santa Maria in early 1968. Once again, N3713G is painted to match "Memphis Belle" footage. Farmer

Chapter Twenty: 44-83690

GRISSOM AIRPARK
GRISSOM AFB, INDIANA

■ ■ ■ ■ ■ ■

44-83690	B-17G-95-DL TO DB-17G TO DB-17P			

USAAF/USAF

DATE	LOCATION	UNIT	CMD	REMARKS
09 MAY 45	LONG BEACH		ATS	ACCEPTED
12 MAY 45	PATTERSON	4100 BASE UNIT	ATS	STORAGE
(15 OCT 45)	(declared excess)		– –	
(07 NOV 45)	(returned to military use)		– –	
14 NOV 45	SOUTH PLAINS	4168 BASE UNIT	ATS	STORAGE
24 JUN 47	PYOTE	4141 BASE UNIT	AMC	STORAGE
17 FEB 50	PYOTE	2753 ACFT STOR SQ	AMC	STORAGE
04 MAY 50	OLMSTED	MIDDLETOWN AIR DEPOT	AMC	
(07 JUL 50)	(FR: B-17G TO: DB-17G)			
19 JUL 50	EGLIN	3200 DRONE GROUP	APG	
30 NOV 50	EGLIN	3200 PROOF TEST GROUP APG		
28 FEB 51	ENIWETOKA	3200 PROOF TEST WING	APG	
31 MAY 51	EGLIN	3200 DRONE GROUP	APG	
02 DEC 51	EGLIN	3205 DRONE GROUP	APG	
06 SEP 54	HOLLOMAN	3205 DRONE GROUP	APG	
55	WRI-PAT	2750 AIR BASE WING	AMC	
55	EGLIN	3205 DRONE GROUP	APG	
55	OLMSTED	MIDDLETOWN AIR DEPOT	AMC	
(55)	(FR: DB-17G TO: DB-17P)			
55	EGLIN	3205 DRONE GROUP	APG	
56	PATRICK	3205 DRONE GROUP	APG	
JUN 59	DAVIS-MONTHAN		AMC	
AUG 60	DAVIS-MONTHAN	2704 ACFT STOR/DIS GP	AMC	
(61)	(transferred to Bunker Hill AFB for display)			

44-83690

44-83690 is on outdoor display at Grissom AFB in Indiana. It was flown to the base in 1961 after fifteen years of Air Force use and is now part of the Grissom AFB Heritage Museum.

44-83690 was accepted at Long Beach on 09 May 1945. As a B-17G-95-DL it was in the final block of the Douglas-produced Fortresses. Flown from Long Beach to Patterson Field, Ohio, 690 was placed in storage along with most of the other factory-fresh B-17s. It was declared excess on 15 October 1945 but returned to military use on 07 November 1945. Shortly thereafter, 83690 was moved to South Plains, Texas, assigned to the 4168th Base Unit, and placed in storage again. It was reassigned once again, on 24 June 1946, to Pyote Field, Texas for storage with the 4141st Base Unit.

DB-17G 44-83690 in May 1953. Most DB-17s carried large letter marking on tail. Note antenna in former ball turret location. Krieger

Another view of the aircraft at what appears to be a military open house. Date and location of photo are unknown. Krieger

On 17 February 1950, the B-17 was assigned to the 2753rd Aircraft Storage Squadron at Pyote.

In mid-1950 44-83690, along with many of the new B-17s at Pyote, was slated for conversion to a drone director. Reassigned to the Middletown Air Depot at Olmsted AFB, Pennsylvania, the Fortress was subsequently modified to a DB-17G configuration and redesignated as such on 07 July 1950.

As a DB-17G, it was initially assigned to the Air Proving Ground Command and the 3200th Drone Group at Eglin AFB in Florida. During February 1951 83690 was deployed with other DB-17s and QB-17s to Kwajalein in the South Pacific to participate in the "Operation Greenhouse" series of of nuclear tests for the Atomic Energy Commission.

Returning to Eglin on 31 May 51, the B-17 joined the 3205th Drone Group where it would remain for the balance of its active military use, and was attached to the 3215th Drone Squadron while at Eglin.

In 1955, 44-83690 was modified to a DB-17P configuration with the installation of additional drone control equipment. Beginning in 1956 it was assigned to the 3235th Drone Squadron at the Missile Test Center at Patrick AFB, Florida, where it remained until 1959 when retired from service and sent to Davis-Monthan AFB in Arizona. Assigned to the 2704th Aircraft Storage and Disposal Group, it was stricken from the Air Force inventory in August 1960.

As one of the last Air Force B-17s, 44-83690 found a new home at Bunker Hill AFB in Indiana. It was flown to the base in 1961 for permanent static display and became the nucleus around which a memorial air park would form. The Fortress and a host of other preserved Air Force aircraft (B-25 Mitchell, B-47 Stratojet, B-58 Hustler, and F-104 Starfighter, among others), came to be displayed near the main gate of the AFB. The base was renamed Grissom AFB in May 1968 in memory of Lt. Col. Virgil "Gus" Grissom who died in January 1967 atop a Saturn rocket during pre-launch tests of Apollo I.

Through the years 690 saw alternating periods of neglect and sporadic efforts at restoration. Equipment and instruments slowly disappeared from the interior, and the exterior began to display the visages of time evident in corrosion and skin damage. Various coats of paint and a hodgepodge of markings were applied to the B-17 at the whim of base commanders or restoration crews. Efforts at maintenance were primarily confined to spot problems and prevention of further deterioration. Grossly inaccurate ball and dorsal turrets had been fabricated and attached to the fuselage in an attempt to portray a combat-ready Fortress. The lack of consistent upkeep and planned long-term restoration was apparent.

However, with the advent of the the Air Force Museum Program in 1981 individual Air Force bases were authorized to form local museums with the full support and cooperation of the the Air Force Museum. Under the program the Grissom AFB Heritage Museum Foundation was established. Founded by John Crume, who had long expressed concern over the deteriorating state of the B-17 and other displayed aircraft, the Heritage Museum Foundation brought together civil and military interests whose goal was preservation of the collection. Acting largely as a fundraising source, the Foundation assumed responsibility for the upkeep and operation of the Grissom Air Park. Volunteers from all areas, whose thread of commonalty lay only in their interest in the historical aircraft, have now donated thousands of hours of labor in the restoration and continual care required by all the aircraft at the the Air Park.

About two-thirds of that time has been devoted to 690, not only because it is the oldest vintage aircraft at Grissom but also because it has become the flagship of the museum. Work commenced in the summer of 1983 as a score of dedicated volunteers swarmed over the old bomber, stripping layers of paint, patching metal skin, and performing corrosion control. It was then primed and finished with a a final coat of aluminized paint.

For one particular member of the restoration crew, Captain Frank Ross, the opportunity to work on the B-17 was a dream come true. Otherwise a KC-135 tanker pilot, Ross's first love was the Flying Fortress. He dove into 690 and spearheaded the effort to restore the old bomber. After the exterior was reasonably complete, Ross turned his attention to the gutted interior. Through the years the B-17 had slowly been stripped of many parts, and the group restoring "Shoo Shoo Shoo Baby" at Dover AFB had also been allowed to obtain needed interior equipment. Nonetheless, Ross and his coworkers have been slowly collecting parts, including a new instrument panel, instruments, seats, and a bombardier control panel. They are being installed as limited time and funding permit.

It was decided early in the project to restore the Fortress in 305th Bomb Group markings as operated from Great Bri-

44-83690 at Dallas in August 1956. Letter marking on tail is gone and "U.S. Air Force" marking is larger and moved onto the lower nose. M. Mayborn via Besecker

44-83690 at Grissom in 1970 carrying a mishmash of markings. Menard via Besecker

tain in World War II, as the direct descendant of that bomb group, the 305th Air Refueling Wing, is based at Grissom. Determining an individual aircraft for name and nose art was relatively easy. 44-83690 became "Miss Liberty Belle," appropriate not only in that it was an actual B-17G operated by the 305th, but also because the base's namesake, Virgil Grissom, had flown "Liberty Bell 7" on his Mercury space mission in 1962.

The original "Miss Liberty Belle" (B-17G-10-BO 42-31255) crashed on a wartime training mission in England but its first commander, Lt. (now Lt. Col. USAF ret.) Richard Wolff, was able to provide records, nose art details. and photos of the original. A reunion of the wartime crewmembers occurred some time later around the newly created "Miss Liberty Belle."

As the aircraft stands now, a fiberglass dorsal turret has replaced the hideous replica dome. The new reproduction is quite authentic in appearance and was obtained through trade from Aero Nostalgia of Stockton, CA, which is quickly becoming a major provider of B-17 parts and replica parts for the numerous ongoing restorations. A real ball turret was obtained from the Air Force Museum and the turret mount from the 390th Bomb Group Museum at Pima County, Arizona. The fiberglass chin turret now in place is slated for replacement by an actual unit left over from the "Shoo Shoo Shoo Baby" project.

The Plexiglas blown nose piece is also to be replaced. The one on 690 is a locally produced replica and is noticeably of the wrong shape. A new blown nose molded from an actual unit is to be obtained, also from Aero Nostalgia. Additional work in the nose section will include reinstallation of cheek window fairings and their accompanying flexible guns. The original left cheek window fairing was removed during conversion to DB-17G configuration, while the right window fairing was given to the "Shoo Shoo Shoo Baby" project. As no authentic fairings are now available, fiberglass units will be used. With metal rivets added, the reproduction can't be told from the original.

The B-17 had been placed on pylons early in its display history. The pylons had presented the B-17 in a very unnatural attitude which tended to spoil the distinctive lines of the airplane. Beyond that, the internal drainage system, designed to work in a conventional attitude, was defeated and water collected in the internal structure promoting unwelcome corrosion. 690 has now been removed from the pylons, allowing water to flow as Boeing intended and bringing the "humpbacked bird" back to its familiar pose.

Restorative work began in 1983 improved the condition of the B-17. Seen here in 1986 it carries new nose art, a chin turret, and a inaccurate blown nose. Parrow

By 1986 44-83690 had been cleaned up but still sat on the pylons and retained a poor replica of a dorsal turret. Parrow

CHAPTER TWENTY-ONE: 44-83785

PINAL AIRPARK, ARIZONA

■■ ■■■■

(alternative 1)

44-83785   B-17G-95-DL to CB-17G to VB-17G to CB-17G to VB-17G to N809Z to N207EV

USAAF/USAF

DATE	LOCATION	UNIT	CMD	REMARKS
22 JUN 45	LONG BEACH		ATC	ACCEPTED
24 JUN 45	CHEYENNE	MODIFICATION CENTER	ATC	
02 JUL 45	KAUAI			
(24 JUL 45)	(departed U.S.)	— —		
(30 APR 47)	(fr: B-17G to: CB-17G)		— —	
(30 APR 47)	(fr: ATC to: Pacific Air Command)			
18 JUL 47	HICKAM		PAC	
(26 OCT 48)	(fr: CB-17G to: VB-17G)		— —	
14 DEC 48	HICKAM	6506 BASE UNIT	PAC	
31 MAY 49	HICKAM	1500 BASE UNIT	PAC	
(09 JUN 49)	(fr: VB-17G to: CB-17G)		— —	
(09 JUN 49)	(fr: PAC to: Military Transport)			
09 JUN 49	HICKAM	6506 BASE UNIT	MTO	
29 JUN 49	HICKAM	1500 MIL SUPPLY GP	MTO	
(29 SEP 49)	(fr: MTO to: Far East Air Forces)			
29 SEP 49	HANEDA	FEA		
07 OCT 49	KOMAKI	6106 BASE UNIT	FEA	
(18 JUL 51)	(fr: CB-17G to: VB-17G)		— —	
28 JAN 52	KOMAKI	6101 BASE WING	FEA	
08 MAR 53	OLMSTED	MIDDLETOWN AIR DEPOT	AMC	OVERHAUL
02 JUN 53	KOMAKI	6101 BASE WING	FEA	
OCT 54	KOMAKI	5 AIR FORCE	FEA	
DEC 56	TACHIKAWA	AIR DEPOT	FEA	
	(record ends)			

CIVIL

DATE	TRANSFER DETAILS
01 SEP 60	FR: MILITARY DISPOSAL FACILITIES, DOD
	TO: ATLANTIC-GENERAL, WASHINGTON D.C.
(19 MAY 61)	(military serial changed from 44-85531 to 44-83785)
04 OCT 62	TO: INTERMOUNTAIN AVIATION, PHOENIX, AZ
01 MAR 75	TO: EVERGREEN HELICOPTERS, MCMINNVILLE, OR
11 JAN 77	TO: EVERGREEN AIR OF MONTANA, MISSOULA, MT
(06 MAR 79)	(registration changed from N809Z to N207EV)
31 MAR 79	TO: EVERGREEN HELICOPTERS, MCMINNVILLE, OR
19 JUL 85	TO: EVERGREEN EQUITY, MCMINNVILLE, OR

44-85531   B-17G-95-VE to TB-17G to SB-17G to TB-17G to N809Z to N207EV

USAAF/USAF

DATE	LOCATION	UNIT	CMD	REMARKS
12 MAR 45	BURBANK		ATC	ACCEPTED
15 MAR 45	CHEYENNE	MODIFICATION CENTER	ATC	
22 MAR 45	HUNTER FIELD			
(30 MAR 45)	(departed U.S.)		– –	
30 JUN 45	SOUTH PLAINS		ATC	STORAGE
04 FEB 46	CLOVIS	234 BASE UNIT	CAF	
07 MAY 46	MARCH	40 BOMB GROUP	SAC	
23 MAY 46	DAVIS-MO	40 BOMB GROUP	SAC	
03 JUN 46	DAVIS-MO	238 BASE UNIT	SAC	
25 AUG 46	LONG BEACH	556 BASE UNIT	ATC	
30 SEP 46	SOUTH PLAINS	4168 BASE UNIT	AMC	
08 JUN 47	OLMSTED	4112 BASE UNIT	AMC	
(21 AUG 47)	(fr: B-17G to: TB-17G)		– –	
26 AUG 47	KADENA	FEA		
(15 FEB 48)	(fr: TB-17G to: SB-17G)		– –	
15 FEB 48	KADENA	2 RESCUE SQ	FEA	
08 JUN 49	KADENA	2 RESCUE SQ	MTO	
21 OCT 51	OLMSTED	MIDDLETOWN AIR DEPOT	AMC	
(22 JAN 52)	(fr: SB-17G to: TB-17G)		– –	
17 FEB 52	UNKN	6400 AIR DEFENSE WG	FEA	FEAMCOM
11 FEB 53	UNKN		FEA	TOP SECRET
	(record ends)			

CIVIL

DATE	TRANSFER DETAILS
01 SEP 60	FR: MILITARY DISPOSAL FACILITIES, DOD
	TO: ATLANTIC-GENERAL, WASHINGTON D.C.
(19 MAY 61)	(military serial changed from 44-85531 to 44-83785)
04 OCT 62	TO: INTERMOUNTAIN AVIATION, PHOENIX, AZ
01 MAR 75	TO: EVERGREEN HELICOPTERS, MCMINNVILLE, OR
11 JAN 77	TO: EVERGREEN AIR OF MONTANA, MISSOULA, MT
(06 MAR 79)	(registration changed from N809Z to N207EV)
31 MAR 79	TO: EVERGREEN HELICOPTERS, MCMINNVILLE, OR
19 JUL 85	TO: EVERGREEN EQUITY, MCMINNVILLE, OR

44-83785

One of the more mysterious of the surviving B-17s, 44-83785 had the distinction of being operated by the Central Intelligence Agency on a number of covert operations. There is, in fact, a large question as to the actual identity of the aircraft, now operated as N207EV by Evergreen International, as details of the operational use of this B-17 are still shrouded behind classified doors.

The story behind N207EV is intriguing. What is known for sure is that this particular B-17 emerged into view in 1962 being operated by Intermountain Aviation as N809Z. Intermountain had purchased N809Z from Atlantic-General Enterprises of Washington D.C. on 04 October of that year. Both Atlantic-General and Intermountain were later revealed to have been proprietary corporations controlled by the Central Intelligence Agency in support of international covert operations.

The CIA had operated at least one, and possibly two, B-17s in the mid-1950s from Clark AFB in the Philippines. One Fortress, known to be B-17G-95-VE 44-85531, was apparently borrowed from the Air Force and used for photo reconnaissance, agent insertion, and other unspecified covert activities against several Asian countries including North Korea, North Vietnam, and China. The aircraft was gloss black overall and carried a minimum of markings, which included a slide on serial number for easy identification changes apparently essential in such specialized work. Other modifications included a exit hatch in place of the ball turret and exhaust suppressers for each engine. The aircraft did not carry any defensive armament.

The CIA and its cover organizations were adept at concealing aircraft identities and had whole departments whose only function was to create fictitious aircraft in duplicates and triplicates to confuse and confound anyone trying to track ongoing CIA operations. The CIA would operate two or three identically marked aircraft on circuitous routes from overseas bases to provide viable covers. Internally, the aircraft were stripped of any identification numbers or plates, thus making it "non-attributable" in the event of it falling into the wrong hands.

When filing paperwork to initially register N809Z with the Federal Aviation Administration, Atlantic-General identified their B-17 as 44-85531 and it was carried on the books identified as such for ten months. At that time a newly "discovered" document was submitted by Atlantic-General which "correctly" identified the bomber as B-17G-95-DL 44-83785, and the FAA changed their paperwork.

However, photographic evidence displays identical exhaust suppressers on 44-85531 in 1958 and N809Z in 1962. Also, the photos reveal a number of unique antennas identically attached to the forward nose section on each aircraft. Thus, it is but a short step to presume that N809Z/N207EV

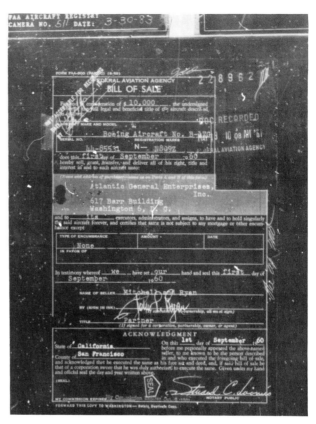

This bill of sale between the B-17s first two civil owners still shows the military serial of 44-85531. Ten months later the FAA was notified that the serial number was in error. Mitchell and Ryan, Atlantic-General Enterprises, and Intermountain were all later revealed to have close ties with the Central Intelligence Agency.

is actually 44-85531 and that security-conscious intelligence officers decided the new aircraft identity was more appropriate for the as-yet uncloaked CIA cover corporations. This is wholly conjecture, though, for it would be difficult to prove the actual identity of the Fortress given the nature of the CIA and the lack of any available documents. A close examination of the interior of N207EV reveals nothing as it was long ago "sanitized" and virtually all identification marks and plates are missing. So, much is left to speculation but both the histories of 44-85531 and 44-83785 are provided here for the curious of heart.

44-85531 rolled from the Burbank production lines of Vega on 10 March 1945 and was accepted by the Army Air Force two days later. It was flown to Cheyenne, Wyoming for modification at the United Airlines Modification Center, and was available for service on 22 March 1945. It departed the U.S. on 30 March, presumably for a replacement depot in Great Britain. It was back in the country in late June, and placed in storage at South Plains, Texas on 30 June 1945. It remained there until 04 February 1946 when flown to Clovis Field, New Mexico and assigned to the 234th Base Unit. On 07 May 1946 it went to March Field in California and the 40th Bomb Group (Very Heavy), where it remained

44-85531 at Clark AFB in October 1957. RB-17G had the unique feature of a slide-in tail number. All black Fortress was used for clandestine activities Olmstead

Same aircraft with different tail serial. Reputed uses included agent insertion into Korea, Vietnam, and China for the Central Intelligence Agency. Olmstead

44-85531 on a boneyard in June 1958. Photographer Olmstead recalled the carburetors and windshield were removed and sent to Wright-Patterson for an unspecified reason. Olmstead

until 23 May 1946 when it was deployed to Davis-Monthan Field in Arizona. On 03 June 1946 44-85531 was assigned to the 234th Base Unit at Davis-Monthan. On 25 August 1946 44-85531 went to the 556th Base Unit at Long Beach Field, and then back to South Plains for storage on 30 September 1946. It remained in storage until June 1947 when assigned to a Base Unit at Olmsted Field in Pennsylvania where it was redesignated as a TB-17G on 21 August 1947. It was subsequently assigned to the Far East Air Forces and stationed at Kadena Air Base on Okinawa.

44-85531 was redesignated as a SB-17G on 15 May 1948 while based at Kadena and assigned to the 2nd Rescue Squadron with the Far East Air Forces. On 08 June 1949 it was reassigned to the Military Air Transport Service, but remained with the 2nd Rescue Squadron at Kadena. It remained with the unit through October 1951, well into the Korean War, with the exception of a short assignment with the 1503rd Base Unit at Haneda, Japan. 44-85531 was also operationally based at Clark Field with the 2nd Rescue Squadron for a short period in 1950.

On 21 October 1951 44-85531 was returned to Olmsted AFB in Pennsylvania for overhaul at the Middletown Air

Depot and was assigned to the Air Materiel Command. At Olmsted, it was redesignated again as a TB-17G and deployed back to the Far East as part of the Far East Air Materiel Command beginning in February 1952. The aircraft would remain with the command for one year, after which the aircraft record card notes the assignment of 44-85531 to a Top Secret project on 11 February 1953. Presumably it began its CIA utilization shortly thereafter, though no indications of its fate are recorded in its military record.

Aviation historian Merle Olmstead was stationed Clark Field in 1957, and he photographed that Fortress during different phases of its use. He recalls last seeing the B-17 languishing in the weeds, devoid of carburetors, windshield, and other items which had been shipped to Wright-Patterson AFB for an unspecified reason. The exact fate of the Fortress beyond that has yet to be absolutely established.

The other Fortress, the one presently listed on the registration documents for N207EV, was 44-83785. It was built by Douglas at Long Beach and accepted by the Army Air Force on 22 June 1945. It was flown to Cheyenne, Wyoming for modifications at the United Airlines Modification Center

N809Z at San Francisco Airport in June 1962. Of particular note are the exhaust suppressors and nose antenna identical to that carried by 44-83551. Note also the "Skyhook" nose equipment. Larkins

and was ready for service on 02 July 1945. It was flown to Hawaii for assignment to the Hawaiian Air Wing, departing the mainland on 24 July. Its use during the following two years is obscure, but it was redesignated as a CB-17G on 30 April 1947 in Hawaii. On 18 July 1947 44-83785 was assigned to Hickam Field and the Pacific Air Command, a joint Army-Navy command.

On 26 October 1948, 44-83785 was redesignated as a VB-17G and was shortly thereafter assigned to the 6506th Base Group at Hickam. It remained with this unit and the 1500th Military Supply Group until September 1949 when it was assigned to the Far East Air Force and once again redesignated back to a CB-17G. It remained with the 1500th Military Supply Group when the unit moved to Haneda, Japan. On 07 October 1949 the CB-17G went to the 6106th Base Group at Komaki, and remained with that unit for nearly a year and a half, and was redesignated as a VB-17G again in July 1951. On 28 January 1952 it was assigned to the 6101st Base Wing at Komaki, and apparently remained at Komaki until 1956, though it was assigned to the 5th Air Force's Headquarters Command in October 1954. Released military records end in December 1956, so the fate of this aircraft is also unconfirmed.

Detail of "Skyhook" equipment carried by N809Z in June 1962. Exact details and purpose have not been confirmed but apparently involved lifting men and equipment directly from the ground. Larkins

Thus, it is apparent that either 44-83551 or 44-83785 eventually wound up in the hands of Mitchell and Ryan, Inc., who sold it to Atlantic-General of Washington D.C. on 01 September 1960. FAA registration records indicate that it was 44-85531 which was purchased from the military disposal facilities of the Department of Defense, and that documents relating to its sale were "lost". In any event, the FAA issued a civil registration of N809Z to the aircraft and, as related earlier, the filed military serial number was changed on 19 May 1961. On 04 October 1962 N809Z was sold to Intermountain Aviation of Phoenix, Arizona. Registration papers filed for that sale indicate a military serial of 44-85531 circled and replaced by the new serial of 44-83785.

Intermountain Aviation was a little known company which moved into Arizona and settled at the Marana Air Park, about thirty miles northeast of Tucson and far from the prying eyes of everyone. Marana was an ex-military airfield and Intermountain put most of the desolate facilities to use, including the guard shacks. Intermountain came to be well-known for their specialized capability for dropping smoke-jumpers into hot spots of forest fires. They also were capable of modifying any aircraft for any purpose. Airlines came to store their unused airliners at Marana and paid Intermountain a fee for the service. It was only in the late seventies that the truth about Intermountain was confirmed. It was revealed that Intermountain was a proprietary organization for the CIA, which wholly owned it and a number of similar companies. The specialties for what Intermountain was well known slotted right into capability the CIA needed, and it would appear Marana was the focal point for a number of covert operations undertaken south of the border. As noted in another chapter, both Intermountain Aviation and Aero-Associates of nearby Ryan Field were implicated in gun-running efforts in the mid-sixties as planes prepared by Intermountain and crewed by Aero-Associates pilots were attempting to ferry Douglas A-26s to Africa in violation of a United Nations weapons embargo.

N809Z sported some strange modifications in 1962. A large boom affair was attached to the nose section, forming a giant "Y" extending forward from the nose. Intermoun-

N809Z at Marana in January 1965. "Skyhook" equipment is still in place, and a tail modification has been added. Note what appears to have been a serial number holding tray on the vertical stabilizer.
C. Jansson via Peltzer

tain explained the device as a system under development whereby the B-17 could swoop in and recover smokejumpers when they were done putting out fires. The daring firefighters would somehow be suspended from tall trees or poles and the Fortress would make a low pass to snag the line. The smokejumper would then work his way into the nose section of the Fortress. N809Z also sported a padded exit chute in the former tail gun position, also for the smoke-jumpers. Though first photographed on the aircraft in 1962, Intermountain continued to develop the Skyhook project, for as late as 1967 they were petitioning the FAA for permission to "conduct exhibition pick-ups of objects and/or cargo from the ground by an airplane in flight". Unconfirmed rumors have N809Z being used to pick up a presumably un-willing "rescued" Soviet "fisherman" from a CIA ship in the Bering Sea.

Perhaps in keeping with the spirit of things, N809Z was graciously lent to United Artists in 1964 to be used for a bit part in "Thunderball," a James Bond epic released that year.

Intermountain kept telling everyone they were in the forest-fire fighting business, so perhaps it seemed a good idea to have some forest-fire fighting equipment on hand. Thus, in July 1969 two 1000 gallon retardant tanks were installed in the bomb-bay of N809Z and the B-17, dubbed Tanker 22, made it to a number of western forest fires in the seventies. Intermountain's little cover story began to unravel, however, along with much of the CIA's conglomeration of companies in the early seventies as Americans in general began to wonder just what was going on with some of our intelligence operations. Intermountain eventually went out of business, and the ownership of N809Z and Intermoun-tain's other assets went to Evergreen Helicopters of McMinn-ville, Oregon. Evergreen obtained N809Z on 01 March 1975, but ownership transferred to Evergreen Air of Montana, located in Missoula, on 11 January 1977. The company had

the registration changed to N207EV on 06 March 1979, and the B-17 went back to Evergreen Helicopters in Oregon on 31 March 1979. During all these changes the Fortress re-mained at Marana Airpark (which would shortly become Pinal Airpark) as Evergreen also absorbed Intermountain's aircraft maintenance and storage business. N207EV made it to the rare fire once in awhile, but largely remained parked on Evergreen's ramp.

Beginning in 1985, an effort was begun to restore the For-tress to a standard configuration. By this time, there were numerous little extras all over the fuselage, including added windows in the waist area, numerous antennas and patches where equipment and other goodies had been added and deleted. The tail sported a unique fabric covered shell and the nose was streamlined fiberglass in place of Plexiglas.

By late 1987 the Fortress remained at Pinal Airpark and was stripped of paint and much equipment. The retardant tanks had been removed, as had the fuselage tail section. Work was underway and, in fact, Evergreen had run an ad in "Trade-A-Plane" for sheet-metal mechanics to assist in the restoration project. The skin on the bomb bay doors and the aft lower fuselage was replaced. Corrosion control efforts were performed in the fuselage interior, especially around the bomb bay area. Fiberglass turrets were installed pend-ing the acquistion of the actual units. Modern radios and navigation equipment are utilized, though following a trend of other B-17 restorations, the original non-working dummy radios will remain installed in their original location to en-sure a measure of accuracy.

N207EV retains a bare metal skin but carries the combat colors of the 490th Bomb Group as operated in England with the Eighth Air Force. Evergreen is underwriting the costs of the restoration and projected flight operations from company funds. It is anticipated that the Fortress will log about 75 hours of flight time annually flying to and from air shows. Final plans envision the B-17 joining the air show circuit in the summer of 1989, and this most unconventional of B-17s will assume its presumably final guise as a combat veteran Fortress.

N809Z in the employ of the Johnson Flying Service. Though carried as an air tanker the Fortress was rarely employed as such in the sixties. The retardant tanks carried a much lower profile than that on most B-17 tankers. Note the additional fuselage windows.
H. Davidson via AAHS

On the fire line at Medford, Oregon in June 1970, a shiny N809Z with retardant tanks installed. Note the Intermountain logo on the fuselage. Peltzer

Little corrosion damage was found on the airframe, and was primarily due to the fire-fighting chemicals used.
Geis

Chapter Twenty-two: 44-83814

NATIONAL AIR AND SPACE MUSEUM
WASHINGTON, D.C.

■ ■ ■ ■ ■ ■

44-83814 B-17G-95-DL to N66751 to CF-HBP to N66751

USAAF

DATE	LOCATION	UNIT	CMD	REMARKS
20 JUN 45	LONG BEACH		ATC	ACCEPTED
22 JUN 45	SYRACUSE		ATC	STORAGE
(12 OCT 45)	(declared excess)		– –	
05 NOV 45	ALTUS		RFC	DISPOSAL

CIVIL

DATE	TRANSFER DETAILS
47	FR: WAR ASSETS ADMINISTRATION
	TO: NORTH DAKOTA PUBLIC SCHOOL DISTRICT NO.3 HAZEN, ND
20 JUN 51	TO: CALIFORNIA-ATLANTIC AIRWAYS, ST. PETERSBURG, FL
12 MAY 53	TO: KENTING AVIATION, TORONTO, CANADA
15 MAY 57	TO: PHOTOGRAPHIC SURVEY CORPORATION, TORONTO, CANADA
11 FEB 60	TO: HUNTING SURVEY CORPORATION, TORONTO, CANADA
09 APR 62	TO: KENTING AVIATION, TORONTO, CANADA
03 DEC 68	TO: KENTING LTD., TORONTO, CANADA
06 MAY 69	TO: KENTING AIRCRAFT, TORONTO, CANADA
01 APR 71	TO: ARNOLD KOLB, DBA BLACK HILLS AVIATION, ALAMOGORDO, NM
20 MAR 74	TO: BLACK HILLS AVIATION, ALAMOGORDO, NM
19 JAN 81	TO: NATIONAL AIR AND SPACE MUSUEM, WASHINGTON, D.C.

44-83814

44-83814 was one of the few Fortresses to escape the immediate post-war scrapyards, enter the civil market, and survive through the ensuing years. Initially registered as N66571, the B-17 was sold to a Canadian survey firm in 1953 but returned to the U.S. for use as an air tanker beginning in 1971. In 1981 it was traded to the National Air and Space Museum and is presently in long-term storage at Dulles International Airport in Washington D.C.

As were many of the Fortresses which survived into the post-war period, 44-83814 was in the last block of Douglas-produced B-17s built at Long Beach. Accepted for service on 20 June 1945, it was flown directly to Syracuse, New York and placed in short term storage. It was declared excess to

military requirements on 12 October 1945 and flown to the Reconstruction Finance Corporation disposal lot at Altus, Oklahoma, arriving in early November 1945. 44-83814 remained at Altus until late 1947 when the North Dakota Public School District Number 3 obtained the aircraft for an unspecified purpose. Though not confirmed by aircraft records, it is likely the arrangements provided that the B-17 was donated to the School District for instructional purposes but title was not transferred. The government did not release its interest in the aircraft and specified that it was not to fly again. A fair number of B-17s and other types were similarly placed on display in communities or made available for use at technical institutions.

Difficulties would ensue, however, in subsequent years as communities and schools sought to dispose of what had become eyesores or liabilities. Many local jurisdictions assumed they owned the aircraft and attempted to sell them on the civil market. It often required years of litigation and eventual cash settlements made to the federal government to gain clear title.

It is not evident from the record the actual use 44-83814 was put to with the North Dakota School District Number 3, but the aircraft was probably flown to Hazen, North Dakota from Altus and remained until 1951. In any event, the Fortress was purchased from the District by Owen F. Williams of California-Atlantic Airways of St. Petersburg, Florida.

Williams apparently made good use of the brewing confusion about legal title and purchased five B-17s from institutions who, it later turned out, didn't actually legally own the airplanes. Nonetheless, Williams was able to register his airplanes with the Civil Aeronautics Administration in a block of numbers between N66568 and N66574 (with the exception of N66569 and N66572 which were applied to other California-Atlantic Airways aircraft). N66571 was applied to 44-83814.

Williams was able to neatly sidestep the title problem by selling N66571 to a Canadian survey company located in Toronto, Canada. Sold to the Kenting Aviation Company, N66571 was given the Canadian registration of CF-HBP. Based at Oshawa, CF-HBP arrived on 12 May 1953 with 855 hours of flight time logged on the airframe. It would eventually be joined by two additional B-17s, CF-ICB (B-17E 41-9210) and CF-JJH (B-17G-95-DL 44-83873).

Kenting Aviation employed CF-HBP in a variety of projects over the years which included air survey operations in the Canadian arctic and around the world. It was also reportedly used in support of construction of the Distant Early Warning Line in Canada and Greenland in 1955. Registration records indicate ownership was transferred to Photographic Survey Corporation of Toronto on 15 May 1957 and then to the Hunting Survey Corporation of Toronto on 11 February 1960 before returning to Kenting Aviation on 09 April 1962. It is not known if ownership actually

transferred to different companies or if these firms operated as subsidiary units to Kenting Aviation. CF-HBP remained active on the Canadian aircraft register until 01 April 1971 when it was sold to Arnold Kolb of Alamogordo, New Mexico. CF-HPB was deleted from the Canadian registry on 16 April 1971.

The FAA reassigned 44-83814 its original registration number of N66571. Kolb operated Black Hills Aviation at Spearfish, South Dakota and later at Alamogordo, New Mexico, and owned a number of B-17s, including N66573 (B-17G-55-BO 42-102715), N73648 (B-17G-95-DL 44-83864), and N6694C (B-17G-110-VE 44-85813*), all of which he employed as air tankers. Kolb put N66571 right to work after making necessary modifications to an air tanker configuration. N66571 remained active as a tanker through 1981 when Kolb finally traded his B-17 to the National Air and Space Museum for a pair of surplus Navy P-2s (SP-2H BuNo 144681 and SP-2H BuNo 150282) from Davis-Monthan AFB.

Ownership was transferred on 19 January 1981 at Davis-Monthan AFB. N66571 was stripped of paint and had its original military serial number applied before being placed on temporary display at the Pima Air Museum near Davis-Monthan AFB.

44-83814 remained at Pima until April 1984 when the NASM arranged to have Kolb and his son fly the bomber to Dulles International via Alamogordo, New Mexico. At Dulles, the NASM prepared it for long-term outdoor storage into which the Fortress was place in July 1984.

Future plans for the B-17 are uncertain. Lacking suitable display space, plans are underway to construct an annex facility at Dulles to supplement the main NASM building in Washington D.C. The NASM also owns the historically significant "Swoose" (B-17D 40-3097*) which is in long-term indoor storage with no restoration scheduled. It is hoped that if the new annex is constructed the NASM will place on display both its B-17D and B-17G as prime examples of American aviation at its best.

N66571 operating as an air tanker with Black Hills Aviation on duty at Omack, Washington in 1978. Note cargo door at left waist position. Peltzer

Arnold Kolb and his son flew N66571 to Dulles International Airport in April 1984 for long term storage with the National Air and Space Museum. Here is the aircraft on arrival on 25 April. National Air and Space Museum

The Fortress in storage at the Dulles Airport in the NASM compound. All large openings are sealed, similar to the process used at Davis-Monthan AFB. Mikesh

The NASM has no plans to display 44-83814 until a new museum facility is built at Dulles. Mikesh

44-83814 in Kenting colors as CF-HBP. Note the numerous added antennas and the left waist cargo door. Photo was taken at Watson Lake, British Columbia in 1966. Gowans

44-83863   B-17G-95-DL to PB-1W 77231 to N6464D to N5233V

USAAF

DATE	LOCATION	UNIT	CMD	REMARKS
05 JUL 45	LONG BEACH		ATC	ACCEPTED
08 JUL 45	SYRACUSE		– –	TO USN

USN

DATE	LOCATION	UNIT		REMARKS
16 JUL 45	NAS JOHNSVILLE	NAMU		ACCEPTED
FEB 47	NAS QUONSET PT.	VX-4		
02 FEB 50	NAS NORFOLK	O&R BUAER M&S		OVERHAUL
27 MAR 50	LITCHFIELD PARK			STORAGE
31 MAR 51	NAS NORFOLK	O&R BUAER M&S		OVERHAUL
09 APR 52	NAS SAN DIEGO	O&R BUAER M&S		
21 APR 52	NAS MIRAMAR	VC-11 (DETACHMENT)		
18 JUN 52	NAS BARBERS POINT	VW-1		
16 FEB 53	ATSUGI	VW-1 (DETACHMENT)		
AUG 53	NAS SAN DIEGO	VW-1		
NOV 53	NAS BARBERS POINT	VW-1		
FEB 54	ATSUCI	VW-1 (DETACHMENT)		
15 APR 54	NAS BARBERS POINT	VW-1		
10 MAY 54	NAS SAN DIEGO	O&R BUAER M&S		
14 JUN 54	LITCHFIELD PARK			STORAGE
(25 AUG 55)	(retired)			
(10 JUL 56)	(stricken)			

CIVIL

DATE	TRANSFER DETAILS
02 DEC 57	FR: USN, NAS NORTH ISLAND
	TO: AMERICAN COMPRESSED STEEL, DALLAS, TX
26 FEB 60	TO: MARSON EQUIPMENT AND SALVAGE COMPANY, TUCSON, AZ
27 SEP 61	TO: AERO UNION, ANDERSON, CA
03 JAN 62	TO: ROGUE FLYING SERVICE, MEDFORD, OR
*01 APR 63	TO: AERO AG, INC, MEDFORD, OR
*71	TO: IDAHO AIRCRAFT COMPANY, BOISE, ID
06 JUN 71	TO: AERO UNION, CHICO, CA
19 JUN 75	TO: USAF MUSEUM

* no indication of legal ownership change on file in FAA records for these operators

44-83863

44-83863 is one of three ex-Navy PB-1Ws to survive in the U.S. today. After being retired from USN service, it operated as N5233V and was used exclusively as an aerial applicator and air tanker until obtained by the Air Force Museum for display at Eglin AFB in Florida.

44-83863 rolled from the Long Beach assembly lines of the Douglas Aircraft Company on 04 July 1945. Though earmarked for the U.S. Navy it was accepted by the Army Air Force on 05 July and flown to Syracuse, New York, arriving on 08 July 1945. It was made available to the Navy on 11 July, but not delivered to NAS Johnsville, Pennsylvania until 16 July 1945.

863 became part of a group of roughly twenty-four Fortresses at NAS Johnsville which were placed into the Naval Aircraft Modification Pool (NAMU) for conversion to PB-1Ws with the installation of search radar and other equipment. 44-83863 was issued Navy serial 77231 and remained with the NAMU until February 1947 when it was assigned to VX-4 at NAS Quonset Point, Rhode Island.

77231 was attached to VX-4 until 1950 when assigned to NAS Norfolk and the Overhaul and Repair shops there. It was then placed in storage at the Naval Aircraft Storage Center at Litchfield Park, Arizona on 27 March 1950, remaining for one year.

It was pulled from storage on 31 March 1951, and after going through the overhaul shops at Norfolk again, was assigned to VC-11 at NAS Mirimar near San Diego. When VC-11 was incorporated into VW-1 on 18 June 1952, 77231 went to NAS Barbers Point in Hawaii as one of four PB-1Ws attached to the new squadron. It was sent to Atsugi, Japan on 16 February 1953 along with several other PB-1Ws, but 77231 would remain with VW-1 for the balance of its Navy utilization which ended on 10 June 1954. At that time it was again placed in storage at Litchfield Park.

77231 was formally retired from Navy service on 25 August 1955, as were most of the Navy PB-1Ws. It and the other PB-1Ws were stricken from the inventory on 10 July 1956, after which they were placed up for disposal by auction.

77231 and twelve other surplus PB-1Ws were purchased by American Compressed Steel Corporation of Dallas, Texas, 77231 being obtained for $9,333.33 on 02 December 1957. Twelve of the Fortresses were initially issued a block of CAA registration numbers between N6460D and N6471D, but they were voided in the initial registration paperwork and never applied to the aircraft. Instead, registration numbers between N5225V and N5237V were issued to all thirteen Fortresses. The numbers were randomly assigned to the Fortresses with no attempts at applying them to sequential USAAF or USN serial numbers. 77231 was issued N5233V.

The surplus PB-1Ws were ferried from Litchfield Park to Dallas-Love Field, one aircraft (N5236V) suffering a minor landing accident upon arrival. The thirteen Fortresses were parked in a remote part of the airport to await further use.

American Compressed Steel Corporation had apparently purchased the Fortresses with the intention of converting them to executive transports. As noted in other chapters, American Compressed Steel would purchase other Fortresses from the Air Force and both it and its succeeding corporation, Aero-American, was generally in the business of converting surplus military aircraft for civil use. One rumor making the rounds at Love Field in 1958 had the whole batch of Fortresses bought by Cuba's Fidel Castro in his bid to form

Early photo of N5233V as a tanker while operated by Rouge Flying Service at Medford, Oregon in September 1962. Larkins

N5233V had its blown nose painted over while with Aero Ag. Peltzer

N5233V was fitted with the fiberglass nose cone characteristic of Aero Union B-17s. T. Piedmonte via Besecker

Tanker number changed to 18 in its later use with Aero Union. B-17 suffered a spar failure in June 1973. MAP

a rebel air force as a counter to then-Cuban dictator Batista's military forces. That account had federal agents stepping in to prevent delivery of the bombers.

In any event, all plans for the PB-1Ws apparently fell through and they languished in their corner of the airport for several years. They began to trickle out as various civil buyers were found. Several went to Bolivia and a few were used in the film "The War Lover". 77231 was purchased on 26 February 1960 by Marson Equipment and Salvage Company of Tucson, Arizona. Whether the PB-1W remained at Love Field after the sale or flown to Arizona is not clear from the record. In any event, Marson Equipment sold it on 27 September 1961 to Aero Union, then of Anderson, California.

Aero Union retained N5233V for four months and then sold it to Rouge Flying Service, of Medford, Oregon. At the time of the sale, 44-83863 had accumulated 2,473 hours of flight time. Rouge Flying Service was evidently an investment company, for they never appeared to have ever operated the aircraft. The Fortress was converted to an air tanker/aerial applicator with the installation of two 1000 gallon tanks in July 1962, after which it was operated as Tanker F71. On 01 April 1963 it was transferred to Aero Ag, Inc., also of Medford, who apparently operated it until 1971 when it was sold to Idaho Aircraft Company of Boise.

On 06 June 1971 N5233V made a complete circle and returned to Aero Union, now based at Chico, California. Aero Union officially gained title, the first legal transfer of ownership in the ten years since they sold the bomber to Rouge Flying Service. Aero Union initially operated N5233V as Tanker D1, joining four other B-17 air tankers Aero Union had in their tanker fleet at the time.

On 28 June 1973, while operating as Tanker 18, N5233V suffered a broken "A" frame assembly in the bomb bay.

Reports at the time indicated the tanker crew had felt something "snap" while dropping a load, and flew the B-17 back to the tanker base. An exterior inspection of the fuselage revealed buckled skin on the wings and around the radio compartment behind the wings. Upon dropping the retardant tank from the bomb bay, the cracked assembly was located. It was determined that the aluminum skin had carried the aerodynamic loads for the return flight.

The FAA immediately suspended the airworthiness certificates of all B-17s pending investigation of the failure. This had a dramatic effect, naturally, on both air tanker operators and fire fighting efforts. It was later determined that the concentrated load of retardant in the bomb bay area overstressed the structure, even though the maximum allowable weight of the material never exceeded design limitations. The FAA downgraded the certificated load from 2000 gallons to 1800 gallons.

N5233V was subsequently repaired and all the B-17s had their airworthiness certificates restored. Nonetheless, the structure failure, plus a rash of crashes, would cause the Forest Service and tanker operators to begin a serious search for equipment to replace the aging B-17s, and the type would generally be gone from the tanker fleets by 1980.

N5233V would take an early retirement, however. Aero Union negotiated a trade with the Air Force Museum which provided that a surplus C-118 go to Aero Union while N5233V would be placed on display at the Armament Museum at Eglin AFB, Florida. At the time of the trade (late 1974) N5233V had amassed about 3600 hours of flight time.

Aero Union stripped the tanker paint scheme from the Fortress. The retardant system was also removed, and a set of bomb-bay doors (no doubt cast aside many years earlier) reinstalled. Aero Union had operated their tankers with fiberglass nose cones in place of the blown Plexiglas nose piece. They now installed a glass nose, and the ex-PB-1W, ex-tanker was ready to return to its first owner, the Air Force.

Aero Union President Dale Newton and tanker buff Jim Babcock flew the Fortress to Eglin by way of Coolidge, Arizona, and Addison, Texas. Their ferry flight, which also included as passengers their respective wives, enjoyed a low level run across the runways at NAS Pensecola, Florida, perhaps as a tip of the hat to the aircraft's Navy past.

The Fortress arrived at Eglin AFB and the Armament Museum on 19 June 1975 and was initially marked as an aircraft of the 95th Bomb Group, 8th Air Force as operated from Britain in World War II. It was displayed without turrets and other armament and was placed on blocks to preserve the tires.

With the establishment of the Air Force Museum Program in 1980, the Air Force Armament Museum was reorganized to better provide for the upkeep and restoration of the assigned aircraft. The new museum officially opened its doors as a Class B Museum on 15 November 1985. A concerted effort was begun to restore the Fortress with the reinstallation of military equipment including turrets, astrodome, and antennas.

By 1987, 44-83863 had been repainted in an olive-drab paint scheme, though still retaining the 95th Bomb Group markings. Replica turrets had been reinstalled in the dorsal and chin positions. Other military equipment had also been reinstalled which brought the appearance of the Fortress back to a combat configuration. The aircraft as displayed is no longer on blocks, which greatly adds to its appearance. At this time, no final decision has been made on individual aircraft markings or nose art to be carried by the bomber.

44-83863 went to Eglin AFB's Armament Museum in 1974. Civil paint was stripped by Aero Union and the museum applied 95th Bomb Group markings. Here displayed as "Wanda the Witch" in July 1978. Weather via AAHS

44-83872　B-17G-95-DL to PB-1W 77235 to N7227C

USAAF

DATE	LOCATION	UNIT	CMD	REMARKS
12 JUL 45	LONG BEACH		ATC	ACCEPTED
16 JUL 45	NAS JOHNSVILLE		– –	TO USN

USN

DATE	LOCATION	UNIT	REMARKS
16 JUL 45	NAS JOHNSVILLE	NAMU	ACCEPTED
MAY 47	NAS QUONSET PT.	VX-4	
18 APR 50	NAS NORFOLK	O&R BUAER M&S	
22 NOV 50	NAS PATUXENT RIVER	FASRON103	
28 MAR 51	NAS PATUXENT RIVER	VX-4	
18 JUN 52	NAS PATUXENT RIVER	VW-2	VX-4 TO VW-2
03 JUN 53	NAS NORFOLK	O&R BUAER M&S	
18 JAN 54	NAS SAN DIEGO	O&R BUAER M&S	
04 FEB 54	ATSUGI	VW-1	
15 JAN 55	LITCHFIELD PARK	NASC	STORAGE
(25 AUG 55)	(retired)		
(10 JUL 56)	(stricken)		

CIVIL

DATE	TRANSFER DETAILS
01 OCT 57	FR: USN, NAS NORTH ISLAND CONTRACTING OFFICER
	TO: AERO SERVICE CORPORATION, PHILADELPHIA, PA
22 SEP 67	TO: CONFEDERATE AIR FORCE, MERCEDES, TX

44-83872

44-83872 is one of the best known surviving B-17s as it is part of the first and largest of the "flying museums." Operating under the civil registration of N7227C, the bomber flies as "Texas Raiders" with the Confederate Air Force in Harlingen, Texas. Prior to the its acquisition by the CAF in 1967, 44-83872 had operated as a Navy PB-1W for ten years, and performed aerial survey work between 1961 and 1967.

44-83872 was accepted by the Army Air Force at the Douglas Long Beach plant on 12 July 1945. One of twenty-seven B-17s to be transferred to the U.S. Navy for conversion to PB-1Ws, 44-83872 was flown directly from Long Beach to NAS Johnsville, Pennsylvania. The Navy formally accepted delivery on 16 July and assigned Navy serial 77235 to the Fortress. 77235 was placed in the Naval Aircraft Modification Unit supply pool at NAS Johnsville for conversion to PB-1W status. It would remain until May 1947 when assigned to VX-4 at NAS Quonset Point, Rhode

N7227C in Aero Service colors at Burbank Airport, California in March 1958. Note the wing-tip antenna, believed to be part of the magnetometer equipment. Opened ball turret location probably contained mapping cameras at the time. C. Jansson via Peltzer

77226 as purchased by Aero Service to serve as a parts source for their B-17 fleet. Registered as N7228C, aircraft is shown here at Philadelphia in 1962. N7228C appears to have the rudder from N7227C installed. The ex PB-1W was later sold first to Bob Sturges in Oregon, and later Aero Flite of Cody, Wyoming for use as an air tanker. It was destroyed in a 1967 crash. San Diego Aerospace Museum

Island. 77235 was attached to VX-4 and its succeeding unit, VW-2, for seven years with the exception of overhauls and modifications conducted at NAS Norfolk with the Overhaul and Repair, Maintenance and Supply unit. It also was assigned for five months, between 22 November 1950 and 28 March 1951, at NAS Patuxent River, Maryland and Fleet Aircraft Service Squadron 103. It then rejoined VX-4 which had moved to NAS Patuxent River.

In April 1952 77235 was assigned to test work to evaluate the Airborne Moving Target Indicator system which had been developed by the Naval Aircraft Development Center at NAS Johnsville. The equipment was designed to detect moving ground targets, air targets moving over land and water, and surface targets at sea. A Douglas AD-4W Skyraider was similarly modified to obtain comparative results.

On 03 June 1953 the PB-1W was assigned to overhaul shops at NAS Norfolk and NAS San Diego. On 04 February 1954 77235 was assigned to the west coast early warning squadron, VW-1, and detached to Atsugi, Japan. On 15 January 1955 77235 was withdrawn from service and flown to the Naval Aircraft Storage Center at Litchfield Park, Arizona, for storage. 77235 had amassed 3,257 hours of logged flight time to that date. It was formally retired from

N7227C played a key role at the retirement ceremonies held for General Curtis LeMay at Andrews AFB on 01 February 1965. Markings from the 305th Bomb Group were temporarily added over the civil markings. USAF

the Navy on 25 August 1955, and stricken from the Navy inventory on 10 July 1956. 77235 was then placed up for sale along with the other surplus Navy PB-1Ws.

On 01 October 1957 Aero Service Corporation of Philadelphia, Pennsylvania purchased 77235 from the Contracting Officer at NAS San Diego for $17,510. Perhaps a function of the competitive bidding process, or just indicative of Aero Service's desire to obtain a Fortress, this amount is substantially higher than the amounts paid for other surplus PB-1Ws sold at the same time, which varied between $7,000 and $10,000.

Aero Service Corporation, a subsidiary of Litton Industries, was an aerial survey firm which eventually would operate as many as four Fortresses. (In addition to 44-83872, Aero Service also operated B-17G-50-BO 42-102542 N5845N, B-17G-105-VE 44-85740* N5017N, and B-17G-110-VE 44-85829* N3193G.) Aero Service registered 77235 as N7227C and ferried the aircraft to Philadelphia.

On 01 October 1957 Aero Service also purchased Bu77226 (44-83857) from the Navy for $15,010 for use as a parts source. Registered concurrently with N7227C, it was issued the civil registration of N7228C and was ferried to Philadelphia. It remained until February 1962 when Aero Service sold it to Bob Sturges of Troutdale, Oregon and after several more ownership changes was destroyed in an air tanker accident in August 1967.

N7227C, meanwhile, went into the shops for conversion to a high altitude magnetometer platform in late 1957. Over the next year it was extensively modified with the installation of a wide variety of radios, sensing equipment, antennas, and a cargo door on the left side of the fuselage waist. It entered service with Aero Service, which employed it on numerous projects over the next seven years for survey work such as North Sea oil field mapping, assignments in South America, and mapping of the U.S. west coast. In July 1963 N7227C was loaded down with two tons of scientific survey equipment and flown to the northern reaches of Canada to survey the solar eclipse then occurring. Operations in excess of 31,000 feet of altitude were undertaken during that project.

In early 1965 N7227C was remarked as an Eighth Air Force Fortress briefly as it became the star attraction at the retirement ceremony conducted for General Curtis LeMay at Andrews AFB in Maryland on 01 February 1965.

Meanwhile, the Confederate Air Force was busily searching for a B-17 to add to its growing collection. Though a well known organization now, in the early 1960s the Confederate Air Force was a small group of pilots which had almost accidentally obtained a good cross-section of American fighters used during World War II. They had started as a loose, fraternal organization of crop dusters and ex-service pilots who had gone together to purchase a Mustang in the mid-fifties. Soon other types were added, someone scrawled

"Confederate Air Force" across an airplane, and everyone started calling everyone else "Colonel" as a lark. Lacking long range goals or basic organization, the CAF gained the reputation of a bunch of crazy pilots spending good money on junk airplanes and flying them in what could be called a haphazard manner from a small duster strip near Mercedes, Texas. The fighters came to be painted overall white with red and blue trim, and became a common sight at local airshows and demonstrations. But as the group grew, a metamorphosis slowly occurred. Wiser heads in the organization recognized the potential of the Confederate Air Force and their ability to preserve and protect a long-ignored and now vanishing species – the American World War II military aircraft. What had been a bunch of pilots out to have some fun matured into a professionally run flying museum earnestly trying to obtain examples of each of the major American combat types flown in World War II.

The fighters were relatively easy. There were still a number of run-out Wildcats and Warhawks around which could be bought and operated for a relative pittance. But the real heavy iron, the medium and heavy bombers, offered new financial and logistical challenges. By 1965 the CAF was rising to those challenges and were seeking examples of the three American heavy bombers of World War II; the B-17, the B-24, and the B-29.

There were a number of Fortresses around, operated by air tanker or aerial survey companies. As has been noted elsewhere, by the early 1960s the Fortress had settled into a small but stable niche in the civil market, performing a job few other aircraft were capable of. The CAF had not found a company which would consider parting with a B-17 on the only terms the CAF could offer: a small amount of scrounged cash and the opportunity to feel good about helping the CAF achieve its goals.

Nonetheless, the Confederate Air Force had been involved with continuing negotiations about Aero Service's Fortress. It was one of the few which might be available and a deal was finally consummated on 22 September 1967 when ownership of 44-83872 was transferred to the Confederate Air Force. Sources give varying amounts, but apparently the CAF was able to scrounge $50,000 to purchase the old bomber.

Through the sixties and early seventies, the CAF was primarily interested in acquisition of aircraft and other tasks involved in running an air force, such as restoration and even maintenance, took a back seat. Thus, the Confederates gained a reputation for operating a pretty ratty collection of aircraft, and came under a fair amount of criticism for maintaining civil paint schemes on their bombers and fighters. Somewhat warranted, the criticism nonetheless failed to accommodate either the time frame or the logistics of operating such a diverse and growing collection of aircraft as a flying museum. No one had ever attempted to privately operate

Departing Boeing Field while operating with Aero Service, N7227C has several additional antennas installed on the fuselage beneath the nose and aft of the wing.
Bowers Collection

N7227C was obtained by the Confederate Air Force in September 1967. The ex PB-1W retained the Aero Service markings for several years but had rebel flags added. Photo taken at Brownsville in July 1967.
Krieger

Note the cargo door in place of the left waist position. Origin of the "Spirit" marking painted on the tail is unknown. Krieger

vintage aircraft on a scale as large before, and the resources of the group were limited. The CAF was on the forefront of preserving the World War II bombers and fighters at a time when most people and the government considered them worthless. Few, if any, other organizations or individuals gave thought to restoring these aircraft back to their original configuration and maintaining them in flying condition. Indeed, N7227C was the first B-17 to be purchased and operated solely for the sake of preservation.

The CAF continued to maintain N7227C in its Aero Service Corporation paint scheme for a number of years. The only markings concession made to its new owner was a number of rebel flags which dotted the aircraft, a last vestige of the CAF's old Southern guard which was slowly losing ground to the maturing ideals of the organization.

N7227C was one of the first CAF aircraft to come under the paint gun, however. It lost it civil markings in 1970, replaced with a glossy military scheme, complete with markings of the 305th Bomb Group and a serial number, 41-24592, from a B-17F-27-BO. Nose markings were applied as "Texas Raiders" with a Texas state flag. The B-17 was devoid of gun turrets or other combat equipment, and still contained civil modifications such as the cargo door and numerous metaled over windows, but the Fortress at least approximated the appearance of its combat brethren.

N7227C operated in this configuration for over a dozen years. Slow progress was made toward adding combat equipment, and a dorsal and ball turret were added in September 1977, as was more accurate paint. A major step was taken in September 1980 when the large cargo door was removed and replaced with conventional waist gun positions.

However, in 1983 the old Fortress was pulled from the CAF flight line to undergo a complete restoration to bring it back to full combat configuration, overhaul the engines and other systems, and apply accurate combat paint. The aircraft was transferred to the Confederate Air Force's Gulf Coast Wing, based in Houston, and they assumed opera-

tional control of the Fortress. N7227C was partially disassembled, thoroughly inspected with each flight and control system rebuilt, and the electrical system was replaced. Along the way the bomb bay doors were made operable again and each of the defensive gun positions restored. When the bomber finally emerged from the CAF hangar in June 1986, it sported a new, more accurate, paint scheme with markings of the 381st Bomb Group, 533rd Bomb Squadron, and its own original serial number, 44-83872. Pin-up nose art now accompanies the Texan flag on the nose as N7227C once again resumes its place on the Confederate Air Force's flight line.

N7227C was repainted again in 1977, and dorsal and ball turrets were added. It retained the cargo door and the bomb bay doors were inoperable until the 1983 restoration effort. Photo taken at Chino in August 1978. Author

CAF B-17 on the ramp at Harlingen, Texas during Airsho76. Note absence of military equipment. Author

EIGHTH AIR FORCE MUSEUM
BARKSDALE AFB, LOUISIANA

■■■■■■

44-83884   B-17G-95-DL to PB-1W 77244 to N6471D to N5230V

USAAF

DATE	LOCATION	UNIT	CMD	REMARKS
12 JUL 45	LONG BEACH		ATC	ACCEPTED
16 JUL 45	NAS JOHNSVILLE		– –	TO USN

USN

DATE	LOCATION	UNIT		REMARKS
25 JUL 45	NAS JOHNSVILLE	NAMU		ACCEPTED
MAY 47	NAS QUONSET PT.	VX-4		
16 JAN 50	NAS NORFOLK	O&R BUAER M&S		OVERHAUL
29 SEP 50	NAS PATUXENT RIVER	VX-4		
18 JUN 50	NAS PATUXENT RIVER	VW-2		
02 FEB 53	NAS NORFOLK	O&R BUAER M&S		OVERHAUL
21 JUL 53	NAS PATUXENT RIVER	VW-2		
24 FEB 54	NAS NORFOLK	O&R BUAER M&S		RETIRED
12 MAR 55	LITCHFIELD PARK			STORAGE
(10 JUL 56)	(stricken)			

CIVIL

DATE	TRANSFER DETAILS
02 DEC 57	FR: USN, NAS NORTH ISLAND CONTRACTING OFFICER
	TO: AMERICAN COMPRESSED STEEL, DALLAS, TX
18 OCT 60	TO: MARSON EQUIPMENT AND SALVAGE COMPANY, TUCSON, AZ
27 SEP 61	TO: AERO UNION, ANDERSON, CA
19 JUL 80	TO: USAF MUSEUM (registration cancelled)

44-83884

44-83884 was transferred to the U.S. Navy and operated as a PB-1W. After Navy service 44-83884 was sold into the civilian market and used as an air tanker between 1965 and 1979. The bomber was then obtained in trade by the USAF Museum and placed on display with the Eighth Air Force Museum at Barksdale AFB, Louisiana. It is one of three surviving ex PB-1Ws in the United States today.

44-83884 was the second to the last Douglas-built Fortresses, and was one of the twenty-two late block B-17s to be transferred to the Navy. It was accepted by the Army Air Force at Long Beach on 12 July 1945 but flown directly to NAS Johnsville, Pennsylvania, delivery being accomplished on 25 July. At NAS Johnsville it was assigned Navy serial 77244 and placed in the Naval Aircraft Modification Unit for conversion to PB-1W configuration with the installation of radar and other special equipment. It remained at NAS Johnsville through May 1947 when assigned to VX-4 at NAS Quonset Point, Rhode Island.

77244 remained with VX-4 until 16 January 1950 when sent to the Overhaul and Repair, Material and Service Group at NAS Norfolk. 77244 rejoined VX-4 at NAS Patuxent River nine months later on 29 September 1951. When VX-4 was incorporated into VW2 on 18 June 1952, 77244 was attached to the newly formed unit.

On 03 February 1953 the PB-1W returned to NAS Norfolk for assignment to the Overhaul and Repair Group, but was once again assigned to VW-2 at Patuxent River on 21 July 1953. 77244 was retired from USN service on 24 February 1955 and flown to Norfolk. From Norfolk it was moved to Litchfield Park, Arizona for storage on 13 March 1955. 77244 was formally stricken from the Navy inventory on 10 July 1956 with 3,751 hours of logged flight time.

77244 and the other surplus Navy PB-1Ws were made available in sales from Litchfield Park. It, and a block of twelve other PB-1Ws, were sold to American Compressed Steel Corporation of Dallas, Texas on 02 December 1957. 77244 was obtained for $8,333.33. It and eleven of the other twelve Fortresses were initially issued a block of FAA registration numbers between N6460D and N6471D. (The other B-17 was issued N7726B.) The numbers were withdrawn, however, and never applied to the aircraft. Instead, the thirteen PB-1Ws were assigned a block of registration numbers between N5225V and N5230V, 77244 becoming N5230V. The American Compressed Steel Fortresses were ferried to Dallas and parked, awaiting future plans.

As noted elsewhere, American Compressed Steel apparently purchased the Fortresses to convert them to executive transports. American Compressed Steel and its successor, Aero American, converted surplus military aircraft

to civilian specifications. There also exists the possibility that the PB-1Ws were slated for Cuban revolutionary Fidel Castro, immersed in a rebellion against Cuban dictator Batista in the late fifties and in desperate need of an air force. In any case, the Fortresses didn't go anywhere for years and suffered the fate of abandoned airplanes as they sank into the mud of dereliction.

However, by the early sixties new civil owners, particularly Bolivian air cargo interests and American air tanker operators, were coming to rescue the faded blue Fortresses from oblivion. N5230V had been purchased by Marson Equipment and Salvage Company of Tucson, Arizona on 18 October 1960. The Fortress continued to rot at Dallas-Love Field, however, until Marson Equipment and Salvage sold it to Aero Union Corporation (which also purchased 44-83863* N5230V on the same date) of Anderson, California. N5230V was ferried to California and underwent conversion to an air tanker with the installation of two 1000 gallon tanks in the bomb-bay. The conversion process must have taken a few years, however, as FAA records indicate the aircraft had only amassed an additional ten hours of flight time between July 1956, when the Navy flew the Fortress to Litchfield Park, and June 1965.

Beginning in 1965 N5230V joined the Aero Union tanker fleet in the annual battle against western forest and range fires. Operating as Tanker 19, N5230V would faithfully perform each fire season, assigned to a Forest Service tanker base such as Redding or Lancaster, California, to await the rushed call for its 2000 gallons of fire retardant. 33V

44-83884 as part of the Aero Union fleet at Redding Airport in August 1966. N5230V was purchased by Aero Union in 1961 but did not become operational until 1965. Larkins

Later photo of N5230V at Chico. Aero Union operated it through the 1979 fire season. Larkins

became, in fact, the last B-17 air tanker to be operated by Aero Union, which had, by then, moved to Chico Airport. N5230V operated through the 1979 fire season and was then traded to the Air Force Museum.

The Air Force, under the auspices of the Air Force Museum Program, assigned N5230V to the new Eighth Air Force Museum located at Barksdale AFB, Louisiana, headquarters of the Eighth Air Force. The museum was understandably eager to get ahold of an example of the aircraft which contributed so much to its history. Jim and Lora Babcock, who had been instrumental in preparing and delivering several of Aero Union's air tankers to various Air Force Bases, went to work on N5230V at Chico. The tanker modifications were stripped, and available equipment, such as bomb-bay doors, were reinstalled. A blown nose glass piece, which had been removed from all of Aero Union's

tankers in 1966 in favor of available fiberglass nose cones, was located and obtained for installation on N5230V. The airplane was cleaned and painted in the Air Force requested colors of the 303rd Bomb Group, Eighth Air Force.

An Aero Union crew, including the Babcocks, ferried N5230V to Barksdale by way of Tucson, Arizona; Kerrville, Texas; and Carswell AFB, Texas. The bomber arrived at Barksdale in early 1980. Museum workers have slowly restored 44-83884 to an Army Air Force combat configuration. Power turrets or fiberglass replicas have been reinstalled and other combat equipment has been replaced as available. The Fortress has been named "Yankee Doodle II" in honor of General Ira Eaker, initial wartime commander of the Eighth Air Force's Bomber Command who led the first American B-17 bombing mission over Europe while aboard "Yankee Doodle", B-17E 41-9023, on 17 August 1942.

Rollout of the 2999th Douglas-built B-17 — 44-83884 in mid-July 1945. The last B-17, 44-83885, was delivered to the Army Air Force some two weeks earlier. The delivery delay for this aircraft may have had something to do with its assignment to the Navy. NASM

CHAPTER TWENTY-SIX: 44-85599

DYESS AFB, TEXAS

■■■■■■

44-85599 B-17G-100-VE to EDB-17G to DB-17G to DB-17P

USAAF/USAF

DATE	LOCATION	UNIT	CMD	REMARKS
30 MAR 45	BURBANK		ATC	ACCEPTED
05 APR 45	CHEYENNE	MODIFICATION CENTER	ATC	
29 APR 45	SOUTH PLAINS	4168 BASE UNIT	ATC	STORAGE
24 JUN 47	PYOTE	4168 BASE UNIT	ATC	STORAGE
01 AUG 50	PYOTE	2753 ACFT STORAGE SQ	ATC	STORAGE
21 SEP 50	TINKER	OKC AIR DEPOT	AMC	
17 JUL 51	WRI-PAT		ARD	
(15 AUG 51)	(fr: B-17G to: EDB-17G)		– –	
19 NOV 51	EGLIN	3200 DRONE GP	APG	
02 DEC 51	EGLIN	3205 DRONE GP	APG	
09 DEC 51	HOLLOMAN	3205 DRONE GP	APG	
(01 FEB 54)	(fr: EDB-17G to: DB-17G)		– –	
(NOV 56)	(fr: DB-17G to: DB-17P)		– –	
DEC 57	HOLLOMAN		APG	
DEC 59	DAVIS-MONTHAN		AMC	STORAGE
OCT 60	DYESS	TO MUSEUM	– –	

44-85599

44-85599 was utilized in a typical manner by the post-war Air Force. It was stored for five years, to be pulled for conversion to a drone director. It was utilized as such for ten years before retirement to Davis-Monthan AFB in 1959. It remained in storage for a year but was then sent to Abilene, Texas for use as a memorial, and was parked at the municipal airport for a number of years, suffering the ravages of vandals and exposure to the elements. It was moved to Dyess AFB, also in Abilene, in 1975 and cosmetically restored to display condition. It now greets visitors at the main gate of the base.

44-85599 rolled from the Burbank production lines of the Vega Corporation on 29 March 1945 and accepted by the Army Air Force the next day. It was immediately flown to the United Airlines Modification Center at Cheyenne, Wyoming, arriving on 05 April. It underwent modifications there and was deemed ready for service on 26 April. The Fortress was unneeded, however, and was flown to South Plains, Texas for storage and arrived on 29 April. It was probably among the first of the B-17s to be placed in storage at South Plains, and would remain in storage for over five years. It was moved, however, in June 1947 to Pyote Field, Texas along with the other South Plains Fortresses.

On 21 September 1950, 44-85599 was pulled from storage and assigned to the Oklahoma City Air Materiel Area at Tinker AFB. It remained there for nearly a year though its utilization is unknown. On 17 July 1951 it was assigned to the Air Research and Development Command at Wright-Patterson AFB in Ohio. A month later it was redesignated an EDB-17G, suggesting use in a long-term test program developing drone control equipment. As noted in Part 2, the designation could also suggest bailment to a extra-service group such as a defense contractor. At least one other DB-17G, 44-85738*, was similarly designated.

As an EDB-17G, the Fortress was assigned to the 3200th Drone Group and the Air Proving Ground Command at Eglin AFB, Florida on 19 November 1951. A few weeks later it would become part of the 3205th Drone Group, and would remain with the unit most of its remaining Air Force utilization.

Shortly after its assignment to the Group, 44-85599 went to the group's Detachment 1 at Holloman AFB in New Mexico. Detachment 1 became the 3225th Drone Squadron in 1953 and provided key support at the Holloman Air Development Center, which specialized in the development and testing of short range missiles.

In February 1954 44-85599 was redesignated a DB-17G, losing the "exempt" designation. It became a DB-17P in November 1956, indicating additional modifications of control equipment for its drone controller role. The aircraft remained at Holloman for the balance of its active use, and was retired to Davis-Monthan AFB in August 1959 as the second to the last active Air Force B-17.

44-85599 remained at Davis-Monthan as other surviving Air Force B-17s were sold or dispersed to museums until it was among the last three remaining. Then, in October 1960, 44-85599 was permanently loaned to the 96th Bomb Group Memorial Association for display at the municipal airport at Abilene, Texas. It was flown to the field where it would eventually carry the markings of the 96th Bomb Group's "Blackhawk."

As other such memorialized Fortresses, 44-85599 soon fell victim to the ravages of both the elements and vandals. Protected by a meager fence, the Fortress quickly went downhill.

New life was injected into the bomber, however, when the 96th Bomb Wing at Dyess AFB stepped in and moved the B-17 to the base in 1975 for restoration and protection. It was stripped, cleaned, and polished. Cosmetic repair was completed, and the Fortress was refinished in the colors of the Eighth Air Force's 96th Bomb Group. Still carrying "485599" as its serial, the aircraft was placed on display near the main entrance to the air base. Efforts are presently underway to obtain replica gun turrets for installation on the bomber, and it would now appear that the future of the Fortress has been secured.

44-85599 on the flight line at Davis-Monthan AFB in October 1960 in preparation for its final flight to Abilene, Texas for display. Crew reviewing pre-flight planning are, from left to right, Col. Shower, Lt. Col. Herman, MSgt Oler, and MSgt Channel. USAF via Criss

The ex DB-17 is externally complete and in fair condition given its outdoor display status. Hade

44-85599 in 96th Bomb Group colors at Dyess AFB in May 1984. Kerr via Gougon

Looking well worn, 44-85599 at the local airport at Abilene in September 1966 before it was moved to Dyess AFB for safer keeping. Peltzer

Chapter Twenty-seven: 44-85718

LONE STAR AIR MUSEUM
HOUSTON, TEXAS

■■■■■■

44-85718   B-17G-105-VE to F-BEEC to ZS-EEC to F-BEEC to G-FORT to N900RW

USAAF

DATE	LOCATION	UNIT	CMD	REMARKS
10 MAY 45	BURBANK		ATC	ACCEPTED
13 MAY 45	LOUISVILLE	MODIFICATION CENTER	ATC	
06 JUL 45	SYRACUSE		ATC	STORAGE
(12 OCT 45)	(declared excess)		– –	
21 NOV 45	ALTUS		RFC	DISPOSAL

CIVIL

DATE	TRANSFER DETAILS
10 DEC 47	FR: WAR ASSETS ADMINISTRATION
	TO: INSTITUT GEOGRAPHIQUE NATIONAL
	(registered as F-BEEC)
(AUG 65)	(carried South African registration ZS-EEC)
(AUG 66)	(again carried registration of F-BEEC)
12 JUN 84	TO: WARBIRDS OF GREAT BRITAIN (as G-FORT)
?	TO: STEVEN GREY
09 JUN 87	TO: AIR-SRV, ANDERSON, TX (as N900RW)
NOV 87	TO: LONE STAR FLIGHT MUSEUM, HOUSTON, TX

44-85718

44-85718 was another "Syracuse" Fortress, one of hundreds of new B-17s stored at the Syracuse replacement depot through the summer and early fall of 1945 before being released for disposal to the Reconstruction Finance Corporation. 44-85718 went to Altus, and was transferred to the French Institut Geographique National (IGN), which would own fourteen B-17s during the post-war years for use as survey aircraft. 44-85718, operating as F-BEEC, continued to perform commercially until 1984 when sold to an English aircraft collector. He operated the aircraft for three years before selling it to American collector Robert Waltrip, owner of the Lone Star Aviation Museum in Texas. The Fortress was brought back across the Atlantic in a much heralded flight in July 1987. The Fortress is now slated for a complete restoration back to combat configuration.

44-85718 rolled from the Burbank production lines on 08 May 1945 and accepted for duty by the Army Air Force on 10 May. It was immediately flown to the Lockheed modification facility at Louisville, Kentucky, arriving on 13 May. It remained there for nearly two months, and was flown into storage at Syracuse, New York, on 06 July. 44-85718 was stored until 12 October 1945 when it and the other Syracuse Fortresses were declared excess. They were released to the RFC and flown to a disposal site at Altus, Oklahoma, 44-85718 arriving on 21 November 1945.

The aircraft remained at Altus for over two years before it was transferred, either directly or through a broker, to the IGN in France. A total of four new B-17s were selected for service by the IGN from Altus during the winter of 1947-1948 as the first group of B-17s obtained for the French survey company. The batch also included B-17G-100-VE 44-85643 (F-BEEA), B-17G-105-VE 44-85733 (F-BEEB), and B-17G-95-DL 44-83729 (F-BEED). All were sold complete with gun turrets (sans guns) and other military equipment. The only item to set the IGN B-17s from the standard military Fortress were the French registrations applied for the ferry flights.

The four were ferried to France and put through overhaul shops at Villacoublay. Initial modifications converted the aircraft to photo-mapping platforms though several, including F-BEEC, were later outfitted to carry additional equipment such as magnetometers for survey work. Missions of the aircraft varied but the IGN Fortresses were seen around the world in the three decades which followed their initial acquisition. F-BEEC was registered briefly in South Africa as ZS-EEC between August 1965 and August 1966. It is presumed that a long-standing assignment caused the aircraft to need the South African registration before regaining its French registration. Log books with the aircraft indicate long-term assignments in both Africa and South America.

As noted before, fourteen B-17s were obtained by the IGN. One was purchased at the outset for spares. Of the thirteen others, two crashed in the course of their survey work. An additional four were scrapped between 1962 and 1973, leaving seven remaining aircraft. Six have now been preserved.

44-85718 was retired from IGN work on 12 June 1984 when it was sold to English aircraft collector Doug Arnold. Arnold had his B-17 registered as G-FORT and it was operated by Warbirds of Great Britain while based at Bitteswell. It was subsequently sold to collector Steven Grey, who sold it to Bob Waltrip on 09 June 1987.

Waltrip's vintage aircraft collection has congealed into the Lone Star Flight Museum, which was based at Houston, Texas when the B-17 was ferried back across the Atlantic in 1987. It has since moved its operation to Galveston, Texas. The B-17, which was issued the civil registration of N900RW, was initially owned by Air-Srv of Anderson, Texas but Waltrip transferred his collection to the Lone Star Flight Museum in November of 1987.

While the B-17 was still in England, the Lone Star Flight Museum decided to have the Fortress painted as "Thunder Bird", a famous 303rd Bomb Group bomber. The Fortress was ferried by a nine man crew, including Gene Girman, radio operator of the original Thunder Bird. The aircraft left Duxford 14 July 1987, and followed the old wartime North Atlantic Ferry Route via Iceland, Greenland, and New Foundland. On 15 July the aircraft touched down at Nashua, New Hampshire for a little politicking, as Vice President George Bush, hot on the campaign trail, put in an appearance in Thunder Bird's cockpit. A photo opportunity, as it were.

A much publicized cross-country sweep across to Texas followed, with N900RW arriving in Houston on the afternoon of 16 July. The B-17 was then grounded and towed into the shop for a complete restoration. Jim Fausz, Lone Star Flight Museum Director, found his new charge in remarkably good condition. The fuselage, despite its world wide treks, was virtually free of corrosion. The IGN mods were well engineered, with little structure being cut or removed.

The wings came off the Fortress and were disassembled for complete corrosion control. The electrical, fuel, and hydraulic systems were removed and overhauled or replaced with new components. Four overhauled engines have been obtained. As the Fortress comes back together, three original, operable gun-turrets are going back into the airframe. A 'stinger' tail compartment, replacing the "Cheyenne" tail, has also been found and placed on the bomber. All military systems, such as bomb bay doors, are now operable. Every effort is being taken to bring N900RW back to as stock condition as possible. It will remain as Thunder Bird, and completion date is expected to be sometime in late 1990. It will then join the growing list of authentically restored B-17s, and should be flying well into the next century.

44-85718 in service with the Institut Geographique National under the French registration of F-BEEC. Obtained directly from the War Assets Administration in late 1947, 44-85718 operated regularly with the IGN through 1983. MAP

F-BEEC on the ramp at Creil, France in September, 1964. Marson

CHAPTER TWENTY-EIGHT: 44-85738

TULARE, CALIFORNIA

■■■■■■

| 44-85738 | B-17G-105-VE to DB-17G to EDB-17G to DB-17G | | | |

USAAF/USAF

DATE	LOCATION	UNIT	CMD	REMARKS
17 MAY 45	BURBANK		ATC	ACCEPTED
20 MAY 45	LOUISVILLE		ATC	MOD CENTER
25 JUN 45	SYRACUSE		ATC	STORAGE
04 OCT 45	GARDEN CITY	4132 BASE UNIT	ATS	STORAGE
13 FEB 46	KELLY	SAN ANTONIO AIR DEPOT	ATC	MODIFICATION
25 MAR 46	CLOVIS	1.5 TASK GROUP	SAC	CROSSROADS
(16 JUN 46)	(depart U.S. to Eniwetok Atoll)		– –	CROSSROADS
01 AUG 46		509 VERY HEAVY BOMB GP	SAC	CROSSROADS
(14 AUG 46)	(return to U.S.)		– –	CROSSROADS
14 AUG 46	ROSWELL	509 VERY HEAVY BOMB GP	SAC	
31 OCT 46	WRIGHT	4000 BASE UNIT	AMC	
(18 JUN 48)	(fr: B-17G to: DB-17G)		– –	
(02 JUN 49)		(fr: DB-17G to: EDB-17G)		
28 MAR 50	EGLIN	550 GUIDED MISSILE WG	APG	
01 JUN 50	WRI-PAT	2750 BASE WING	AMC	
01 MAR 51	EGLIN	3210 SUPPORT GP	APG	
03 MAY 51	WRI-PAT		ARD	
24 JUL 51	EGLIN	3203 MIS SUPPORT GP	APG	
03 AUG 51	HOLLOMAN	3200 PROOF TEST WG	APG	
02 DEC 51	HOLLOMAN	3205 DRONE GP	APG	
13 JAN 54	EGLIN	3205 DRONE GP	APG	
(25 JAN 54)	(fr: EDB-17G to: DB-17G)		– –	
14 SEP 54	HOLLOMAN	3205 DRONE GP	APG	
56	EGLIN	3205 DRONE GP	APG	
(AUG 58)	(placed on permanent display with AMVETS, Tulare, CA)			

44-85738

44-85738 is parked on public display alongside Highway 99 in the Central California town of Tulare. Its major distinction is that it is, apparently, the sole survivor of a number of B-17s which were involved in Operation Crossroads, the first series of atomic testing undertaken in the South Pacific.

A Lockheed-built model, 44-85738 was accepted at Burbank on 18 May 1945. It was immediately flown to

Louisville, Kentucky, for modifications, and deemed ready for operational use on 25 June. The European war long over, the B-17 was flown to Syracuse, New York, and placed in storage along with several hundred other factory-fresh Fortresses.

Many of these B-17s would eventually be flown to Altus, Oklahoma for disposal or scrapping, but 85738 remained in storage. On 04 October 1945 it was moved to Garden City, Kansas, where it remained until 13 February 1946 when it

Line-up of Operation Crossroads B-17s at Eniwetok Atoll on 16 May 1946. 44-85738 is the third B-17 on the line (Number IV). All aircraft carried the Operation Crossroads insignia their nose. USAF

44-85738 and other 'mother' ships being reworked at the San Antonio Air Depot at Kelly AFB in March 1946. Six B-17s were used as mother ships and ten were utilized as 'baby' drones for Operation Crossroads. The required modification work was completed in three weeks. USAF

was assigned to the 1.5 Task Group, part of Operation Crossroads. Modification to drone director status followed at the San Antonio Air Depot, located at Kelly Field in Texas, followed by assignment to Clovis Field in New Mexico on 26 March 1946.

Operation Crossroads provided for the first of many massive post-war detonations to test and further develop nuclear weapons. Though steeped in controversy now, the world of 1946 held few reservations about nuclear testing and both the military and scientific communities massed around tiny Bikini Atoll in the South Pacific for the inaugural detonation scheduled that summer. The residents of Bikini were evacuated to a new home and the atoll's lagoon soon became the anchoring point for a giant fleet of ships. Many of the soon-to-be targets were captured German and Japanese vessels, though there were also a fair number of large American warships, including a carrier and battleship, considered expendable in the name of science. All told, there over 100 ships anchored in the lagoon, targets for two scheduled tests. One weapon would be dropped from an overflying B-29 Superfortress to detonate above the fleet, while the second would be detonated from the floor of the lagoon a few weeks later. Attached to the decks of the ships were countless experiments, measuring instruments, and various types of military equipment including naval aircraft.

The Army Air Force would contribute radio-controlled drone B-17s to fly through and near the resultant mushroom clouds for sample collection and photographic survey. The "mother" B-17s, of which 44-85738 was one, would shepherd the "baby" drones from the safety of distance from the atomic detonations. In early May 1946, ten drones and six direc-

tor B-17s deployed to Eniwetok Island, some 170 miles west of Bikini. They were attached to the 509th Composite Group, famed for dropping the two atomic bombs during the war and now responsible for handling the first device during Crossroads. The balance of the 509th, including the B-29 which would drop the first bomb, was based at Kwajalein Island, located 200 miles southeast of Bikini. Successive series of practice missions to coordinate schedules, adjust photo angles, and perfect techniques were conducted.

Finally, on 01 July 1946, Test Able took place. The first device was dropped from a B-29 flying at 35,000 feet over the atoll, and detonated 1000 feet above the anchored fleet. The resultant blast and cloud was subjected to intense scrutiny from all manner of cameras and instruments, including those aboard the B-17 drones. An extensive post-

44-85738 at Castle AFB in August 1958 en route from Eglin AFB to Visalia, California. Hennion

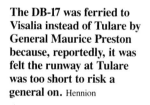

The DB-17 was ferried to Visalia instead of Tulare by General Maurice Preston because, reportedly, it was felt the runway at Tulare was too short to risk a general on. Hennion

44-85738 arriving at Tulare on 04 August 1958 with Capt. Zurlingen at the controls. Hennion

test examination of the fleet was conducted (with minimal radiation protection for inspectors, according to published sources). Two weeks later Test Baker took place, with the detonation of the submerged weapon. Similar measurements and inspections were conducted.

Its mission completed, 44-85738 returned to the U.S. in August 1946 and assigned to Roswell Field in New Mexico, where it continued to operate as a drone controller. It was assigned to the Air Materiel Command on 31 March 1947 and redesignated, with the newly created drone prefix, as a DB-17G on 18 June 1948.

On 02 June 1949, 44-85738 was again redesignated, this time with a second prefix, as an EDB-17G. The "E" prefix probably denoted assignment to a long-term test program where it was desirable to exempt the aircraft from routine maintenance and modifications as established by technical orders. It is possible the airplane was loaned to a contractor or other government agency for test work, though this is not clear from the record. As an EDB-17G, 738 was assigned to the Air Proving Ground Command and, on 28 March 1950, based at Eglin AFB in Florida. It was assigned to the 3210th Support Group until 02 May 1951 when it was transferred to the Air Research and Development Command at Wright-Patterson AFB in Ohio. It remained with ARD for six weeks and then went back to Eglin and the 3203rd Missile Support Group. On 03 August 1951 738 went to Holloman AFB, home of the Holloman Air Development Center and located near Alamogordo, New Mexico. It served first with the 3200th Drone Group, and then, on 02 December 1951, joined the 3205th Drone Group.

Most of the DB-17s (and QB-17s) eventually came to be assigned to the 3205th, and the unit had squadrons based at Eglin AFB, Holloman AFB, Patrick AFB, and NAS Point Mugu. Aircraft were moved around depending upon test schedules and requirements, but 85738 would remain with the Group for the remainder of its military utilization. The EDB-17G designation reverted to DB-17G on 05 December 1954.

As the supply of QB-17 drones was depleted, the number of DB-17s required for director work was similarly reduced. Some DB-17s were themselves converted to QB-17 drones and used as targets. For the most part, however, the DB-17s were withdrawn from service and sent to storage or for disposal at Davis-Monthan AFB. Many found their way to museums or, eventually, the civil market.

44-85738 circumvented the process somewhat and in 1958 became the second of the DB-17s to be slated for preservation. (The USAF Museum had obtained the first in June, 1957.) As it happened, the central Californian town of Tulare was engaged in a search for a memorial to grace their fair community. The city was not specifically looking for a war memorial, but rather an item which would relate to the city's past. The town council had agreed to obtain an old Southern Pacific locomotive when the suggestion of an airplane was considered. The city had a famous native son in the person of General Maurice Preston, wartime commander of the 379th Bomb Group and in 1958, Air Force Deputy Chief of Staff. Inquiries were made of General Preston, who enthusiastically endorsed the idea and arranged to have a B-17 set aside for the town memorial. Officially, the Fortress would be permanently loaned to the local AMVETs chapter for public display.

The Air Force selected 44-85738, still at Eglin, for Tulare and a ferry flight was arranged. A three man crew, consisting of Captain Herbert Zurligen (pilot), Captain John Rohr (copilot), and Sgt. James Touchton (flight engineer) flew the aircraft to Davis-Monthan AFB. There, General Preston joined the crew as pilot and flew the Fortress to Castle AFB in California via Colorado Springs (to pick up Preston's son, then at the Air Force Academy) and March AFB in Riverside, California. On 03 August 1958 Preston made the short flight from Castle to Visalia Airport, some seven miles from Tulare, with a load of reporters who were treated to a low-level tour of the local area.

The city of Tulare formally accepted the airplane from Preston in a civic ceremony that evening, and the B-17 was ferried to Tulare's small airstrip the following morning with Zurligen at the controls. (Preston had wanted to fly the bomber into Tulare himself, but the Pentagon would not risk him to the short runway available. He had to content himself with flagging the bomber into its final parking spot.)

The ensuing years were not kind to the B-17. Things started off well enough with the attentions of a grateful community. The Air Force provided a set of power turrets to bring the airframe back to the appearance of a wartime bomber (though the post-war Air Force markings remained intact). Initial plans had the B-17 moving to a central town park, but a decision was soon made to leave it at the local airstrip instead, located as it was along Highway 99, a major north-south freeway spanning the state.

Unfortunately, an unceasing attack by vandals against the B-17 began quickly, and with the passing of time the elements also took their toll. By the late sixties the Fortress sat on flat tires, with most of the Plexiglas shattered, the fabric rotted off the control surfaces, and a gutted interior with every loose part along with various once-attached parts such as instruments, seats, and wiring harnesses ripped from the airplane. The meager fence designed to protect the bomber was trampled, allowing easy access to anyone who wanted to get inside the B-17, regardless of their reverent or destructive intent. In short, the airplane was turning to junk.

The AMVET chapter, painfully aware of their responsibility toward preserving the old bomber, yet limited by disinterest and negligible resources, took a major step in 1971 by accepting the offer of a local businessman to move the B-17 to his property for display near his restaurant. Shortly thereafter, a tractor towed the airplane about a mile across some fields to its new home, also visible from Highway 99. A high fence was erected around the B-17 and prospects seemed better that its condition could at least be stabilized.

However, the state of the aircraft had understandably attracted the attention of the public, as well as other museums eager to obtain a Flying Fortress. Efforts were started to have the Air Force Museum, which now controlled the fate of the Tulare B-17, take it back and loan or trade it to a group that had the resources to restore and maintain the aircraft properly. Hill AFB in Utah made several offers of trade for the B-17, as did the Confederate Air Force. And when the Air Force learned that 44-85738 was now on private property (a violation of the original loan agreement), it warned the AMVETs chapter to place the Fortress back on public property and restore it to displayable condition or risk its loss.

Thus, in 1981 the AMVETs ignobly towed the B-17 back to the airpark and its original home. Serious efforts were initiated to restore and protect its exterior. That attempt was sidelined in August 1982 when a semi-truck loaded with grapes was unable to negotiate a nearby off-ramp and slammed into the bomber, damaging its tail and shoving it thirty feet into a fence and some poles. Years of protracted legal battles ensued, but damage to the B-17 was eventually repaired.

Finally, years of work by the AMVETs group are paying off. The airframe is intact and externally complete. Some of the work was performed by Aero Nostalgia, of Stockton, California, which has become a supplier of B-17 parts and replica parts. Aero Nostalgia installed new fuselage glass,

detailed the engines and props, and performed some miscellaneous maintenance and painting in exchange for some interior equipment and the damaged dorsal and chin turrets which were replaced by Aero Nostalgia with fiberglass reproductions. Aero Nostalgia will also replace the crazed Plexiglas blown nose with a new piece when one comes available.

The AMVETs skinned the control surfaces with aluminum as a necessary concession to short-lived fabric. The post-war markings were removed and replaced with the wartime markings of the 379th Bomb Group, as commanded by General Preston. Inexplicably, the "triangle K" on the tail was applied out of line with the aircraft and the serial, applied as 0-485738, represents the serial as applied during the 1950s. (The "0" preceding the serial number indicates an aircraft more than ten years old.)

Other markings on the aircraft include 44 bomb symbols, indicating combat missions flown, which have led many to believe this aircraft is a combat veteran. The painted bomb symbols were added prior to its arrival at Tulare to represent General Preston's wartime record, but have come to ascribe wartime action to this B-17's otherwise peacetime heritage.

The inside of 738 will remain as is—gutted and stripped. It is perhaps a fitting testament in itself to the thoughtless vandal and his destructive capability. Nonetheless. 44-85738 has regained a measure of its former stature and, though it has not undergone what could be considered a professional restoration, become a fitting memorial to those veterans who have served our nation though the years.

44-85738 retained DB-17 markings until 1985. Note the absence of the chin turret fairing in this November 1965 photo. Larkins

44-85738 shortly after arrival. Power turrets were reinstalled later. The bomb symbols, representing General Preston's wartime record, were applied prior to the B-17 arriving at Tulare. Carter via AAHS

The Tulare B-17 on display in November 1965. Aircraft is still in relatively good condition but the sign of things to come is the main entrance door wide open. Larkins

CHAPTER TWENTY-NINE: 44-85740

EAA AIR MUSEUM
OSHKOSH, WISCONSIN

■■■■■■

44-85740   B-17G-105-VE to N5017N

USAAF

DATE	LOCATION	UNIT	CMD	REMARKS
17 MAY 45	BURBANK		ATC	ACCEPTED
21 MAY 45	LOUISVILLE	MODIFICATION CENTER	ATC	
29 JUN 45	SYRACUSE		ATC	STORAGE
(12 OCT 45)	(declared excess)		– –	
07 NOV 45	ALTUS		RFC	DISPOSAL

CIVIL

DATE	TRANSFER DETAILS
10 JUN 47	FR: WAR ASSETS ADMINISTRATION
	TO: METAL PRODUCTS, AMARILLO, TX
10 JUL 47	TO: UNIVERSAL AVIATION, TULSA, OK
02 AUG 47	TO: CHARLES WINTERS, MIAMI, FL
16 AUG 47	TO: VERO BEACH EXPORT AND IMPORT CO., VERO BEACH, FL
27 JUN 49	TO: AERO SERVICE CORP., PHILADELPHIA, PA
10 AUG 62	TO: C.D. STOLTZFUS, COATSVILLE, PA
16 DEC 66	TO: DOTHAN LEASING AND EQUIPMENT RENTAL, DOTHAN, AL
06 FEB 70	TO: DOTHAN AVIATION CORP., DOTHAN, AL
20 FEB 78	TO: W.E. HARRISON, TULSA, OK
21 MAY 79	TO: B-17 AROUND THE WORLD, INC., TULSA, OK
31 MAR 81	TO: EAA FOUNDATION, FRANKLIN, WI

44-85740

44-85740 had a long a varied civil career after a brief military use which consisted primarily of ferry flights from factory to modification center to storage yard to scrap yard. Civil use included utilization as a aerial survey platform and sprayer. It now resides at the EAA Air Museum located at Oshkosh, Wisconsin.

44-85740 was accepted by the Army Air Force at the Burbank Vega factory on 17 May 1945. It was flown to a modification center at Louisville, Kentucky, arriving on 21 May. It spent a little over a month there before being ready for service. However, the Army Air Force had no use for it and hundreds like it, so 44-85740 joined a growing number of new Fortresses at a storage depot at Syracuse, New York,

arriving on 29 June 1945. It and most other new B-17s were declared excess to military requirements on 12 October 1945 and slated for disposal. It was flown to Altus, Oklahoma on 07 November and assigned to the Reconstruction Finance Corporation for sale.

44-85740 remained parked at Altus for nearly eighteen months before being purchased by Metal Products of Amarillo, Texas. The net sales price for the B-17 was $750. A month later, however, the Fortress went to Universal Aviation of Tulsa, Oklahoma, which was able to purchase the aircraft for $1800. Universal Aviation was an aerial survey company and the first to use the Fortress in a money-making civil role. Universal already owned one Fortress, B-17G-95-DL 44-83811 which had been registered by

44-85740 in storage at Coatsville, Pennsylvania in 1964 or 1965. The B-17 had been purchased for conversion to a sprayer which was not accomplished until after Hugh Wheelless purchased the B-17 in 1966.
MAP

Universal as N5014N. It had obtained 44-85740 and registered it as N5017N, but instead of putting it to work, sold it instead to Charles Winters of Miami, Florida on 02 August 1947.

N5017N was the first of three Fortresses purchased by Winters in 1947. Winters was intent on starting a Caribbean cargo air line, but instead turned and sold N5017N only two weeks after its purchase. The new owner was the Vero Beach Export and Import Company of Vero Beach, Florida, which had purchased the B-17 for $3500. Winters' other two B-17s, NL1098M (44-83851) and N5024N (44-83753), were later sold to a Jewish purchasing agent surreptitiously equipping the desperate new Israeli Air Force for their fight for independence.

A ferry crew delivered the B-17 from Oklahoma to Melbourne Florida. A pilot for the company, Thomas Cobb, then ferried the B-17 to Sebring, Florida to a modification shop which converted the airframe for air cargo. The bulkhead between the radio room and the waist area was removed, and provisions for securing cargo was installed.

In December 1947 the B-17, with a total of only 37 hours of flight time, entered service carrying beef from a cattle ranch west of Melbourne, Florida to Puerto Rico.

Vero Beach Export and Import Company operated N5017N for two years before they sold the B-17 to Aero Service Corporation of Philadelphia on 27 June 1949 for $28,000. As noted elsewhere, Aero Service came to operate a number of B-17s during the post-war period, primarily as high-altitude photo mappers.

Aero Service converted N5017N for high altitude mapping at its Mercer County Airport facility near Trenton, New Jersey. Beginning in late 1949 N5017N was dispatched for mapping duties in the Middle East, where it remained until May 1953.

Aero Service completely rebuilt N5017N in August 1953, at which point the airframe had accumulated 1389 hours of flight time. The airframe was disassembled and all components overhauled. New fuel tanks were installed, and the aircraft was rewired. New instruments and avionics were installed, and fresh engines and props replaced the original powerplants. At the completion of the overhaul N5017N

returned to the middle east for assignment in Libya. The aircraft later went to Thailand and back to Libya. The Fortress was extensively used, as just over three years later it showed nearly 3325 hours of flight time. It logged flight time over Iran, Laos, Vietnam, Cambodia, Egypt, and Jordan on its far-flung mapping and photo missions.

Aero Service operated N5017N until August 1962 when they sold it to Chris Stoltzfus and Associates of Coatsville, Pennsylvania. Stoltzfus had intended to modify N5017N for use as an aerial sprayer, but his economic situation never allowed it. He kept the B-17 at the Coatsville Airport under shrouded engines and glass, but was forced to move his B-17 when the airport was expanded. He made the short flight to his own private airport, despite his lack of experience in the type.

On 16 December 1966 N5017N was sold to Dothan Aviation Corporation of Dothan, Alabama. Dothan Aviation was owned by Hugh Wheelless, who came to operate three Fortresses during the sixties. Besides N5017N, Wheelless also owned N3701G (44-8543*), N4710C (44-85812) and N9323R (44-85828). Dothan Aviation used the Fortresses under contract to the U.S. Department of Agriculture and various state agencies in the southeast for their constant attacks against the fire ant. N5017N was equipped with a hopper and spray bars in March 1967 and began operations which lasted until 1976. During this period the Fortress was finished in silver paint with a yellowish-orange dorsal fin. By January 1969 the Fortress had logged 6051 hours. In 1976 the spraying program had ended and the two surviving Fortresses, N5017N and N3701G, were parked with no apparent future.

Wheelless broke up his company in 1980, but sold N5017N to Dr. William Harrison of Tulsa, Oklahoma on 20 February 1978. Harrison, long a warbird supporter, had plans to fly the Fortress around the world on a goodwill mission and to rekindle memories of the past by visits to wartime bases in England. On 21 May 1979 ownership of the Fortress was transferred to a new corporation, B-17 Around the World, Inc., formed by Harrison and five other warbird owners. Combat markings were added to the B-17, becoming the "Aluminum Overcast" with fictitious bomb group markings. The Fortress was otherwise not restored and continued to carry many of its civil modifications. Plans for the round-the-world flight quickly fell through, however, as realities of the cost and political climate became apparent.

The corporation instead decided to donate their airplane to the Experimental Aircraft Association Foundation for display at the EAA Museum, and the donation was accomplished at the EAA convention at Oshkosh in the summer of 1980. Legal transfer occurred on 31 March 1981.

The EAA maintained N5017N in airworthy condition and the Fortress occassionally toured parts of the country, putting in appearances at numerous airshows. Its appearance remained much the same, sporting a marginally accurate paint scheme with no armament installed. However, it remained popular and was a big draw for the EAA at its musuem.

In October 1988 the EAA Foundation's Board of Directors decided to place N5017N on static display, severely limiting its flights to special displays. Along with that decision came one which provided for some restorative work and a new paint scheme. In late spring 1989 the B-17 was flown from Wisconsin to, ironically enough, Dothan, Alabama where Hayes Aircraft repainted it. An overall glossy aluminized paint with white tones was applied, with markings of the 398th Bomb Group added. (The white tones in the paint, unfortunately, tend to detract from the accuracy of the markings and the attempt at a realistic appearance.) Two gun turrets were obtained, consisting of a ball turret shell and a fiberglass chin turret. These were installed once the aircraft had returned to Wisconsin. Other military equipment, such as radios and bomb racks will be added as they become available, as will a replica top turret. Nose markings have not been determined at this time.

EAA officials feel that the effective grounding of the Fortress is the best course for the Museum to take, as the aircraft has become such a draw it would be unfair to take it from the facility for months at a time. As it is, N5017N will form an integral part of the display at the new EAA Eagle Hangar, and may still take to the skies on the odd occasion.

N5017N, still in Aero Service markings, at Chris Stolzfus' private airport in late 1965. It was sold the following year.
Besecker Collection

N5017N at Oshkosh in July 1985. Note the abbreviated military serial and lack of armament. Restoration effort was primarily the application of military markings. Krieger

CHAPTER THIRTY: 44-85778

STOCKTON, CALIFORNIA

■■■■■■

44-85778   B-17G-105-VE to TB-17G to VB-17G to N3509G

USAAF/USAF

DATE	LOCATION	UNIT	CMD	REMARKS
06 JUN 45	BURBANK		ATC	ACCEPTED
08 JUN 45	DALLAS	MODIFICATION CENTER	ATC	
09 SEP 45	SOUTH PLAINS		ATC	STORAGE
01 FEB 46	OLMSTED	4112 BASE UNIT	ATS	
14 MAR 46	BORINQUIN		CAC	
(01 JAN 48)	(fr: B-17G to: TB-17G)		– –	
01 JAN 48	BORINQUIN	24 COMPOSITE GROUP	CAC	
19 APR 48	BORINQUIN	48 SR	CAC	
21 JUN 48	RIO DE JANIERO		BMC	
(01 SEP 50)	(fr: TB-17G to: VB-17G)		– –	
OCT 54	BOLLING	1100 OP	HQC	
DEC 56	DAVIS-MONTHAN		AMC	STORAGE
(APR 59)	(reclamation authorized) – –			

CIVIL

DATE	TRANSFER DETAILS
14 AUG 59	FR: 2704TH ACFT STORAGE AND DISPOSTION GROUP
	TO: ACE SMELTING, PHOENIX, AZ
20 SEP 60	TO: SONORA FLYING SERVICE, COLUMBIA, CA
25 MAY 61	TO: LEO DEMERS, MADRAS, OR
29 APR 66	TO: AERO UNION, CHICO, CA
02 JUN 72	TO: WILLIAM DEMPSEY, RANTOUL, KS
06 JUL 78	TO: WESTERN AVIATION CONTRACTORS, AMERICAN FORK, UT
15 JUN 81	TO: WESTERNAIRE, ALBUQUERQUE, NM
28 MAY 82	TO: ACFT COMPONENT EQUIPMENT SUPPLIES, KLAMATH FALLS, OR

44-85778

44-85778 is a lesser known example of the Fortress, though it served in the Air Force through the post-war period and was put to use as an air tanker under the civil registration of N3509G. The B-17 was retired from tanker use in 1981 and is currently in semi-storage awaiting restoration at Aero Nostalgia of Stockton, California.

44-85578 was accepted by the Army Air Force on 06 June 1945 at Burbank, California. It was flown to Dallas and the Lockheed modification facility where it spent nearly three months, somewhat longer than most Fortresses. It was available for service on 05 September and was flown into storage at South Plains, Texas, arriving on 09 September. 44-85778 remained at South Plains until 23 January 1946 when it was pulled for assignment to the 4112th Base Unit at Olmsted Field in Pennsylvania. It arrived for duty on 01 February.

A month later it was dispatched to the Caribbean Air Command, passing through Morrison Field, Florida en route to assignment at Borinquin Field in Puerto Rico. Though information contained in the aircraft records is sketchy, it would appear that the Fortress either was assigned Air-Rescue duties or was variously assigned to units performing that function. Though never designated as a TB-17H, 44-85778 was assigned to the 24th Composite Group and the 48th Search and Rescue Group, both of the Caribbean Air Command. That the Fortress passed through Morrison Field enroute to assignment is also indicative that it may have been assigned air-rescue functions as that base was the headquarters of the Air Rescue Service beginning in July 1946. 44-85778 was redesignated as a TB-17G on 01 January 1948.

On 20 June 1948 the Fortress was released from the Caribbean Air Command at Ramey AFB, Puerto Rico, assigned to the Brazilian Military Command, and assigned to Rio de Janeiro, Brazil. It would remain with that unit for six years, being redesignated at a VB-17G on 01 September 1950. Exact duties assigned to the aircraft are unknown, but it can be presumed that it was used by the American embassy for VIP transport within Brazil and in trips to the U.S.

44-85778 returned to the U.S. for assignment with Headquarters Air Force at Bolling AFB, Washington D.C. in October 1954. The VB-17G was attached to the 1100th Operational Group at Bolling until retirement to Davis-Monthan AFB in 1956.

The Fortress remained in storage for three years before authorization for disposal was given in April 1959. It was placed up for sale by auction and was purchased by the Ace Smelting Company for $2888.88 on 14 August 1959. Ace Smelting had the aircraft registered as N3509G and sold it to the Sonora Flying Service of Columbia, California on 20 September 1960.

Sonora Flying Service purchased N3509G with the intent to convert it to a tanker configuration, but the conversion never occurred as the company went out of business. Instead, they sold the aircraft to Leo Demers of Madras, Oregon, on 25 May 1961. Demers brought it to Madras for conversion, with bomb-bay tanks and spray bars on the trailing edge of the wings being installed. At the completion of the work in April 1962 the airframe had amassed 4,014 hours of flight time. The aircraft was utilized both as a forest sprayer of insecticide and as an air tanker by Demers until 1966 when N3509G was again sold. Demers operated the aircraft as Tanker 97.

On 29 April 1966 N3509G was purchased by Aero Union at Chico, joining their fleet of Fortresses. It operated as Tanker 16 in the Aero Union livery, and the spray bars were deleted from the wings. In June 1968 it received the distinctive Aero Union fiberglass nose cone in place of the standard Plexiglas blown nose.

Aero Union sold N3509G on 02 June 1972 to William Dempsey of Rantoul, Kansas, who operated Central Air Services of Wenatchee, Washington. Dempsey also ran D&D Aero Spraying in Kansas. The Fortress became Tanker 42 under Dempsey, who continued to operate it as an air tanker in Washington State. By August 1973 the aircraft had 5,021 hours of logged flight time.

Dempsey sold N3509G to Western Aviation Contractors of American Fork, Utah on 06 July 1978. Western Aviation Contractors continued to utilize N3509G as a tanker with the tanker code of 102 applied. It was sold three years later to Westernaire, Inc. of Albuquerque on 15 June 1981. Westernaire, an aviation sales broker, placed the Fortress up for sale. It was listed in an ad for Trade-A-Plane in July 1981 with a sales price of $325,000 and the notation that one could "make lots of money fire fighting or spraying" with the aircraft.

It was purchased on 28 May 1982 by Aircraft Component Equipment Supplies of Klamath Falls, Oregon. That company is owned by Richard Vartanian, a Los Angeles businessman who purchased the Fortress largely as an investment.

N3509G in September 1965 at Madras, Oregon. Note the installation of both spray bars and retardant tanks. The B-17 was sold the following April to Aero Union where it was used exclusively as a tanker. Larkins

The Fortress was moved to Mojave Airport on the high California desert, where it was placed in storage with Wally MacDonald for several months. It continued to carry the tanker colors as applied by Central Air Services. In early 1983 it was moved to Stockton and initial plans for the Fortress called for a documentary film to be developed around a trip to Hawaii. The bomber was stripped of paint and a logo of "America's Queen" applied to the nose. Initial efforts toward restoration were begun, but plans for the documentary fell through, and restoration work stopped. N3509G now rests inside the large hangar of Aero Nostalgia awaiting a decision on its fate.

A determination has been made that to insure trouble free operations the fuselage of the Fortress should be reskinned. Years of use of corrosive fire-fighting chemicals have taken their toll on the aluminum skin aft of the bomb bay. A careful inspection of the skin reveals a few areas where the corrosion has gone through the skin, but much of the aluminum appears in quite good condition. However, it may be that the skin is not beyond use and repairs to specific areas would suffice to keep the bomber airworthy.

Vartanian has several options as the fate of N3509G. He can go the whole route and reskin the fuselage, believed the first such large-scale job on a civil restoration. Or, he can spot repair the skin and maintain the bomber in an airworthy condition. Or, as has been suggested, the aircraft may become the basis of a trade to the Air Force or other organization seeking a museum-bound Fortress. No decision seems imminent, and the Fortress is parked in a partially disassembled state. Two of the engines are off the nacelles, and the cowlings are off the other two. Part of the tail section is removed, and Aero Nostalgia owner Jim Ricketts has used some components of N3509G as a basis for fiberglass molds he constructs to duplicate parts for other Fortress restorations. Thus, the fate of N3509G is undetermined, but it seems unlikely that the aircraft will return to the air on a regular basis in the near future.

Tanker 16 at the Aero Union base at Chico in April 1972. Note the addition of the fiberglass nose cone. Menard via Besecker

N3509G retained Aero Union's nose cone and much of its paint scheme in this view taken in 1979 at Chandler, Arizona. The B-17 went through three tanker operators before retirement in 1982. Lawson

N3509G in indefinite storage at the Aero Nostalgia hangar at Stockton Airport. Some components are off the aircraft for use as molds for fiberglass replica parts. Author

Chapter Thirty-one: 44-85790

Milwaukee, Oregon

■ ■ ■ ■ ■ ■

44-85790   B-17G-105-VE

USAAF

DATE	LOCATION	UNIT	CMD	REMARKS
13 JUN 45	BURBANK		ATC	ACCEPTED
16 JUN 45	DALLAS	MODIFICATION CENTER	ATC	
19 JUL 45	ROME		ATC	STORAGE
08 OCT 45	SCOTT		ATC	
(12 OCT 45)	(declared excess)		– –	
07 NOV 45	ALTUS		RFC	FOR DISPOSAL

OTHER DETAILS

DATE	REMARKS
05 MAR 47	PURCHASED BY ART LACEY, PORTLAND, OREGON, FOR EXHIBITION ATOP HIS GAS STATION

44-85790

Certainly one of the most bizarre fates of a post-war Flying Fortress was that of 44-85790. The Fortress has been on display above a gas station in a suburb of Portland, Oregon, since 1947. Aside from that unusual placement, a number of fanciful stories and histories have come to surround this aircraft, most of them will little basis of fact. The fate of this aircraft lies with Art Lacey, who purchased the aircraft in 1947.

44-85790 was built by Vega at Burbank and was accepted for service by the Army Air Force on 13 June 1945. It was flown to Dallas for modifications and emerged, ready for service, on 19 July. The Army Air Force shunted 44-85790 off with the hundreds of other excess Fortresses into storage, 790 ending up at Rome, New York. Their status remained unchanged until the following October when the Army Air Force found the lot excess to further military use and available for disposal. While that decision was later reconsidered and roughly half of those slated for disposal were reclaimed for future Air Force use, 44-85790 was flown first to Scott Field in Illinois, and then to Independence, Missouri. Final destination was the RFC lot at Altus, where the aircraft joined hundreds of other aircraft, both new and weary combat veterans alike.

The story ended for most of the aircraft at that point, as the majority were later sold in blocks for scrapping. By a

quirk of fate, however, 44-85790 survived. Through the years a number of discrepancies have arisen surrounding the details of its subsequent use, and what follows is an attempt to provide a straight-forward record.

Bob Sturges, who had many dealings with post-war B-17s, recalls that a company in Oklahoma, the H.E. Distributing Company, had salvaged a number of B-17s and had mounted one fuselage above a service station. A representative of the company had spoken to Art Lacey and suggested that he obtain a Fortress for display at his service station in Oregon. Lacey inspected the installation and then proceeded to Altus with the idea of obtaining one of the B-17s for himself. He selected a Fortress and paid the WAA $1500 to obtain it. Lacey did not actually purchase the B-17 for the going price of $13,750, and Sturges recalls that Lacey only obtained permission to move the aircraft and display it. Title remained with the U.S. government as was the case of many post-war transfers of surplus equipment. Lacey maintains that he has a bill of sale which grants him full title to 44-85790.

Lacey couldn't fly the Fortress out himself, but in the process of moving the aircraft around at Altus his B-17 suffered a brake failure and was taxied into another parked aircraft. His new pride and joy was now quite dented, but he was able to persuade a sympathetic official to switch some numbers around to provide him with another undamaged B-17. Thus did the paths of Art Lacey and 44-85790 cross.

Lacey called upon Sturges and George Fuller to fly 44-85790 to Troutdale. This was accomplished over a three day period between 08 March and 10 March 1947, with Lacey along for the ride. Lacey relates that he performed much of the flying himself. Upon arrival at Troutdale, Lacey and a group of his friends took to task and disassembled the Fortress for overland transport to Lacey's gas station, located some twenty miles away. Surprisingly, as few, if any, of the group knew the first thing about disassembling, transporting, and reconstructing such a large aircraft, the Fortress came back together basically complete. It was subsequently mounted on three pylons and formed a superstructure for Lacey's "Bomber Gas" station. The USAAF insignia was painted out, to be replaced by the Texaco star.

Through the years the Fortress has suffered the fate of such a public oddity. Vandals have attacked the interior. Oversized trucks have mangled the belly. Rumors have spread about purchase attempts by Paraguayan rebels and rich collectors, possibly fueled by Lacey himself as the somewhat mundane history of the Fortress fades into the past.

In the early sixties the ball turret was donated to the AMVETS group in Tulare for installation on 44-85738. And in a coup of sorts, the Arizona wing of the Confederate Air Force obtained the complete top turret assembly for installation in 44-83514. The turret was exchanged for a fiberglass replica, new glass, and some cosmetic work performed upon 44-85790.

Lacey has had offers as high as $1.5 million for the B-17, which he has adamantly refused on the basis that his bomber has become something of a local landmark and he intends to keep it as such. Still, the old Fortress has slowly slid into a somewhat sad state, and it seems unfortunate that it suffers from such an ignoble fate while so many of its brethren have enjoyed a pampered rebirth in the hands of dedicated musuems and individuals.

The bomber of Bomber Gas. 44-85790 in all the glory it can muster, fluorescent lights and all. Snider

Aft fuselage in 1986. Note skin wrinkling and metaled over control surfaces. Snider

44-85790 in its current state. The B-17 has suffered the wear and tear of time and vandalism. The ball turret is gone and the dorsal turret is a fiberglass replica. The blown nose is obviously non standard also. Photo taken in 1987. Peltzer Collection

CHAPTER THIRTY-TWO: 44-85828

390TH MEMORIAL MUSEUM
TUCSON, ARIZONA
■ ■ ■ ■ ■

44-85828   B-17G-110-VE to PB-1G 77254 to N9323R

USAAF

DATE	LOCATION	UNIT	CMD	REMARKS
14 JUL 45	BURBANK		ATC	ACCEPTED
16 JUL 45	DALLAS	MODIFICATION CENTER	ATC	
31 AUG 45	SOUTH PLAINS		ATC	STORAGE
01 MAR 46	ROME	4104 BASE UNIT	AMC	STORAGE
09 SEP 46	MEMPHIS	554 BASE UNIT	AMC	TRANSFER
(09 SEP 46)	(to USCG)		– –	

USCG

DATE	LOCATION	REMARKS
SEP 46	NAS JOHNSVILLE	CONVERSION
48	(assigned to U.S. Coast and Geodetic Survey)	
OCT 59	CGAS ELIZABETH CITY	STORAGE

CIVIL

DATE	TRANSFER INFORMATION
08 MAR 60	FR: USCG, CGAS ELIZABETH CITY, NC
	TO: JOE E. MARRS, OPA LOCKA, FL
09 APR 60	TO: SERV-AIR, INC., WESTCHESTER AIRPORT, WHITE PLAINS, NY
23 MAY 62	TO: TROPICAL EXPORT TRADING CO., FT. LAUDERDALE, FL
17 JUL 62	TO: HUGH WHEELUS, DOTHAN, AL
04 OCT 62	TO: BLACK HILLS AVIATION, SPEARFISH, SD
03 JAN 64	TO: AERO FLITE, INC., CODY, WY
29 DEC 75	TO: BRUCE KINNEY, RICHEY, MT
18 MAY 78	TO: AFG INC.
07 JUL 78	TO: AIRCRAFT SPECIALTIES, MESA, AZ
07 DEC 80	TO: USAF MUSEUM, WRIGHT-PATTERSON AFB, OH
	(for display at the 390th Memorial Museum located at the Pima Air Museum, Tucson, AZ)

44-85828

44-85828 performed its military service as a Coast Guard PB-1G and earned the distinction of being the last Flying Fortress to be operated by the U.S. military. Much of its utilization as a PB-1G was as a photo mapper on assignment to the U.S. Coast and Geodetic Survey, a role which it performed between 1948 and 1959. After being sold surplus into the civil market, 44-85828 was converted to an air tanker and was actively employed until 1980 when a trade placed it into the hands of the 390th Memorial Museum located at the Pima Air Museum near Davis-Monthan AFB in Arizona.

Arizona.

44-85828 was accepted for service by the Army on 14 July 1945 at Burbank, and was flown to the Lockheed modification center located at Dallas-Love Field, Texas, on 16 July. Modifications took nearly six weeks and then 44-85828 joined other Fortresses in long-term storage at South Plains, Texas. It remained at South Plains through February 1946 when it and fourteen other Vega built Fortresses, earmarked for Coast Guard service, were drawn from South Plains and flown to Rome, New York. 44-85828 was flown to Rome on 03 March 1946.

Once at Rome the B-17s were assigned to the 4104th Base Unit and placed in short term storage awaiting transfer to the Coast Guard. 44-85828 was formally transferred on 09 September 1946, the location of transfer being Memphis, Tennessee, with the 554th Base Unit being the last USAAF unit holding the aircraft. At the time of transfer, 44-85828 had 55 hours of flight time logged.

Upon acceptance by the Coast Guard, 44-85828 was redesignated as a PB-1G and assigned the Navy Bureau of Aeronautics number of 77254. It is evident that the serial had been set aside prior to the return of the Coast Guard from the wartime Navy to its traditional assignment with the Department of the Treasury. Arrangements had also been made for the PB-1Gs to be reworked at Navy facilities and many were converted to search and rescue configuration at the Naval Aircraft Modification Unit at NAS Johnsville, Pennsylvania.

Based on the limited information available from the Coast Guard, it is probable that 77254 was reworked to the Army Air Force TB-17H air-sea rescue standard, as were the other PB-1Gs. This included the deletion of all armament and other combat equipment, and the installation of search radar in the former location of the chin turret under the nose. Additional radio and navigation equipment was also installed. It is probable that provisions were made for 77254 to carry the A-1 Airborne Droppable Lifeboat on the belly of the aircraft. Whether 77254 ever carried the boat in operational

service is not known from available material.

At some point, possibly as early as 1948, 77254 was modified to become a photo mapper for occasional assignment to the U.S. Coast and Geodetic Survey. Primary modification was the installation of $1.5 million nine lens aerial mapping camera in the former position of the ball turret. The bomb-bay doors were sealed and the bomb-bay was loaded with oxygen bottles for an expanded oxygen system. A Norden bombsight was reinstalled in the nose for camera alignment and sighting. The search radar was retained in the nose section.

Modifications complete, the aircraft was relegated to the U.S. Coast and Geodetic Survey for eight or nine months out of each year. Operating with a six man Coast Guard crew and three man Coast and Geodetic Survey crew (consisting of a navigator and two photographers), 77254 was dispatched on missions covering the width and breadth of North America. The unique camera equipment could photograph 313 square miles of territory with one exposure of the special film at 21,000 feet. The camera weighed 750 pounds when loaded, and the 23 inch wide film was loaded in 200 foot lengths, which provided for 100 exposures.

The aircraft ranged from Puerto Rico to Alaska recording the surface and coastline for the Hydrographic Office of the Coast and Geodetic Survey. Unique among the other postwar uses of the Fortress was that this particular aircraft operated for the eleven-year assignment with the same crew basically intact. The only two incidents to mar the otherwise perfect safety record of the aircraft was a pair of ground handling accidents which occurred, coincidentally, at Hill AFB in Utah.

Details of the special camera installation are shown here with four of the aircraft's nine crewmembers on the final mission in 1959.

USCG via R. Scheina

77254, the last of many, at Boeing Field where the first had started it some twenty-four years earlier. USCG

77254 conducted its last mission in Alaska in the late summer of 1959. The return flight to North Carolina in September 1959 included a stop at Boeing Field in Seattle and CGAS San Francisco. From there it was flown to CGAS Elizabeth City, North Carolina, for retirement on 14 October 1959. The airframe had logged 5,515 hours of flight time at the conclusion of military service.

77254 was placed up for auction by the Coast Guard, and was sold to Joe Marrs of Opa Locka, Florida on 08 March 1960 for $6676.00. A month later Maas sold the Fortress to Serv-Air, Inc. of White Plains, New York, for $13,500. Serv Air owned the aircraft, registered as N9323R, for two years, though details of its operational use are unknown. Serv-Air

sold N9323R to the Tropical Export Trading Company of Fort Lauderdale, Florida on 23 May 1962. Tropical Export owned it for barely two months before selling the aircraft to Hugh Wheelless, operator of Dothan Aviation of Dothan, Alabama. Wheelless installed spray tanks and underwing bars on N9323R, presumably in preparation for use against fire ants in the southeast U.S., a role Wheelless employed a number of surplus B-17s in. N9323R was sold the following October, however, to Black Hills Aviation of Spearfish, South Dakota.

Black Hills Aviation was owned by Arnold Kolb, another operator who owned as many as four B-17s at any one time during the sixties and seventies. Kolb employed his aircraft as air tankers and N9323R was converted to carry retardant tanks. Becoming Tanker B30, N9323R began a long utilization which spanned nearly two decades and five tanker operators.

Kolb sold N9323R to Aero Flite of Cody, Wyoming in January 1964, and the aircraft would remain based at the air tanker facility at Cody through 1975. At that time it was sold to Bruce Kinney of Richey, Montana. It continued to be operated as a tanker using tanker code 37, and was sold to AFG, Inc. on 18 May 1978. AFG was a subsidiary company of Aircraft Specialties of Mesa, Arizona, and N9323R went to Aircraft Specialties the following summer to join four other B-17 tankers employed by the company at that time.

N9323R became the subject of a trade between the company and the Air Force Museum a year and a half later, with N9323R going into storage at the Pima Air Museum near Davis-Monthan AFB in Arizona, while Aircraft Specialties received a C-54 in exchange.

N9323R was assigned by the Air Force Museum to the 390th Memorial Association for their museum, then under development, which commemorated the exploits of the 390th Bomb Group during World War II and afterwards. The 390th Bomb Group had completed 301 combat missions during the war while equipped with B-17s. The unit was reactivated in 1962 and equipped with Titan missiles, becoming the 390th Strategic Missile Wing. The 390th Memorial Museum Foundation was established in 1980 with veterans of the original group and active duty members of the Strategic Missile Wing. The Foundation established a goal to construct a museum/library complex to house a B-17 and a Titan missile. The library opened in May 1985, and the museum was completed in the summer of 1986.

N9323R was painted in the colorful group markings of the 390th Bomb Group. It became "I'll Get Around," and now carries the tail serial of B-17G-30-BO 42-31892, in exception to Air Force Museum policy which suggests aircraft be marked with correct serial numbers. 44-85828 remained on outdoor display at the Pima Air Museum while the 390th Memorial Museum was constructing the museum building on the grounds of the Pima facility. 44-85828 was moved into the building where it now remains as a memorial to the Bomb Group, its successor unit, and those who served with the unit during the past forty-plus years.

44-85828 received the civil registration of N9323R in 1960 when sold surplus from the USCG. It went through several owners but was bought by Black Hills Aviation of Spearfish, South Dakota, to be converted to an air tanker in 1962. It is shown here as operated by Aero Flite, which had purchased it in 1964. Peltzer Collection

Chapter Thirty-three: 44-85829

YANKEE AIR FORCE
YPSILANTI, MICHIGAN

■■■■■■

44-85829   B-17G-110-VE to PB-1G 77255 to N3193G

USAAF

DATE	LOCATION	UNIT	CMD	REMARKS
16 JUL 45	BURBANK		ATC	ACCEPTED
18 JUL 45	DALLAS	MODIFICATION CENTER	ATC	
03 SEP 45	SOUTH PLAINS		ATS	STORAGE
01 MAR 46	ROME	4104 BASE UNIT		STORAGE
12 AUG 46	TOPEKA	5948 BASE UNIT	AMC	
(15 SEP 46)	(to USCG)			

USCG

DATE	LOCATION	REMARKS
SEP 46	NAS JOHNSVILLE	CONVERSION
MAY 59	CGAS ELIZABETH CITY	STORAGE

CIVIL

DATE	TRANSFER DETAILS
11 MAY 59	FR: USCG, CGAS ELIZABETH CITY, NC
	TO: ACE SMELTING, PHOENIX, AZ
16 NOV 59	TO: FAIRCHILD AERIAL SURVEY, LOS ANGELES, CA
02 AUG 65	TO: AERO SERVICE CORPORATION, PHILADELPHIA, PA
01 OCT 65	TO: BIEGERT BROS., SHICKLEY, NB
19 MAR 66	TO: AIRCRAFT SPECIALTIES, MESA, AZ
18 FEB 81	TO: GLOBE AIR, INC., MESA, AZ
25 JUN 86	TO: YANKEE AIR FORCE, YPSILANTI, MI

44-85829

44-85829 was one of fifteen Vega-produced B-17s which went to the Coast Guard in 1946 for use in air-sea rescue duties as PB-1Gs. As PB-1G 77255, 44-85829 evidently also served in iceberg patrol and was surplused in 1959. It was subsequently used for aerial survey as N3193G by two companies before conversion as an air tanker in 1965. 44-85829 became part of the Yankee Air Force in 1986 and is under gradual restoration to combat configuration by the flying museum, and should return to the air in 1990.

44-85829 was accepted by the Army Air Force on 16 July 1945 at Burbank. It was flown to the Lockheed modification center at Dallas-Love Field, arriving on 18 July. The aircraft was available for service on 28 August, five days before official surrender documents were signed in Tokyo Bay aboard the U.S.S. Missouri. From Dallas, 44-85829 was flown into storage at South Plains, Texas, joining hundreds of other factory-fresh B-17s also stored there. It entered storage on 03 September but was earmarked for the Coast Guard, along with fourteen other Fortresses, on 13 February 1946. 44-85829 was ferried to Rome, New York, on 20 February, and entered short term storage at that facility with the 4104th Base Unit. It remained at Rome through September 1946 when officially transferred to the Coast Guard. The aircraft may have gone through Topeka, Kansas during the transfer, or else was administratively assigned to the 594th Base Unit at Topeka for the transfer while the aircraft remained at Rome. In any event, 44-85829 was assigned the Bureau of Aeronautics serial of 77255 and sent to the Naval Aircraft Modification Unit at NAS Johnsville, Pennsylvania, for modifications similar to those performed on Army TB-17Hs for conversion to air-sea rescue configuration. Though the Coast Guard had administratively returned to the jurisdiction of the Department of the Treasury on 01 January 1946, the PB-1Gs received both Navy serial numbers and the use of Navy conversion facilities.

Specific details of Coast Guard use of 77255 are sketchy. From the record, it would appear that the aircraft was modified to carry the radar installation in place of the chin turret, had other armament deleted, and carried an A-1 lifeboat during some parts of it USCG use. It may have been used in the late forties for iceberg counts conducted from Argentia, Newfoundland. 77255 was operationally based at CGAS San Francisco in 1953, and may have remained at that station until retirement in 1959.

On 11 May 1959 the aircraft was sold by auction at CGAS Elizabeth City, North Carolina, to Ace Smelting of Phoenix, Arizona for $5887.93. Ace Smelting apparently ferried the aircraft to Arizona, though this is not clear from the record. It was registered as N3193G, and sold to Fairchild Aerial Survey of Los Angeles, California on 16 November 1959. Early the following year N3193G was in the shops being reworked to carry aerial survey equipment. A plywood floor was installed in the bomb bay and camera equipment was mounted onto the flooring. Crew positions were also installed, with provisions for nine personnel plus flight crew.

N3193G at Long Beach Airport in January 1964 owned by Fairchild Aerial Survey. Inscription on right waist states "Gravity, Electromagnetics, Magnetometer, Photogrametric Engineers." C. Jansson via Peltzer

N3193G in May 1966 shortly after purchase by Aircraft Specialties. It had been owned by Max Biegert between October 1965 and March 1966. B. Baker via Larkins

44-85829 gained warpaint for the first time in January 1969 for "Tora Tora Tora." After the film it retained the paint scheme for several months, with the addition of some bright orange stripes on the tail and wings. Photo taken at Mesa, Arizona in April 1969. Peltzer

All military equipment was removed. The former fuselage opening for the ball turret was opened up and it, plus openings in the aft fuselage once used for military cameras, were used to mount radomes of various types. A fuselage door was installed on the left side of the fuselage. At that point, in April 1960, the aircraft had amassed 4096 hours of flight time.

Fairchild utilized the aircraft for five years, and then sold it to the Aero Service Corporation of Philadelphia on 02 August 1965. Aero Service may have operated it with their three other Fortresses (N5845N, N5017N*, and N7227C*) in their aerial survey work. Aero Service only owned N3193G for three months, however, as on 01 October 1965 it was sold to the Biegert Brothers of Shickley, Nebraska.

The Biegert Brothers owned a number of B-17s over the years, and had developed the first B-17 sprayer from 42-29782*, registered as N17W. Max Biegert installed a pair of bomb bay tanks and underwing spray bars on N3193G, stripping any remaining aerial survey equipment from the airframe. The aircraft was subsequently sold to Aircraft Specialties on 19 March 1966, and they further modified it for use as an air tanker.

Aircraft Specialties operated one of the largest fleets of B-17 air tankers over the years. Based at Falcon Field in Mesa, Arizona, their tankers would spread out across the southwestern U.S. during the annual fire season on contract to various state and national forest services. N3193G became Tanker 34 in the Aircraft Specialties livery and was based at various Arizona and California tanker bases during the following twenty years.

In January 1969, N3193G joined four other Aircraft Specialties B-17 tankers and flown to NAS Ford Island on Oahu, Hawaii for use in the film "Tora Tora Tora". All five were repainted in 1941-era Army Air Corps colors and ferried to Hawaii via Oakland, California. They represented elements of the 7th Bomb Group, which arrived in the midst of the Japanese attack on Pearl Harbor, in the filmed re-creation of the events of 07 December 1941.

Upon completion of the filming, N3193G returned to Arizona for continued use as an air tanker. By that point the airframe had amassed 4894 hours of flight time. It would fly another thousand hours in the next decade. In the course of air tanker operations, the aircraft landed gear-up in Salmon, Idaho, suffering damage to the retardant tank under the bomb bay, but little else. In 1981, Aircraft Specialties was reorganized as Globe Air and the aircraft paperwork was changed to reflect the new ownership.

In 1985 the owners of Globe Air decided to liquidate their assets and close the company down. The accumulated mass of aircraft, extending far beyond the four remaining B-17s and including six C-54s, two TBMs, ten PV-2s, several Constellations, and a huge assortment of spare parts, engines, and surplus equipment, were all placed on the auction block in October 1985. Two of the B-17s, N17W and N93012 (44-83575*), had been sold prior to the auction. The third Fortress, N9563Z (44-83563*) was sold for $250,000 at the auction. N3193G never made the minimum bid set by Globe Air, so the aircraft was retained by owner Gene Packard for future sale.

Nine months later 44-85828 was sold to the Yankee Air Force of Ypsilanti, Michigan. The Yankee Air Force had been formed in 1981 as a new, non-profit, tax-exempt museum. Its primary goal was to commemorate the contribution of the Ford-built B-24s which had been assembled at Ypsilanti during World War II. Toward that end, they leased a large World War II-era hangar from the county which operated the airport, and began a search for a Ford-

The final paint scheme worn by N3193G as a tanker. Photo taken at Santa Rosa, California in July 1983. Larkins

built B-24 that they could obtain. However, the almost extinct status of the type in general caused a refocusing of the group's aim. The collection of aircraft has grown to over twenty aircraft, a number of which remain flyable. The group, which relies solely on volunteer labor and financial contributions, has slowly built up a substantial facility and continues to expand.

N3193G was ferried from Mesa, Arizona to Ypsilanti between 30 June and 02 July 1986. Shortly after arrival at the Willow Run Airport and with 6,745 hours of flight time, it was rolled into the maintenance hangar and grounded for restoration. Utilizing volunteer labor, the B-17 has been disassembled to component parts and is slowly being rebuilt. The group's first goal is to return N3193G to safe flying condition, with the reinstallation of combat equipment such as

turrets an eventual goal. Corrosion was located in the vertical stabilizer area, requiring an extensive teardown and repair of those components. Each flight system in receiving considerable attention to insure trouble-free operation when the Fortress once again becomes operational.

Tentative plans call for the B-17 to become the "Yankee Lady" and may be marked as a 381st Bomb Group aircraft. Final decision as to paint scheme and markings have yet to be made. Completion of the project is targeted at 1990, though the mechanics working on the aircraft are not under any pressure to complete the work on a particular timetable. The Yankee Air Force wants the aircraft to be a reliable and safe component of their air museum when it finally returns to the air, and all indications point to yet another B-17 which should remain airworthy into the next century.

In the YAF hangar, work continues on 44-85829 during the summer of 1989. Hade

PARTIAL AIRFRAMES

■■■■■

CHAPTER THIRTY-FOUR: 44-83316

OCOTILLO WELLS, CALIFORNIA

■■■■■

44-83316 B-17G-75-DL to VB-17G				

USAAF/USAF

DATE	LOCATION	UNIT	CMD	REMARKS
02 FEB 45	LONG BEACH		ATC	ACCEPTED
17 FEB 45	GRENIER		ATC	
(29 FEB 45)	(departed U.S.)			
	(probably in storage at U.K. and German depot)			
(30 APR 47)	(assigned to Air Forces Europe)			
30 APR 47	RHEIN MAIN	61 TROOP CARRIER	AFE	
24 JUN 48	TULLN	7909 BASE UNIT	AFE	
(01 JUL 48)	(from: B-17G to: VB-17G)		– –	
01 JUL 48	TULLN	7360 BASE UNIT	AFE	
17 APR 50	ERDING	85 AIR DEFENSE SQ	AFE	
24 NOV 50	WEISBADEN	7167 SPCL AIR MSNS SQ	AFE	
14 JUL 52	ERDING	85 AIR DEFENSE SQ	AFE	
26 AUG 52	WEISBADEN	7167 SPCL AIR MSNS SQ	AFE	
03 DEC 52	FAIRFAX	4160 BASE SQ	ADC	
22 FEB 54	GRANDVIEW	4676 AIR DEFENSE GP	ADC	
56	GRANDVIEW	328 FIGHTER GROUP	ADC	
DEC 56	DAVIS-MONTHAN		AMC	STORAGE
APR 59	NORTON		AMC	FOR MUSEUM

44-83316

44-83316 is one of several surviving B-17s which no longer exist as complete airframes. Not only is this particular aircraft disassembled, but it is also incomplete as the wing and nose sections are missing. Nonetheless, it is included here because it is an identifiable aircraft and may yet have a future. It served as a VB-17G and, after being withdrawn from service, was preserved in storage at Norton AFB in San Bernadino, California for a number of years, only to end up as a prop in the TV series "12 O'Clock High," a fate which saw its effective destruction.

The Fortress was assigned to the Air Defense Command on 07 November 1952 and flown back to the United States to join the 4160th Base Squadron at Fairfax AFB, Virginia. Once again providing administrative support, the VB-17G later went to Grandview AFB, Missouri and the 4676th Air Defense Group. 44-83316 remained with the unit for most of its remaining military utilization, but was also assigned to the 328th Fighter Group in 1956, shortly before the VB-17G was retired to Davis-Monthan AFB and placed in storage.

It would remain at Davis-Monthan AFB for nearly two and a half years. In April 1959 it was removed from storage

The remnants of 44-83316 on the Anza desert of California. The fuselage is in three parts and the nose and wings are missing. Author

44-83316 is the second-oldest surviving Douglas-built Fortress, being a B-17G-75-DL, and rolled from the Long Beach production lines on 30 January 1945. It was accepted for service on 02 February and flown to Grenier, New York, arriving on 17 February 1945. The aircraft apparently departed the U.S. on 29 February 1945, probably destined for a replacement depot in Great Britain. The aircraft record card is vague, but it can be presumed that this B-17, as many other Fortresses, was stored in Great Britain until the war was over, and then dispatched to Germany as part of the occupation forces, again being placed in storage.

In any event, 44-83316 was based at Rhein Main, Germany and assigned to Air Forces Europe as of 30 April 1947. It was assigned to the 61st Troop Carrier Squadron at Rhein Main, where it remained until 24 June 1948 when assigned to Tulln, Austria, joining the 7909th Base Unit. Shortly afterwards, it was reassigned to the 7360th Base Unit and was redesignated a VB-17G on 01 July 1948.

44-83316 was utilized for administrative transport at Tulln until 17 April 1950 when it joined the 85th Air Defense Wing at Erding, in Germany. On 24 November 1950 the VB-17 went to Weisbaden and the 7167th Special Air Missions Squadron. The purpose of this unit is not known, but the aircraft remained with the unit through November 1952 with the exception of a short reassignment back to the 85th Air Defense Wing in July 1952.

and flown to Norton AFB in San Bernadino, California, and earmarked for museum display. The late Frank Pine, of Tallmantz Aviation, recalled that some effort was underway at Norton AFB to organize a museum, as a number of retired USAF aircraft, including an F-86, an F-107, and a T-33, were gathered at the base and placed in temporary storage. He remembered that the substantial collection of aircraft was often a source for film studios to borrow aircraft for motion picture productions. The Fortress and other aircraft re-

Origination of the cutouts on the fuselage are unknown, though the studio may have cut them for camera access. Author

mained in storage for several years until the Air Force decided to disperse the unofficial collection. Tallmantz Aviation, located at Orange County Airport in Southern California, was authorized to obtain, on loan, many of the aircraft for the International Flight and Space Museum which had been organized as a non-profit auxiliary museum to their Movieland of the Air Museum. The Air Museum (later to become Planes of Fame) was also able to obtain a number of exhibits for their collection which was then located at Ontario Airport.

Tallmantz Aviation had been authorized 44-83316 as part of the group for their non-profit museum. Paul Mantz, perhaps ironically recalling the days when he owned in excess of seventy-eight Flying Fortresses in his post-war "air force," had long sought to obtain a B-17 again both for display at his museum and for motion picture production use. He and his partner, Frank Tallman, had finally negotiated a loan of the surplus B-17 at Norton.

Tallmantz mechanics who inspected the Fortress in 1964 found it nearly airworthy and removed the control surfaces to have them recovered at Tallmantz's Santa Ana facility. Other projects took precedence, however, and it took several months before additional efforts were made to prepare the B-17 for the short ferry flight to Orange County Airport.

When the Tallmantz crew returned to Norton to continue work on the B-17, they were surprised to discover that a crew from Twentieth Century Fox studios and been allowed to strip the cockpit of 44-83316 to help the studio construct a sound stage mock-up for their production of the new TV series "Twelve O'Clock High." The cockpit had been literally gutted, Frank Pine recalling that bolt cutters had been used to remove the throttle quadrant and wiring harnesses. The wings had been removed and sold to another company, so the aircraft was useless for their museum. Tallmantz turned their attention elsewhere and would pick up the last surplus Air Force B-17, 44-83525*, from the Air Force in a lease agreement worked out two years later.

The fuselage of 44-83316, meanwhile, became a non-operable prop at Chino Airport during the second year (1965) of production of the television series "12 O'Clock High". The Air Museum's B-17, 44-83684* N3713G, was used as set dressing, though it was flyable and was also used for taxiing and operational scenes. 316 came to be used in a less glamorous way, becoming the perennial crashed Fortress and was subject to numerous fires and explosions at the hands special effects people from the studio. When "12 O'Clock High" was canceled in 1966, the hulk was towed off to a corner of the airport and abandoned.

Part of 44-83316 would take to the air again, however. Arnold Kolb, owner and operator of Black Hills Aviation of Spearfish, South Dakota, was actively involved in rebuilding 44-85813 N6694C, the five-engined test bed once operated by the Curtiss-Wright Aeronautical Corporation.

N6694C had been obtained by Kolb for his air tanker fleet but needed extensive rebuilding of the nose section and cockpit. Kolb obtained the forward fuselage of 44-83316 from Twentieth Century-Fox and incorporated it into N6694C. Using the parts from 44-83316, Kolb moved the cockpit of N6694C forward to that of a standard Fortress and grafted the new nose onto his tanker. N6694C eventually became a cornerstone in Kolb's tanker fleet, which also included 44-83814* N66571. Unfortunately, N6694C was nearly destroyed in an accident at the tanker base at Bear Pen Airport near Supply, South Carolina in April 1980 and never flew again, though parts from that airframe will be used to rebuild another Fortress in the next few years.

The remainder of 44-83316 now lies stored at Carl Scholl's ranch near Ocotillo Wells, California. It and two other Fortresses, 44-83542* and 44-83722*, are owned by warbird restorer and museum operator Kermit Weeks, who may eventually use them as the basis for building up a flyable B-17. The remains of the B-17 consist of the fuselage aft of the top turret location. The disposition of the wings are unknown. The hulk shows the last vestiges of TV production paint schemes and artificially inflicted combat damage. The interior of the fuselage, which rests in several sections, is gutted. It is obvious the structure could only be used for parts or for the basic framework of the aft fuselage.

Aft fuselage section of 44-83316 still retains studio paint. Author

44-83316 at Chino in February 1967. Wings had been removed prior to 20th Century Fox obtaining the airframe. Double radio compartment windows characteristic of many VB-17Gs. Peltzer Collection

Chapter Thirty-five: 44-83542

Ocotillo Wells, California

■■■■■■

44-83542   B-17G-85-DL to DB-17G to DB-17P to N9324Z

USAAF/USAF

DATE	LOCATION	UNIT	CMD	REMARKS
03 APR 45	LONG BEACH		ATC	ACCEPTED
23 APR 45	SOUTH PLAINS		ATC	STORAGE
15 JUN 45	PATTERSON		ATC	STORAGE
(15 OCT 45)	(declared excess)		– –	
02 NOV 45	SOUTH PLAINS		ATC	
(07 NOV 45)	(returned to military use)		– –	
17 JUN 47	PYOTE	4141 BASE UNIT	AMC	STORAGE
01 MAY 50	PYOTE	2753 ACFT STORAGE SQ	AMC	STORAGE
23 MAY 50	OLMSTED	MIDDLETOWN AIR DEPOT	AMC	
(29 JUN 50)	(fr: B-17G to: DB-17G)		– –	
30 NOV 50	EGLIN	3200 DRONE SQ	APG	
28 FEB 51	ENIWETOK	3200 PROOF TEST GP	APG	
31 MAY 51	EGLIN	3200 PROOF TEST WG	APG	
02 DEC 51	EGLIN	3205 DRONE GP	APG	
06 OCT 54	PT. MUGU	3205 DRONE GP	APG	
(56)	(fr: DB-17G to: DB-17P)			
DEC 56	HOLLOMAN	3205 DRONE GP	APG	
DEC 58	DAVIS-MONTHAN	AMC STORAGE		
(MAY 59)	(reclamation authorized)		– –	

CIVIL

DATE	TRANSFER DETAILS
10 SEP 59	FR: 2704TH AIRCRAFT STORAGE AND DISPOSITION GROUP, DAVIS-MONTHAN AFB, AZ TO: ACME AIRCRAFT PARTS, INC., COMPTON, CA
17 NOV 60	TO: WESTERN AIR INDUSTRIES, ANDERSON, CA
06 JUN 62	TO: AERO UNION, ANDERSON, CA (LATER CHICO, CA)
(12 JUL 71)	(N9324Z severely damaged in accident while operating as an air tanker. Subsequently used for parts.)

44-83542

44-83542 was placed in storage for five years after rolling from the production lines. It then served for nearly eight years as a director aircraft for unmanned QB-17 drones. After being withdrawn with the other few remaining DB-17s, it was sold surplus and was quickly put to use as an air tanker. It was nearly destroyed in an accident in 1971, afterwhich it became a parts source to keep other tankers flying. The picked over hulk was sold to Kermit Weeks, who may use it as the basis for an eventual restoration of an airworthy Fortress.

44-83542 was built at Long Beach and accepted by the Army Air Force on 03 April 1945. It was immediately flown to South Plains, Texas for storage along with the majority of new Douglas B-17s. It remained at South Plains for six weeks before being flown to Patterson Field, Ohio. It was again placed in storage at Patterson, where it was declared excess to military use on 15 October 1945.

Most of the new Fortresses were declared excess on or about 15 October. Many, at that point, were flown to disposal yards dotted around the country to join combat veteran B-17s for scrapping. Several hundred B-17s were returned to military use and rejoined the inventory in early November, however. 44-83542 was one of those, and returned to South Plains on 02 November 1945. It remained in storage for nearly five years, first at South Plains and then, beginning on 17 June 1947, at Pyote Field, Texas, where all the stored B-17s were moved.

44-83542 was withdrawn from the storage depot on 23 May 1950 for assignment to the Air Proving Ground Command and conversion to a DB-17 director. It was flown to the Middletown Air Depot at Olmsted AFB, Pennsylvania, for the necessary modifications. The Fortress was redesignated as a DB-17G on 29 August 1950 and flown to Eglin AFB for assignment to the 3200th Drone Squadron on 27 September 1950.

The 3200th Drone Squadron, as noted elsewhere, was part of the 3200th Proof Test Wing at Eglin, and was instrumental in the development of the drone program. The 3200th Proof Test Wing, with 44-83542 and a number of other drones and drone controllers, was assigned to Eniwetok Atoll in the South Pacific on 28 February 1951 for use in the Greenhouse Series of nuclear testing undertaken to test the new hydrogen bomb. That series had the aircraft actually based at Kwajelein for the operational tests at Eniwetok.

The deployment of the unit ended in late May and the Wing returned to Eglin. In December 1951 the 3205th Drone Group was established and most of the B-17 drones and directors went to the new group. 44-83542 remained at Eglin with the 3205th Drone Squadron until 06 October 1954 when it was assigned to Detachment Two at the U.S. Naval Air Missile Test Center located at NAS Pt. Mugu on the California coast. Detachment Two of the 3205th Drone Group soon became the 3235th Drone Squadron, and elements of the unit were used not only at NAS Pt. Mugu, but also at the U.S. Naval Ordinance Test Station at Inyokern, California, and the Flight Test Center at Edwards AFB, California. The 3235th Drone Squadron performed developmental work on weapons such as the Falcon air-to-air missile and Terrier ship-to-air missile systems. Drone and drone controllers assigned to NAS Pt. Mugu, as well as Patrick AFB and Eglin AFB, experienced high levels of

N9324Z shortly after conversion to an air tanker configuration. Photo taken at Chico in June 1964. Larkins

44-83542 on tanker duty in Anchorage in August 1969.
N. Taylor via Besecker

corrosion and overhaul facilities at the Middletown Air Depot in Pennsylvania spent much time reskinning B-17s to repair the damage. 44-83542 spent several months at the depot in 1955 for an overhaul, and then returned to NAS Pt. Mugu. 44-83542 remained with the squadron until late 1956, when it was assigned to the 3225th Drone Squadron at Holloman AFB, New Mexico.

Holloman AFB was home of the Holloman Air Development Center and specialized in short range missiles. At Holloman 44-83542 was redesignated as a DB-17P, indicating additional modifications to drone control equipment. The aircraft remained with the squadron for the balance of its military utilization before retirement to Davis-Monthan AFB in December 1958. It joined a growing number of retired DB-17s and VB-17s gathering at the base.

44-83542 was released for sale in May 1959 and sold by auction for $5,289.99 on 10 September 1959. Its first civil owner was Acme Aircraft Parts of Compton, California, but they quickly resold the aircraft to Western Air Industries of Anderson, California, for $8,000. Western Air Industries was the precursor of Aero Union, which also was initially based at Anderson. Aero Union operated a number of air tankers which included a fleet of B-17s which usually varied between three and six at any one time.

44-83542 had been purchased by Western Air on 17 November 1960 along with stablemate 44-83514*, with the former becoming N9324Z and the latter N9323Z. Both underwent conversion to air tanker configuration, with N9323Z getting the initial work. N9324Z received two 1,060 retardant tanks in its bomb bay in October 1961, at which point records indicated the aircraft had amassed 3,259 hours of flight time. N9324Z became Tanker 18 and served for nearly ten years in the annual battles against the forest and range fires of the western U.S. It remained in service with Aero Union, which had moved to Chico Airport.

However, luck ran out for N9324Z on 12 July 1971 near Benson, Arizona. While fighting a fire, the Fortress lost power and crashed. Though the crew emerged uninjured, the airframe was twisted and broken aft of the wings. The right wing outboard section was folded up and over the inboard section, and the remains were thought only good for salvage. The FAA registration was canceled, and the

wreckage was hauled to Desert Air Parts of Tucson for storage and dismantling.

For many years 44-83542 became a source of parts for a number of B-17s. The rear spar of the wing apparently went into N9323Z at one point, and the center section of the wings complete with the engine nacelles went into 42-32076*, "Shoo Shoo Shoo Baby" to replace the laterally sliced wings the group at Dover AFB was working with.

In the late seventies, the remaining hulk was purchased by the New England Air Museum of Hartford, Connecticut, with the intent of using parts to rebuild the remnants of their B-17, 44-85734*, (the ex-Pratt & Whitney five-engined test bed) which had been nearly destroyed aft of the wing when a SA-16 Albatross had been flipped onto the back of the B-17 by a tornado in 1979. It apparently had not occurred to those who arranged the purchase that both aircraft were merely wreckage aft of the wings, and that few parts from N9324Z would in any way assist in the rebuilding of 44-85734. N9324Z was never transported east as wiser heads prevailed and recognized the obvious.

Instead, the remains of N9324Z were sold to Kermit Weeks for his new Weeks Air Museum at Tamiami Airport in Florida. Weeks had the hulk transported to Carl Scholl's storage yard near Ocotillo Wells on the Anza desert of California. Here it was joined by two other partial B-17 airframes owned by Weeks: 44-83316* and 44-83722*. Weeks, in his more ambitious moments, apparently considers the possibility of rebuilding at least one flyable B-17 from the Fortress hulks he owns. Looking over the material, it seems he has nearly an entire fuselage available. The forward fuselage of N9324Z is intact, with a fairly complete cockpit, albeit missing an instrument panel and other controls. Damage appears to be minimal to that part of the airframe. Aft of the wing attach points and forward of the horizontal stabilizer is little but twisted wreckage, but aft of the main crew entry door the airframe appears intact. Still, he appears to be short a few wings and their attached accessories such as engines. Nonetheless, if Kermit Weeks decides to try and pull an airplane together out of the material he has, it can be assumed that an flyable airplane will eventually emerge. Thus, N9324Z may again take to the air.

Remains of N9324Z on the California desert in October 1987. Nose section to left is from 44-83722, also in storage. Note fire damage above wing root. Forward fuselage is remarkably intact. Author

Chapter Thirty-six: 44-83722

Ocotillo Wells, California

■ ■ ■ ■ ■

44-83722   B-17G-95-DL to B-17H to TB-17H to SB-17G

USAAF/USAF

DATE	LOCATION	UNIT	CMD	REMARKS
16 MAY 45	LONG BEACH			ACCEPTED
18 MAY 45	CHEYENNE	MODIFICATION CENTER		ATC
22 JUN 45	KEESLER			
10 OCT 45	SANTA ROSA	434 BASE UNIT	CAF	
18 NOV 45	SANTA ROSA	475 BASE UNIT	CAF	
01 DEC 45	MCCLELLEN	4127 BASE UNIT	ATS	
19 FEB 46	HAMILTON	475 BASE UNIT		
21 MAR 46	HAMILTON	460 BASE UNIT	CAF	
(25 MAR 46)	(fr: B-17G to: B-17H)		– –	
28 MAR 46	HAMILTON	475 BASE UNIT	CAF	
20 MAY 46	HAMILTON	62 BASE UNIT	CAF	
(08 DEC 46)	(fr: B-17H to: TB-17H)		– –	
01 MAR 48	DHAHRAN	1414 BASE UNIT	ATO	
01 JUN 48	DHAHRAN	1060 AIR RESCUE SQ	MTO	
02 SEP 48	DHAHRAN	2153 AIR RESCUE SQ	MTO	
03 SEP 48)	(fr: TB-17H to: SB-17G)		– –	
20 APR 49	OLMSTED	MIDDLETOWN AIR DEPOT	AMC	
31 JUL 49	KINDLEY	6 AIR RESCUE SQ	MTO	
31 JUN 50	KINDLEY	1 AIR RESCUE SQ	MTO	
52	YUCCA FLATS			TO TARGET

OTHER INFORMATION

DATE	TRANSFER DETAILS
MAY 65	FR: ATOMIC ENERGY COMMISSION COMMERCIAL CONTRACT OFFICE, REYNOLDS ELECTRICAL ENGINEERING COMPANY (PROJECT MANAGEMENT BRANCH), U.S. AEC NEVADA OPERATIONS OFFICE TO: VALLEY SCRAP METAL, PHOENIX, AZ
MAY 65	TO: AIRCRAFT SPECIALTIES, MESA, AZ
FEB 81	TO: GLOBE AIR, INC, MESA, AZ
OCT 85	TO: WEEKS AIR MUSUEM, TAMIAMI AIRPORT, FL

44-83722

44-83722 is a Fortress which may eventually become part of an effort to create a flyable B-17 out of three incomplete hulks. It now lies in disassembled storage on the California desert, and is one of two B-17s hauled off an atomic test site in 1965 after being subjected to several atomic blasts in 1952. Prior to its use as a target, it served for five years as an air-sea rescue B-17H, and later SB-17G.

44-83722 was accepted by the Army Air Force at Long Beach on 16 May 1945. It was flown to the United Airlines Modification Center at Cheyenne, Wyoming, emerging on 22 June 1945. From Cheyenne, it was flown to Keesler Field, Mississippi for assignment to the air-sea rescue unit being formed there. 44-83722 remained at Keesler until 10 October 1945 when assigned to the 4758th Base Unit at Santa Rosa, California.

On 01 December 1945, it went to McClellen Field in Sacramento, California and attached to the 4127th Base Unit, most likely for overhaul or modifications at the Sacramento Air Depot. The B-17G then went to Hamilton Field and the 4601st Base Unit, under the command of the Continental Air Force. At Hamilton, the Fortress provided air-sea rescue service for the eastern Pacific. On 25 March 1946, 44-83722 was redesignated as a B-17H, the designation for lifeboat-carrying Fortresses. A few days later it was attached to the 475th Base Unit, and, on 20 May 1946, the 62nd Base Unit. As is apparent, the air-sea rescue structure of the Army Air Force was under constant change and reorganization in attempts to develop a effective network of service.

44-83722 became a TB-17H on 08 December 1946, though this was only a paperwork change indicating a refinement of the designating system in use. In early 1948 the aircraft was transferred to Saudi Arabia and assigned to Dhahran Air Field to provide air-rescue service to the Middle East. It and another TB-17H, 44-85746, were attached to the 1414th Base Unit, the only unit based at Dhahran and literally about as far from the U.S. as one could get. The U.S.

military was allowed 225 personnel at Dhahran by the Saudi government, who also imposed severe restrictions on movement and rotation of those Americans assigned.

On 01 June 1948 the air-rescue service was assigned to the Military Air Transport Command, and months of additional reorganization of the roughly fifty air-sea rescue units spread around the world followed. What emerged by late 1949 was the establishment of seven Air Rescue Squadrons, each consisting of a headquarters unit and four detachments lettered "A" through "D". The 1414th Base Unit at Dhahran became the 2153rd Air Rescue Unit, officially Flight D of the 7th Air Rescue Squadron. Headquarters of the Squadron was located at Weisbaden, West Germany, along with its Detachment A. Detachment B was located at Lajes Air Base in the Azores Islands, and Detachment C was located at Wheelus AFB in Libya. Reorganization would again follow, as the Headquarters unit would eventually go to Wheelus and the Detachment at Weisbaden would become part of the 9th Air Rescue Squadron.

Detachment D at Dhahran was equipped with only two B-17s, unlike most units which had four of the aircraft. The unit also came to be equipped with a Sikorsky H-5 helicopter, and provided a Land Rescue Team with three vehicles for overland travel.

44-83722 was redesignated as an SB-17G on 03 September 1948 in accord with the modified designation system established by the new USAF. In early 1949 the aircraft was rotated back to the United States for overhaul at the Middletown Air Depot located at Olmsted AFB, Pennsylvania. Back in Dhahran, the SB-17Gs were being phased out in favor of the new Grumman SA-16 Albatross, which offered the utility of being able to land on water to effect rescues. The first two SA-16s to be deployed overseas went to Dhahran, and 44-83722 was not returned to the unit.

TB-17H 44-83722 shortly after the war. TB-17Hs became SB-17Gs in 1948, and also gained a red stripe in the national insignia. Location and date unknown. Larkins

Instead, the SB-17G was assigned to Kindley Field on Bermuda and attached initially to the 6th Air Rescue Squadron, and then to the 1st Air Rescue Squadron. The Fortress remained at Kindley until early 1952 when it and another SB-17G (44-83575*) was detached and sent to Nevada for use as a target in the first series of nuclear tests to be performed by the Atomic Energy Commission at their new Test Site.

The two Fortresses, plus five other B-17s and 21 other aircraft, were parked at varying distances from the planned explosions to determine blast and radiation effect for Operation Snapper. While 44-83575 was parked roughly two miles from the blasts, 44-83722 was parked much closer and suffered great damage during the test. The fuselage was broken into two parts. A large amount of compression effect occurred, as aluminum skin was molded and pressed into the underlying aircraft structure. Other blast and heat damage also took place, and the aircraft was irradiated.

At the completion of the tests, the B-17s were towed off with other test material and left to cool off. Forgotten for the next ten years, the accumulated material was eventually deemed safe for handling and was put up for disposal as scrap. The Atomic Energy Commission auctioned the lot, and the two B-17s were sold for pennies a pound to Valley Scrap Metal of Phoenix, Arizona.

Aircraft Specialties of Mesa, Arizona, purchased both hulks from Valley Scrap. They intended to rebuild 44-83575 to flyable condition for use as an air tanker, but it was obvious 44-83722 was useful only for parts. In May 1965 it was ignobly disassembled and hauled out on the back of a truck.

Over the span of the next twenty years, 44-83722 took up residence in the back lot of Aircraft Specialties. With the fuselage laying on its side, parts from the B-17 found their way into Aircraft Specialties' fleet of Fortresses which numbered as many as six at one point. Laying as it was among the remains of dozens of airplanes, engines, discarded and stored parts, and the many bits of airplane flotsam accumulated through the years, the B-17 slowly faded from view. The military serial was apparently never determined by its owners or the aviation community at large. It became known only for the sad sight it presented.

When Aircraft Specialties' successor company, Globe Air, went out of business in 1985, the hulk for 44-83722 was purchased by Kermit Weeks, an aviation collector and organizer of the ever growing Weeks Air Museum in Florida. Weeks already owned B-17G 44-83525*, and he purchased 44-83722 to provide a parts source or become the basis for a diorama for his museum showing the effects of a crashed Eighth Air Force Fortress. Weeks had the hulk hauled off to storage in the Anza desert of California to await his call.

Now, Weeks has gathered the remains of three B-17s: 44-83542, 44-83316, and 44-83722. Based upon the available material, he is considering the possibility of constructing an airworthy B-17 from the three. He is lacking many parts, such as B-17 center sections, and the parts he has are in poor shape having been picked over for the past twenty years by other Fortress operators. Nonetheless, Weeks has produced some fine restorations over the past few years, and given the resources and time required, it may be possible that part of 44-83722 may indeed return to the sky at some undetermined point in the future.

44-83722 and the results of Operation Snapper. Here the wreckage of several aircraft, including a P-47, lie in the mid-sixties after 'cooling off' for over a decade. Reynolds Electrical via Leon

Effect of compression damage and remnants of Air-Sea Rescue markings evident here. Reynolds Electrical via Leon

The cockpit section has been well picked over in the past twenty years. Identity of the airframe wasn't firmly established until recently. Author

44-85734   B-17G-105-VE to N5111N

USAAF

DATE	LOCATION	UNIT	CMD	REMARKS
16 MAY 45	BURBANK		ATC	ACCEPTED
27 MAY 45	LOUISVILLE	MODIFICATION CENTER	ATC	
06 JUL 45	SYRACUSE		ATC	STORAGE
(12 OCT 45)	(declared excess)		– –	
12 NOV 45	ALTUS		RFC	

CIVIL

DATE	TRANSFER DETAILS
25 JUN 47	FR: WAR ASSETS ADMINISTRATION
	TO: ESPERADO MINING COMPANY, ALTUS, OK (as part of lot of 423 aircraft for scrap)
19 NOV 47	TO: PRATT & WHITNEY AIRCRAFT, HARTFORD, CT
16 JUN 67	TO: CONNECTICUT AVIATION HISTORICAL ASSOCIATION
87	TO: TOM REILLY, KISSAMEE, FLORIDA

44-85734

44-85734 was one of three B-17s modified to accept a fifth engine in the nose section for test work. 44-85734's was the only modification undertaken by a private corporation, the other two having been completed while the aircraft were still operated by the Air Force. Pratt & Whitney tested a number of large turboprop engines on the test bed before retiring the aircraft to the Connecticut Aviation Historical Society which operated a museum at the Bradley Airport. That facility was severely damaged by a 1979 tornado, part of its result being a SA-16 Albatross being lifted from the ground to land inverted on the waist section of 44-85734's fuselage. The museum was reorganized into the New England Air Museum, but repairs of the B-17 were beyond its resources. In 1987 they traded 44-85734 to aircraft restorer Tom Reilly of Florida. He hopes to have his B-17 airworthy by the mid 1990s.

44-85734 rolled from the Burbank production lines on 14 May 1945 and was accepted by the Army Air Force two days later. It was ferried to Louisville, Kentucky for modifications but was flown directly into storage at Syracuse, New York, on 05 July 1945. It remained with several hundred other new B-17s until 12 October 1945 when most Army B-17s were declared excess to military needs. 44-85734 was flown to the RFC lot at Altus, Oklahoma, to join the growing number of B-17s parked on the field for disposal.

It remained in storage until 25 June 1947 when the War Assets Administration sold 423 aircraft on a scrap bid to the Esperado Mining Company of Altus. Presumably, the Esperado company was preparing to scrap their purchase on the field at Altus. However, in November of 1947 the Pratt & Whitney Aircraft Division of the United Aircraft Corporation made arrangements with Esperado Mining and the War Assets Administration to purchase two of the B-17s. The terms of the agreement provided that Pratt & Whitney would pay $5400 for each B-17, and Esperado would pass $2700 of the purchase price along to the WAA for waiver of the scrap warranty written into the original surplus sale. By this method, Pratt & Whitney obtained 44-85734 and B-17G-105-VE 44-85741 "as is" and "where is." On 31 December 1947 the two Fortresses received CAA registrations of N5111N and N5110N respectively. N5110N was flown directly to Rentscheler Airport, Pratt & Whitney's airport located near East Hartford, Connecticut, where it became a spares source and never flew again. It was finally scrapped

44-85734 with the ferry nose installation at Boeing Field in 1950. Williams via Larkins

N5111N on 'display' at the Bradley Museum in the early seventies. The B-17 was donated without the fifth engine installed. The control surfaces were removed by the museum. MAP

in the late fifties.

44-85734, on the other hand, was ferried to the Boeing factory in Seattle. Pratt & Whitney had Boeing rework the Fortress and convert the nose section to accept the new XT34 turboprop engine then under development. Concurrent with this modification was a similar program underway at the Boeing-Wichita factory to convert B-17G-105-VE 44-85813 to a test bed for use by Curtiss-Wright to test their XT35 turboprop. That aircraft would remain under the jurisdiction of the Air Force, however, and be redesignated as an EB-17G upon completion. Though details of the modifications differed for each aircraft, Boeing designated both aircraft as Model 299Zs.

The B-17 design was particularly attractive for adaptation to an engine test bed for a number of reasons. The primary factor was that the fuselage nose section of a multi-engined aircraft was the obvious location for a large engine to be tested. The Fortress was the largest American aircraft with a conventional landing gear, which would insure adequate propeller clearance for the fifth engine. The B-17 was also strong and predictable, and an adequate parts supply was readily available.

The most distinctive aspect of the modification was moving the cockpit over four feet aft to provide for additional room in the nose section and better establish the weight and balance. This was accomplished be removing a section of the upper decking in vicinity of the dorsal turret and positioning the cockpit aft. The fuselage was beefed up with additional structure to handle the large engine mounts built into

the nose, and the entire fuselage was reskinned with a heavier gauge of aluminum. Excess military equipment was stripped from the airframe in addition to other minor modifications. For ferrying purposes, a large nose cone was installed and 793 pounds of ballast was carried forward of the cockpit. The aircraft was ferried from Seattle to Connecticut in February 1949.

Over the course of the following fifteen months, the XT34 turboprop engine was completed and installed into the nose of N5111N. The XT34 was a Navy funded single-shaft turboprop engine for which design work was begun in 1945. It progressed through several different versions and would eventually power the Douglas C-133 Cargomaster. In that versions it produced 5700 shaft horsepower. A test program of the engine was initiated in May 1950 and continued for several years. By July 1953 N5111N had accumulated 312 hours of flight time. Two years later it had added two hundred hours to that total. In 1957 total hours exceeded 850 hours, and by 1965, as the various test programs drew to a close, N5111N had amassed 994 hours. The T34 had remained the primary engine installation on the airframe, though a Pratt & Whitney T64 turboprop engine had been installed briefly to test engine and propeller combinations.

On 16 June 1967 the B-17 was donated to the Connecticut Aeronautical Historic Association. Located at Bradley International Airport near East Hartford, N5111N was maintained in a non-flying display status. It was kept outdoors with much of the aviation collection, which numbered nearly eighty aircraft by 1974. Its general condition deteriorated through the years as the resources of the museum were not sufficient to maintain such a large collection.

Conditions took a dramatic turn, however, on 03 October 1979 when a tornado cut a swath through the museum. Twenty-three aircraft were destroyed and forty were damaged. Aircraft as large as a Lockheed Constellation were picked up and hurled a hundred yards by the winds. The museum's Douglas C-124 Globemaster reportedly exploded with the rapid changes in air pressure. A Grumman SA-16A Albatross (s/n 51-0025) on display was lifted and carried 600 feet to land inverted on N511IN's mid section. The Fortress was, understandably, badly damaged, with a crushed waist section and other damage to the wings.

A museum nearly strapped even prior to the tornado could not attempt to rebuild the Fortress, and its remains were shunted off to a corner of the museum in a state of semi-storage. As noted elsewhere, one attempt was made to obtain the fuselage of a wrecked air tanker, 44-83542*, from a storage yard in Arizona. However, both fuselages had been destroyed in the same area and the plans quickly collapsed.

Recent events have indicated the possibility that N511IN may yet get back into the air. The museum, now reorganized as the New England Air Museum, had traded the damaged hulk to Tom Reilly, who restored 44-83575* for its civil owner. Tom Reilly, in turn, will restore the Museum's rare North American B-25H-10-NA (43-4999). Reilly has already trucked the Mitchell out, and plans to complete his part of the trade agreement by late 1989. At that point he will receive the hulk of 44-85734, and he foresees a restoration project lasting in excess of six years. He has obtained the remainders of, coincidentally, the other Boeing 299Z, 44-85813 N6694C, which had crashed at Bear Pen, South Carolina while on tanker duty in April 1980. He plans to graft the intact rear fuselage of N6694C onto N511IN. He also will restore the cockpit back to its conventional position, and manufacture a new, standard nose compartment to replace the modified structure now in place. Tom Reilly obviously face a major rebuilding effort but, if successful, he will add yet another restored Fortress to the air.

Details of the modified nose structure. The major attach points for the fifth engine are near the top. Long bar hanging down appears to be part of the remaining support structure. Panel in lower center would be open and provide access to the pilot's compartment in a conventional Fortress. Campbellphoto

Major damage to the trailing edge of the right wing, as well as the aft fuselage, resulted from a 1979 tornado tossing a Grumman SA-16 Albatross intact upon the B-17. Campbell

Forward fuselage and wings are in fair condition given its history. Major damage on wings are on the trailing edge of the center sections. Outboard wing panels suffered little damage. Campbell

44-85813   B-17G-110-VE to EB-17G to JB-17G to N6694C

USAAF/USAF

DATE	LOCATION	UNIT	CMD	REMARKS
27 JUN 45	BURBANK		ATC	ACCEPTED
01 JUL 45	DALLAS		ATC	MOD CENTER
03 AUG 45	ROME		ATC	STORAGE
04 OCT 45	CALDWELL, NJ	CURTISS-WRIGHT	ATS	BAILED
	(MODIFIED BY BOEING-WICHITA)			
MAR 47	WOODRIDGE			
(06 APR 49)	(fr: B-17G to: EB-17G)			
SEP 52	CALDWELL			
56	WOODRIDGE			
(56)	(fr: EB-17G to: JB-17G)			

CIVIL

DATE	TRANSFER DETAILS
30 AUG 57	FR: DEPARTMENT OF THE AIR FORCE
	TO: CURTISS-WRIGHT CORPORATION, WRIGHT AERONAUTICAL DIVISION,
	WOODRIDGE, CT
01 DEC 66	TO: EWING AVIATION, SAN RAMON, CA
15 AUG 69	TO: EWING-KOLB AIRCRAFT, SPEARFISH, SD
30 JUL 70	TO: ARNOLD KOLB, DBA BLACK HILLS AVIATION, SPEARFISH, SD
20 MAY 74	TO: BLACK HILLS AVIATION, SPEARFISH, SD
(16 APR 80)	(aircraft severely damaged in crash near Bear Pen, North Carolina)
(85)	(remains to Tom Reilly, Kissimmee, Florida)

44-85813

44-85813 was one of two B-17s extensively modified during the post-war period to serve as engine test beds. It was lent to the Curtiss-Wright Corporation shortly after the war, and was purchased by the company in 1957 for their own test programs. They sold the B-17 in 1966, and it was later used as an air tanker until badly damaged on a tanker mission in North Carolina. The remains of the aircraft will be used, ironically, to return the former Pratt & Whitney engine test bed, 44-85734, to the air.

44-85813 rolled from the Burbank production lines on 26 June 1945 and was accepted for service the next day. It was flown to the Dallas modification center operated by Lockheed on 01 July 1945, and was available for service a month later. It was flown to Rome, New York for storage.

On 04 October it was withdrawn from storage and assigned to Paterson, New Jersey for use by the Curtiss-Wright Aeronautical Corporation for conversion to a engine test-bed for the XT-35 turboprop engine then under development. It was ferried to the Boeing-Wichita factory for the conversion work, which began in January 1946. The primary feature of the modification was moving the cockpit aft nearly four feet in order to preserve acceptable balance requirements with the installation of the test engine, and provide room for the engine accessories. To accomplish the movement of the cockpit and reinforce the airframe structure for the additional loads, the fuselage was basically

44-85813 was sold to Curtiss-Wright in August 1957 and, registered as N6694C, continued to be used in company test programs largely based at Edwards AFB.
Roby via AAHS

N6694C had the nacelle from a L1049 Constellation grafted onto its nose to test a Wright R3350 engine variation. Maloney

The B-17 fell into disuse as test programs eventually drew to a close. Curtiss-Wright finally sold it without the R3350 installation.

remanufactured. The nose section and upper decking of the forward fuselage was removed. Additional supporting stringers were installed in the structure to receive the anticipated stress, which was also carried by a heavier gauge aluminum skin which replaced the old skin. The lower portion of the fuselage behind the turboprop engine exhausts were skinned with stainless steel. Excess military equipment was removed, and various test instrumentation was installed.

Concurrent with the modifications performed on 44-85813 were those performed by Boeing-Seattle on B-17G 44-85734 for Pratt & Whitney in a privately funded venture for testing of their new XT-34 turboprop engine. Boeing designated both conversions as Boeing Model 299Z, though the conversions were not identical. One additional modification on 44-85813 was the installation of Curtiss electric propellers in place of the Hamilton-Standard hydraulic props normally swung by the Wright R1820s. A large, snub-nosed

fairing was installed over the nose of 44-85813 for test flight and ferry purposes. The Fortress was redesignated as an EB-17G on 06 April 1947, indicating that it was now considered exempt from the standard technical orders for the type.

44-85813 was based at Caldwell, New Jersey, where the XT-35 test program was conducted. The XT-35 was one of a pair of large turboprop engines being developed for the military in the late forties and in final form developed nearly 5500 equivalent horsepower.

With the termination of the XT-35 program, 44-85813 was further modified to carry a Wright XJ65 jet engine in the nose section. The engine was slung below a streamlined nose structure, and its intake was covered by a cap for ferry flights and ground protection.

In October 1956 44-85813 was redesignated as a JB-17G, reflecting the elimination of the "E" for exempt prefix. The

The nose of N6694C was rebuilt to a standard configuration by Arnold Kolb and the reborn aircraft was put to use as a tanker. It entered the fleet in 1971. MAP

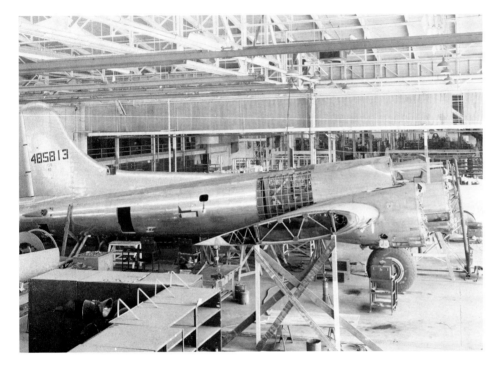

Extensive nature of the rebuild is shown to good advantage in this Boeing-Wichita photo. Besides the obvious movement of the cockpit, less apparent modifications included additonal fuselage stringers and thicker aluminum skin. 44-85813 was virtually new in this photo with only a few ferry flights on the logbooks.
Bowers Collection

Nose job complete, 44-85813 stands ready for its delivery flight to the Curtiss-Wright facility in New Jersey. Nose cone provided a measure of aerodynamic integrity and followed along when N6694C was sold to civil owners. Note also the Curtiss electric props, marked by the smaller hubs.
Bowers Collection

"J" designation indicated the Fortress had been assigned to a temporary test program, something of a misnomer as the Air Force obviously had no intention of ever returning the aircraft to a standard configuration. Designation as an NB-17G would have been more appropriate, indicating permanent test status.

On 30 August 1957 44-85813 was purchased by Wright Aeronautical Division of the Curtiss-Wright Corporation for continued use in its own test programs. The purchase price was $15,000 and included a spare engine and assorted parts. At the time of sale, the Fortress was based at Edwards AFB in California and records indicate total flight time at 579 hours. When 44-85813 was purchased it apparently had been modified to carry the Wright R3350 engine on the nose, and the sale was made because company wanted to continue the test program with the engine. The aircraft was issued a civil registration of N6694C.

To accomplish the engine mounting, the entire nacelle from a Lockheed L1049 Constellation was grafted onto the modified nose. A version of the R3350 Turbo-Compound engine was tested on N6694C, and the company estimated 75 flights and 160 hours of flight time per year in papers filed with the FAA. In 1961 the program was shifted to Wright-Caldwell Airport in New Jersey where the program was continued. Also in 1961, the Fortress was refitted with a Hamilton-Standard propeller in place of one Curtiss electric propeller for vibration testing.

In December 1966 Curtiss-Wright concluded it had no further use for the test bed, and it was refitted with the original snub-nose fairing and sold. At the time of sale the Fortress had nearly 1600 hours of flight time. The first civil owner was Ewing Aviation of San Ramon, California, though its exact use by that owner is not known. What is known is that the aircraft went directly to Spearfish, South Dakota where it was parked. Later, Ewing went into partnership with air tanker operator Arnold Kolb of Spearfish, beginning on 15 August 1969 and ending on 30 July 1970 when Kolb purchased the Fortress outright. On 20 May 1974 Kolb transferred ownership to Black Hills Aviation of Spearfish, which he owned and operated.

Beginning in 1969 Kolb brought the Fortress back to a conventional configuration. Using parts from the hulk of B-17G 44-83316*, late of the TV production "Twelve O'Clock High", the cockpit area was rebuilt and a standard B-17 nose was refitted. The FAA certified the B-17 in the Restricted category on 02 December 1970, at which point Kolb installed two 1200 gallon tanks into the bomb bay. N6694C became Tanker C12 in the Black Hills Aviation fleet, though Kolb moved to Alamogordo, New Mexico in the mid-seventies.

N6694C continued in tanker service through 1980 when it crashed on take off during a tanker mission conducted from Bear Pen Airport in North Carolina. The forward fuselage was burnt beyond use, and the remains of the aircraft were bulldozed off the crash site. They remained at the airport until warbird restorer Tom Reilly of Kissimmee, Florida purchased the remains for use in an eventual restoration. He transported much of the material to his base in Florida, though at this writing some of the airframe still remains at Bear Pen Airport.

Reilly, who was instrumental in the restoration of 44-83575 for owner Bob Collings, plans to use the usable parts to restore the Pratt & Whitney engine test bed, 44-85734, which he is obtaining in trade with the New England Air Museum at Hartford, Connecticut. 44-85734*, as noted elsewhere, was damaged in a tornado which struck the Museum in 1979 as the waist section of the fuselage was crushed by another aircraft. Reilly plans to use the rebuildable remains of both airframes together to produce one airworthy B-17. It is ironic that the two airframes specially modified by Boeing forty years ago for use as unique engine test beds will come together in the end to create one more flying Fortress.

Forlorn but not forgotten at Spearfish, South Dakota, in June 1967. N6694C retains the electric props. It was owned by Ewing Aviation of San Ramon, California at this point, but was stored at Arnold Kolb's facility at Spearfish. via Bowers Collection

Part Five:
Other Fortresses In The World Today

■■■■■■

Overview

■■■■■

While the majority of the surviving B-17s in the world remain in the United States, there are nonetheless a number of Fortresses elsewhere. A few in Europe are flyable, with several others placed on display in museums. One B-17, an ex-air tanker, went to Great Britain from the U.S. for display in 1983. Another Fortress, an ex-IGN machine, recently returned to the United States for a new museum in Texas. Thus, there is still some fluidity in the status of the remaining aircraft. Beyond the preserved examples, there remains at least one derelict B-17 airframe in South America, and five other identified airplanes which have been located around the world but not recovered due to cost, political factors, or other considerations. Two of those are B-17Es which are the subject of recovery from beneath several hundred feet of ice in Greenland, where they have remained since being lost on a wartime ferry mission along with several P-38s. The present condition of those B-17s is unknown. Without a doubt, there are still other parts, pieces, or whole airplanes lurking in the attics of the globe.

What follows is an encapsulated history of the remaining B-17s known to exist.

One of several B-17s transferred to the Free French Air Force by the U.S. was B-17F-BO 42-30177, here shown on Guam in August 1945. 42-30177 later went to the IGN as F-BGSG and was scrapped in 1973.
Peltzer Collection

1. B-17E 41-2446, Abandoned, Papua New Guinea

41-2446 was accepted by the U.S. Army Air Corps at the Boeing factory in Seattle on 06 December 1941 (the day before the Japanese attacked Pearl Harbor). It was rushed to the Southwest Pacific and attached to the 7th Bomb Group based at Townsville, Australia. Its first combat mission was attempted on 23 February 1942 as part of a flight of six B-17s sent to bomb Rabaul, located on New Britain. Weather difficulties, mechanical problems, and attacks from enemy fighters all combined to force the crew of the Fortress to attempt an emergency landing on the north coast of New Guinea near Popondetta. The pilot set up an approach on what appeared to be a flat field, but which turned out to be a grassy swamp. The Fortress suffered little damage in the landing, but sank several feet into the marsh. The uninjured crew began a six-week trek to escape the desolate area and returned to their base. 41-2446 was written off and abandoned. The aircraft was rediscovered in 1972 when an Royal Australian Air Force helicopter crew spotted the overgrown Fortress. As word spread about the presence of the B-17E, several American groups began attempts to extract it and return it to the U.S. for restoration and display. Among the most persistent was the Travis Heritage Museum located at Travis AFB, California. They initiated delicate negotiations with the Papua New Guinea government, the outcome of which seemed to rise and ebb with the swings of New Guinea nationalism. Eventually a tentative agreement was worked out in which the Museum would restore two aircraft for New Guinea's attempt at an air museum in exchange for the Fortress. The fragile nature of New Guinea politics caused the plan to unravel, and it now seems probable that the airplane will continue its reign as the "Swamp Ghost" for the indefinite future.

2. B-17E 41-9101, Abandoned, Greenland

41-9101 was delivered to the Army Air Corps in April 1942. During a ferry flight to England in mid-July 1942 it and B-17E 41-9505 were escorting six P-38s across the North Atlantic Ferry route when bad weather was encountered. Reportedly compounding the weather problems were misleading navigation signals transmitted by a German submarine. In any event, all eight aircraft were forced to land in a remote area of Greenland, the crewmen were rescued, and the aircraft were abandoned. Several unsuccessful expeditions were launched in recent years in an attempt to locate the aircraft. Finally in 1987, using sophisticated metal detection equipment, the aircraft were located encased in ice some 260 feet beneath the surface. Their condition has yet to be established, but it seems unlikely it is anything except twisted wreckage.

3. B-17E 41-9105, Abandoned, Greenland

41-9105 suffered the same fate as 41-9101 above.

4. B-17E 41-9210, Derelict, La Paz, Bolivia

41-9210 was accepted by the Army Air Corps on 16 May 1942, and was thirty-five aircraft from the end of Boeing's production of B-17Es. It was sent to Minneapolis and loaned to the Honeywell Corporation for development work on avionics. It remained as a test-bed until transferred to the Reconstruction Finance Corporation in early 1945. The RFC's Office of Surplus Property transferred the aircraft to the University of Minnesota for educational use in an agreement dated 10 July 1945. 41-9210 had been in storage at Minneapolis and was released to the University on 08 November 1945. The University of Minnesota held the aircraft until 1952, when it amended its agreement with the U.S. government and obtained title to the B-17 for a payment of $7575.00. Once title was received, the Fortress was traded to Jack Lysdale of Lysdale Flying Service on 29 August 1952 in exchange for a Cessna 170. Lysdale, after wading through piles of red tape and paperwork, received the registration of N5842N on 22 December 1952.

Lysdale had already sold the B-17, however, to Albert Leeward of Fort Wayne, Indiana, in a bill of sale dated 03 December 1952. Leeward applied to register the Fortress in his name on 03 December and received the registration on 29 December 1952. Leeward owned 42-9210 until 04 March 1955, when it was sold to Kenting Aviation, Ltd., of Toronto, Canada.

Kenting received the Canadian registration of CF-ICB for 41-9210 and operated it as one of two B-17 survey aircraft. (A third B-17, 44-83873, was also purchased by Kenting as a parts source.) Kenting sold CF-ICB to Four Star Aviation

of Miami, Florida on 22 June 1964.

Four Star re-registered the Fortress as N9720F and sold it to CIA Boliviana de Aviacion of La Paz, Bolivia on 23 July 1964. The Fortress received the Bolivian registration of CP-753 and was assigned to freight runs along with nearly two dozen other old B-17s. It plied along and over the Bolivian Andes until it was damaged in a take-off accident in 1976. 41-9210 became a parts source and now sits, derelict and forlorn, on an air strip in La Paz. It's engines reportedly went to an American air tanker operator, and other components, such as control surfaces, are missing. Efforts at obtaining and restoring the Fortress are underway by numerous parties, so there is the possibility that the old B-17 will someday make its way north once again.

41-9210, as CP-753, at the La Paz airport in January 1986. Engines and control surfaces are off the B-17E and it carries the markings of Frigorifico Reyes, its last civil operator. It appears in fairly good condition and several groups on both sides of the Atlantic are making serious efforts to obtain the airplane. R.F. Arnold

5. B-17G-85-VE 44-8846, Operational, Creil, France

44-8846 was accepted by the Army Air Force on 13 January 1945 at Burbank, sent through the modification center at Cheyenne, Wyoming, and ferried overseas for assignment to the Eighth Air Force in England. It was attached to the 351st Bomb Group and the 305th Bomb Group during the last months of the war. At the conclusion of hostilities, 44-8846 remained in Europe as part of the occupational forces, and was assigned to Air Forces Europe on 30 April 1947. It was redesignated as an RB-17G on 22 March 1949 and was based at Weisbaden, Germany beginning in August 1950. Its last military unit was the 7499th Composite Squadron at Weisbaden, before it was transferred to the Institut Geographique National of France on 05 December 1954.

The IGN registered the Fortress as F-BGSP as it joined a fleet of B-17s which eventually numbered thirteen and which would span the globe on various survey and research missions in the subsequent two decades. F-BGSP would carry equipment as diverse as a laser range-finder, infrared

The last days of 44-83729 which had operated with the IGN. It was scrapped in 1970. MAP

F-BEEA in IGN service. All IGN aircraft were based at Creil, France. MAP

sensors, and sensitive radar equipment for its assignments. F-BGSP was retired from IGN service in the early eighties but continues to operate in a semi-restored condition as "Lucky Lady," carrying 381st Bomb Group markings. Registration was changed to F-AZDX in 1985. The Fortress is operated by a consortium of sponsors, including IGN and the GMF. In July 1989 F-AZDX was repainted and used in the film production of "The Memphis Belle" in England.

6. B-17G-85-VE 44-8889, Musee de l'Air, Paris, France

44-8889 was accepted by the Army Air Force in February 1945 and may have served operationally, or at least placed in a replacement depot, with the Eighth Air Force during the last months of the war. The subsequent military use of the Fortress is not known. It was transferred to the Institut Geographique National in August 1954 and joined another dozen B-17s in the IGN's world wide survey and research work. 44-8889 was registered as F-BGSO and was modified to carry the specific equipment for its survey work. On 08 September 1976 it was donated to the Musee de l'Air at Le Bourget near Paris and is currently on static display.

7. B-17G-95-DL 44-83718, Museu Aerospacial, Rio de Janeiro, Brazil

44-83718 was accepted for service by the Army Air Force on 16 May 1945. It went through the modification shops at

Cheyenne and was then assigned to a unit at Keesler Field, Mississippi. It went to a base unit at Topeka, Kansas in September 1946, and then assigned to Morrison Field, Florida and modified to become an air-sea rescue TB-17H in September 1946. In 1948 it was redesignated as a SB-17G and assigned to Wheelus AFB in Libya with the 5th Rescue Squadron. It returned to the U.S. in 1950 and was assigned to Hamilton AFB in California. In 1951 4483718 was assigned to Davis-Monthan AFB, and then in 1953, to Hill AFB and the Ogden Air Depot. In 1955 it was transferred to the Forca Aerea Brasileira (Brazilian Air Force) in an SB-17G configuration in 1955. It was assigned a FAB serial of 5408 and joined a squadron of twelve SB-17Gs grouped into the 6th Grupo de Aviacao based at Recife. The group performed search and rescue and photo reconnaissance. FAB 5408 was one of the last four B-17s to be retired from Brazilian service in October 1968, to be replaced by Lockheed RC-130H type aircraft. 5408 was placed on display at Natal, Brazil for several years, and then moved to the Museum Aerospacial (Brazilian Air Force Museum) in Rio de Janeiro where it is currently undergoing restoration.

8. B-17G-95-DL 44-83735, Imperial War Museum, London, United Kingdom

44-83735 was accepted by the Army Air Force at Long Beach on 28 May 1945. It was placed in storage and then declared excess to military use in October 1945. It was flown to the RFC disposal lot at Altus, Oklahoma and sold surplus

44-8889 as F-BGSO with the IGN. This Fortress may have served operationally with the Eighth Air Force. It was retired by the IGN in 1976 and placed in the Musee de L'Air in Paris for display. AAHS

on 17 February 1947 to Transocean Airlines of Oakland, California. It was issued the civil registration of N68269. The owner of Transocean Airlines converted the Fortress to an executive transport with the installation of a lounge, lavatory, office space, and other amenities. It was used on trans-Pacific flights between California and Manila for two years before the Fortress was sold to the Assembly of God church on 04 October 1949 for use in transporting missionaries through the Americas, Africa, and the Middle East.

It was sold to Albert Leeward of Fort Wayne, Indiana on

07 November 1951, who sold it to the Institut Geographique National of France on 23 August 1952. It received the French registration of F-BDRS and modified to perform survey and resource research with the organization. It served the IGN until 1975 when it was transferred to the Imperial War Museum at Duxford, England. The B-17 has been undergoing a gradual restoration in the years since, and now carries the colors of the 401st Bomb Group's 615th Bomb Squadron. It carries the tail serial of 42-31983, a B-17G-35-BO, and the nose art of the "Mary Alice."

Another survivor is 44-83735 which operated with the IGN as F-BDRS until 1975 when transferred to the Imperial War Museum in Britain. MAP

N17TE as operated by Euroworld. It was later given a combat paint scheme and re-registered as G-BEDF. MAP

9. B-17G-95-DL 44-83790, Abandoned, Newfoundland, Canada

44-83790 was accepted for service by the Army Air Force on 11 June 1945. It was sent through the Cheyenne modification center and available for use on 14 July. It was briefly assigned to the 3rd Air Force before being placed in storage at South Plains, Texas in October 1945. It remained in storage for nearly a year and assigned to various base units over the next two years. It was being ferried for assignment in Europe when the aircraft made an off-field landing in northeastern Canada in early 1948. The aircraft was bellied in but suffered little damage otherwise. The Air Force authorized reclamation and usable equipment was removed from the airframe. It was rediscovered several years ago by a Canadian who searches out aircraft wrecks. He notes the airframe is still in excellent condition and could be made airworthy again given the expense and complications of removing the aircraft from its present remote and inaccessible location.

10. B-17G-95-DL 44-83868, Bomber Command Museum, Hendon, UK

44-83868 was accepted for service by the Army Air Force in early July 1945. It was transferred to the U.S. Navy for conversion to a PB-1W on 15 July and sent to the Naval Aircraft Modification Pool at NAS Johnsville, Pennsylvania. It was issued the Bureau of Aeronautics serial of 77233 and modified to carry search radar in its former bomb-bay. 77233 was retired from Navy service with the balance of the Navy PB-1Ws in 1955 and sold by sealed bid to the American Compressed Steel Corporation of Dallas, Texas, in 1957 along with twelve other surplus PB-1Ws. 44-83868 was initially issued a civil registration number of N6466D, but the number was canceled and reissued as N5237V. The PB-1G was ferried to Dallas-Love Field and left to rot. It was purchased by Butler Aviation of Redmond, Oregon and was operated as an air tanker through the early eighties. In 1983 N5237V was the subject of a series of trades and it ended up with TBM, Incorporated, of Visalia, California, (part owner of Butler Aviation) which partially restored the bomber with the reinstallation of bomb bay doors, a new Plexiglas nose, and fiberglass replica turrets. The B-17 was repainted to represent a Fortress of the 94th Bomb Group, Eighth Air Force. N5237V was then ferried to Great Britain for eventual display at the RAF· Bomber Command Museum at Hendon. The engines on the Fortress were swapped out with those from 44-85784 "Sally B" in 1983 to help keep that Fortress flyable, and 44-83868 remains on static display at the Bomber Command Museum.

11. B-17G-95-VE 44-85583, Display, Base Aerea De Recife, Brazil

B-17G-95-VE 44-85583 was accepted for service on 27 March 1945 at Burbank. It was sent through modification shops in Louisville, Kentucky and then sent to storage at South Plains, Texas. In August 1945 it was withdrawn from storage and sent to a base unit at Spokane, Washington, and then to Biggs Field, Texas, in February 1946, where it was redesignated as a TB-17H. In May 1947 it was again relegated to storage at Pyote, Texas, where the Air Force declared it excess to requirements in April 1950. Six months later it was withdrawn from storage, sent through overhaul shops at Tulsa, Oklahoma, and redesignated as a SB-17G. In July 1951 it was sent to Rio de Janeiro and then, in June 1953, was among a group of six SB-17Gs transferred to the Forca Aerea Brasileira (FAB) An additional seven were transferred in 1954 and 1955. 44-85583 received the FAB serial of 5402 in 1955 when the twelve surviving (one had crashed in 1952) B-17s were assigned a block of numbers between 5400 and 5411. FAB 5402 served in a search and rescue role with the 6th Grupo de Aviacao based at Recife until withdrawn from service in October 1968. It was placed as a gate guardian for the Base Aerea de Recife on March 31, 1973, where it currently remains on static display.

12. B-17G-105-VE 44-85784, Duxford, United Kingdom

44-85784 was accepted by the Army Air Force at Burbank on 19 June 1945. After undergoing modifications in Dallas, Texas, it was assigned to Wright Field, Ohio, and various test programs. At one point 44-85784 had manned wing-tip turrets installed for test purposes. It was redesignated as an EB-17G in September 1948, and then an ETB-17G in April 1949. In September 1950 it was assigned to development work at Schenectady, New York. After being withdrawn from service, the Fortress was transferred to the Institut Geographique National in France on 31 October 1954. It was issued a civil registration of F-BGSR and became part of a fleet of thirteen B-17s operated by IGN on globe-circling missions. F-BGSR was equipped with various types of survey equipment, and had additional photo equipment, infrared sensors, and radar equipment installed over the years. It was withdrawn from IGN service in 1970 and purchased by Americans Ted White and Duane Egli. The Fortress was re-registered as N17TE and moved to Biggins Hill Aerodrome in England. It became part of White's Euroworld collection and was eventually re-registered as G-BEDF and transferred to B-17 Preservation Ltd. at Duxford, England. New life was injected into "Sally B" when the Royal Air Force Museum donated various parts, including low time engines, off their static-displayed 44-83868 in 1983. 44-85784 was dubbed "Sally B" and carried the colors of the 447th Bomb Group until July 1989 when it was repainted as a B-17F for use in the film production of "The Memphis Belle." That filming took place both at Duxford and the ex-RAF field at Binbrook. The original markings will probably be restored to the aircraft.

PART SIX: APPENDICES

■ ■ ■ ■ ■

APPENDIX ONE: B-17 SERIAL LIST

■ ■ ■ ■ ■

U.S. ARMY AIR CORPS/U.S. ARMY AIR FORCE

The following is a listing of U.S. Army Air Corps/Army Air Force assigned serial numbers. All B-17s were built for that service and any later transfers were accomplished after the aircraft had received its Army serial number. Specific construction block information (i.e. B-17G-95-DL) has been omitted in the listing to clarify serial blocks assigned to the Fortress.

DESIGNATION	SERIAL	DESIGNATION	SERIAL
Y1B-17 (13)	36-149/161	B-17F-BO (2300)	41-24340/24639
			42-5050/5484
Y1B-17A (1)	37-269		42-29467/31031
B-17B (39)	38-211/223	B-17F-DL (605)	42-2964/3562
	38-258/270		42-37714/37715
	38-583/584		42-37717/37720
	38-610		
	39-001/010	B-17F-VE (500)	42-5705/6204
B-17C (38)	40-2042/2079	B-17G-BO (4035)	42-31032/32116
			42-97058/97407
B-17D (42)	40-3059/3100		42-102379/102978
			43-37509/39508
B-17E (512)	41-2393/2669		
	41-9011/9245	B-17G-DL (2395)	42-3563
			42-37716
			42-37721/38213
			42-106984/107233
			44-6001/7000
			44-83236/83885
		(canceled)	(45-7701/8300)
		B-17G-VE (2250)	42-39758/40057
			42-97436/98035
			44-8001/9000
			44-85492/85841
		(canceled)	(44-85842/85941)

Appendix Two: PB-1W and PB-1G Serial Listing

■■ ■■■

U.S. NAVY BUREAU OF AERONAUTICS NUMBERS

The U.S. Navy system of serial numbers as applied to the PB-1 used a sequential series of five digits. All PB-1 aircraft transferred through the Navy and destined for Coast Guard service (which included all but one PB-1G) received Navy serial numbers which carried over to their USCG service. The designation "PB-1" was not assigned until July 1945, shortly before the first large block of aircraft was going to be transferred to the Navy. At that time it appears the Navy Bureau of Aeronautics assigned the sequence between 77225 and 77258 to the PB-1 aircraft. At a later time, two additional sequences, 82855 through 82857 and 83992 through 84027 were set aside.

In July 1945 twenty Douglas-built B-17s were transferred for use by the Navy, and were assigned 77225 thru 77244. A total of eighteen Lockheed-built B-17s were set aside by the AAF for transfer to the USCG thru the Navy. These were, for the most part, transferred to the Navy between April and November 1946 and accepted for service by the USCG beginning in July 1946. Only fifteen were actually transferred, and they were assigned Navy serials between 77245 and 77257, plus two additional (82855 and 82856) from the second serial block. Of the three other B-17s earmarked, two were retained by the AAF and scrapped at South Plains. There is some doubt about the fate of the third B-17 as the Army Air Force record card does indicate it was transferred but its fate is not evident from the available records.

The Navy obtained two additional B-17s for use as XPB-1 test beds for various developmental programs. The first was transferred in June 1945 and given the serial of 77258 while the second was transferred in August 1946 and became 83992.

The USCG obtained one aircraft directly from the USAAF inventory in May 1947. Because it was not transferred through the Navy it never received a Bureau of Aeronautics number, and the aircraft used an abbreviated form of its AAF serial, 44-85832, as its USCG serial. The Navy took back at least one PB-1 from the USCG in 1948 (BuNo 77242) and evidently assigned a new serial number (BuNo 84000) from the remaining block of allocated numbers. Six B-17s were transferred from the USAF to the Navy in May 1948 and issued serials between 83993 and 83998. They were placed into a replacement pool at Corpus Christi and then stricken several months later, unused. Two additional PB-1s were transferred to the Navy in 1950, these coming from the Air Force which had modified two EB-17Gs to PB-1W configuration for test programs. When the tests were completed the aircraft were transferred to the Navy and assigned serials 77137 and 77138, somewhat unusual in that these numbers had once been set aside as part of a block of PB4Y aircraft. It would appear that the Navy serials 83999 and 84001 thru 84027 were allocated for PB-1 aircraft but never assigned. Also of interest are twenty USAF RB-17Gs transferred to the Navy in 1949 and 1950. Their Navy designations and serials, if any, are still undetermined. None of the aircraft appeared on later civil registration records.

PB-1 SERIAL LISTING

The following listing is a compilation of USAF, USN, and USCG serial information. A number of these aircraft are identified here for the first time and is the result of careful research. Some of the serials are at odds with previously published information but a review of all available records would seem to support this listing.

TYPE	USN S/N	USAAF S/N	TYPE	USN S/N	USAAF S/N
PB-1	34106	42-3521	PB-1G	77245	(1)44-85806
			PB-1G	77246	44-85812
			PB-1G	77247	44-85821
PB-1W	34114	44-83538	PB-1G	77248	(2)44-85822
			PB-1G	77249	44-85823
PB-1W	77137	44-83463	PB-1G	77250	44-85824
PB-1W	77138	44-85679	PB-1G	77251	44-85825
			PB-1G	77252	44-85826
PB-1W	77225	44-83855	PB-1G	77253	44-85827
PB-1W	77226	44-83857	PB-1G	77254	44-85828
PB-1W	77227	44-83858	PB-1G	77255	44-85829
PB-1W	77228	44-83859	PB-1G	77256	44-85830
PB-1W	77229	44-83861	PB-1G	77257	44-85831
PB-1W	77230	44-83862			
PB-1W	77231	44-83863	XPB-1	77258	44-85683
PB-1W	77232	44-83864			
PB-1W	77233	44-83868	PB-1G	NONE	(3)44-85832
PB-1W	77234	44-83869	PB-1G	82855	(4)44-85837
PB-1W	77235	44-83872	PB-1G	82856	(5)44-85834
PB-1W	77236	44-83873	PB-1	82857	(5)44-85838
PB-1W	77237	44-83874			
PB-1W	77238	44-83875	XPB-1	83992	(6)44-85571
PB-1W	77239	44-83876			
PB-1W	77240	44-83877	PB-1	83993	(7)NOT KNOWN
PB-1W	77241	44-83878	TO	TO	
PB-1W	77242	44-83879	PB-1	83998	
PB-1W	77243	44-83883	PB-1	83999	NO INFO
PB-1W	77244	44-83884	PB-1	84000	(2)44-85822
			PB-1	84001	(8)NO INFO
			TO	TO	
			PB-1	84027	

NOTES:

1) Most sources list PB-1G 77245 as B-17G-95-DL 44-83885 which is not correct. 44-83885 was a USAF EB-17G and later JB-17G active until 1958.

2) The Navy record cards for 77248 and 84000 suggest that they were the same aircraft. Apparently in July 1948 the USCG returned the PB-1G to the USN, who assigned a new Bureau number. What further service the aircraft performed is not known, nor is its eventual fate.

3) This is the only B-17 transferred directly from USAAF inventory to the USCG. It never was assigned a Navy serial and carried its abbreviated USAAF serial for its Coast Guard duty.

4) Two additional B-17G-VEs, 44-85833 and 44-85835 were earmarked for the USCG but never transferred. They were scrapped at South Plains in 1946.

5) There are some contradictions in the Navy records for BuNo 82856 and 82857. 82856 was transferred from the USCG to the Navy in July 1948 and may have received a new Navy serial. The Navy record card for 82857 shows it was acquired from the USCG in July 1948 but indicates no earlier Navy service. However, 82857 was known to have been under Navy jurisdiction in November 1946 when the Navy delivered it to the USCG originally.

6) The Navy obtained 44-85571 on loan from the War Assets Administration in August 1946 for use by Cornell Aero Labs in a Westinghouse jet engine test program. It was later utilized in other programs until stricken in 1955 at Litchfield Park.

7) These six PB-1s were transferred from USAAF in May 1947 and were stored at Corpus Christi until 31 August 1947 when stricken from the USN. Fate unknown.

8) It is probable that these serial numbers were allocated for PB-1s, though no Navy records have come to light which verify this.

OTHER B-17S TRANSFERRED TO THE U.S. NAVY

USAF S/N	USAF	TRANSFERRED FROM	DATE
44-83404	RB-17G	SAC, OFFUTT AFB	FEB 50
44-83408	RB-17G	SAC, OFFUTT AFB	FEB 50
44-83433	RB-17G	SAC, BARKSDALE AFB	FEB 50
44-83435	RB-17G	SAC, FAIRFIELD-SUSUIN AFB	JAN 50
44-83442	RB-17G	SAC, MARCH AFB	MAR 50
44-83505	RB-17G	SAC, OFFUTT AFB	APR 50
44-83653	RB-17G	SAC, FAIRFIELD-SUSUIN AFB	JAN 50
44-83726	RB-17G	SAC, FAIRFIELD-SUSUIN AFB	JAN 50
44-83749	RB-17G	SAC, MARCH AFB	MAR 50
44-83765	RB-17G	SAC, FAIRFIELD-SUSUIN AFB	JAN 50
44-85495	RB-17G	SAC, FAIRFIELD-SUSUIN AFB	JAN 50
44-85514	RB-17G	SAC, FAIRFIELD-SUSUIN AFB	JAN 50
44-85537	RB-17G	SAC, FAIRFIELD-SUSUIN AFB	JAN 50
44-85542	RB-17G	SAC, FAIRFIELD-SUSUIN AFB	FEB 50
44-85574	RB-17G	SAC, FAIRFIELD-SUSUIN AFB	JAN 50
44-85628	RB-17G	SAC, OFFUTT AFB	JUL 50
44-85657	RB-17G	SAC, FAIRFIELD-SUSUIN AFB	DEC 49
44-85661	RB-17G	SAC, BARKSDALE AFB	MAY 50
44-85665	RB-17G	SAC, OFFUTT AFB	FEB 50
44-85681	RB-17G	SAC, BARKSDALE AFB	FEB 50

APPENDIX THREE: B-17s SURVIVING THROUGH THE POST-WAR PERIOD INCLUDING CIVIL AND PRESERVED EXAMPLES

The following listing includes all B-17s known to have been transferred to civil jurisdiction or set aside by military forces for preservation after withdrawal from service. Asterisk (*) denotes surviving examples. Other abbreviations used are:

S. – scrapped, followed by date, if known
D. – destroyed, followed by date, if known

IAF – Israeli Air Force
FAB – Forca Aerea Brasileira (Brazilian Air Force)
PAF – Portugese Air Force

ABND – Aircraft abandoned
OPRNTL – Aircraft is maintained in flying condition
RSTOR – Aircraft is undergoing restoration
DSPLY – Aircraft is on display and available for public viewing

SERIAL	DESIGNATION	OTHER MILITARY/CIVIL USE	DISPOSITION
40-3097*	B-17D		STORAGE NASM
41-2438	B-17E	RCAF 9206/LV-RTO	S. 1964
41-2446*	B-17E		ABND, NEW GUINEA
41-2595*	B-17E	XC-108A	STORAGE, IL
41-9101*	B-17E		ABND, GREENLAND
41-9105*	B-17E		ABND, GREENLAND
41-9210*	B-17E	N5842N/CF-ICB/N9720F/CP-753/N8WJ	RSTOR, FL
41-9142	B-17E	RCAF 9205/LV-RTP	S. 1964
41-24434	B-17F-5-BO	N60475/CB-79/CP-579	D. DEC 1958
41-24485*	B-17F-10-BO		DSPLY, TN
42-3360	B-17F-50-DL	N67974/CB-70/CP-570	D. SEP 55
42-3374*	B-17F-50-DL		DSPLY, NB
42-3470	B-17F-65-DL	N66574/OB-RAH-346/N9815F/AN-AMI/CP-633/HK-580	D. UNKN
42-3490	B-17F-70-DL	SE-BAN	S. OCT 1948
42-3543	B-17F-75-DL	SE-BAH	S. SEPT 1946
42-6073	B-17F-45-VE	N7942A/CP-686	D. NOV 1968
42-6107	B-17F-50-VE	N1340N	D. AUG 1970
42-29782*	B-17F-70-BO	N6015V/N17W	OPRNTL, WA
42-30177	B-17F-90-BO	F-BGSG	S. AUG 1973
42-30661	B-17F-115-BO	SE-BAK	S. DEC 1946
42-30921	B-17F-125-BO	CB-71/CP-571	D. JAN 1962
42-31163	B-17G-5-BO	SE-BAM	D. DEC 1945
42-32076*	B-17G-35-BO	SE-BAP/OY-DFA/DAF672/F-BGSH	DSPLY, OH
42-97115	B-17G-40-BO	SE-BAO	S. OCT 1948
42-102542	B-17G-50-BO	N5845N	D. 1955
42-102715	B-17G-55-BO	N66573	D. JUL 1979
42-107067	B-17G-35-DL	SE-BAR/OY-DFE	S. JAN 1946
43-37650	B-17G-65-BO	N66570/CB-97/CP-597	D. SEP 1955
43-38322	B-17G-85-BO	N66568/CB-80/CP-580/CP-936	D. FEB 1972
43-38635*	B-17G-90-BO	N3702G	DSPLY, CA
43-38978	B-17G-100-BO	N4960V	S. 1962
43-39281	B-17G-110-BO	N7043C	S. 1959
43-39304	B-17G-110-BO	N9407H/F-BDAT	D. 1950
43-39307	B-17G-110-BO	CP-625	D. NOV 1957
43-39356	B-17G-110-B	N39356	UNKN
44-6332	B-17G-50-DL	CB-88/CP-588	D. MAY 1963
44-6393*	B-17G-50-DL	CP-627/CP-891	DSPLY, CA
44-6556	B-17G-55-DL	CP-624	D. FEB 1963
44-8543*	B-17G-70-VE	N3701G (#2)	OPRNTL, TX
44-8846*	B-17G-85-VE	F-BGSP/ZS-DXM/F-BGSP/F-AZDX	OPRNTL, FRANCE
44-8889*	B-17G-85-VE	F-BGSO	DSPLY, FRANCE
44-8990	B-17G-90-VE	N3678G	D. OCT 1962
44-83316*	B-17G-75-DL		PARTIAL, STORAGE
44-83439	B-17G-80-DL	N6180C/N131P	D. UNKN
44-83512*	B-17G-85-DL		DSPLY, TX
44-83514*	B-17G-85-DL	N9323Z	OPRTL, AZ
44-83525*	B-17G-85-DL	N4520/N83525	OPRTL, FL
44-83538	B-17G-85-DL	PB-1W 34114/N5235V/N7726B/OB-SAB-576	D. JUN 1963
44-83542*	B-17G-85-DL	N9324Z	PARTIAL, STORAGE
44-83546*	B-17G-85-DL	N3703G	OPRNTL, CA
44-83559*	B-17G-85-DL		DSPLY, NB
44-83563*	B-17G-85-DL	N9563Z	OPRNTL, NY
44-83575*	B-17G-85-DL	N93012	RSTOR, PA

44-83587	B-17G-90-DL	N7046C	S. 1959
44-83600	B-17G-90-DL	N7044C	S. 1959
44-83624*	B-17G-90-DL		DSPLY, DL
44-83634	B-17G-90-DL	N7042C	S. 1959
44-83663*	B-17G-90-DL	FAB 5400/N47780	DSPLY, UT
44-83684*	B-17G-90-DL	N3713G	DSPLY, CA
44-83690*	B-17G-95-DL		DSPLY, IN
44-83718*	B-17G-95-DL	FAB 5408	DSPLY, BRAZIL
44-83722*	B-17G-95-DL		PARTIAL, STORAGE
44-83728	B-17G-95-DL	F-BGOE	S. 1970
44-83729	B-17G-95-DL	F-BEED	S. 1962
44-83735*	B-17G-95-DL	N68269/F-BDRS	DSPLY, ENGLAND
44-83750	B-17G-95-DL	CP-623	D. JUL 1958
44-83753	B-17G-95-DL	N5024N/IAF	S. AUG 1962
44-83757	B-17G-95-DL	N5198N/F-BDRR	S. 1962
44-83763	B-17G-95-DL	N7041C	S. NOV 1959
44-83778	B-17G-95-DL	N7040C	S. 1959
44-83785*	B-17G-95-DL	N809Z/N207EV	RSTOR, AZ
44-83790*	B-17G-95-DL		ABND, CANADA
44-83809	B-17G-95-DL	CP-626	D. OCT 1959
44-83811	B-17G-95-DL	N5014N/IAF/N9814F/IAF	S. AUG 1961
44-83814*	B-17G-95-DL	N66571/CF-HBP/N66571	STORAGE, NASM
44-83842	B-17G-95-DL	N1212N/N7712M/PAF	UNKN
44-83851	B-17G-95-DL	N1098M/IAF	S. AUG 1961
44-83857	B-17G-95-DL	PB-1W 77226/N7228C	D. AUG 1967
44-83858	B-17G-95-DL	PB-1W 77227/N6461D/N5226V/CP-742	D. FEB 1965
44-83859	B-17G-95-DL	PB-1W 77228/N6462D/N5228V/OB-LIN-623/OB-SAC-623/OB-R-623/CP-767	D. APR 1967
44-83861	B-17G-95-DL	PB-1W 77229/N6463D/N5227V/CP-741	D. OCT 1965
44-83863*	B-17G-95-DL	PB-1W 77231/N6464D/N5233V	DSPLY, FL
44-83864	B-17G-95-DL	PB-1W 77232/N6465D/N5234V/XB-BOE/N73648	D. DEC 1972
44-83868*	B-17G-95-DL	PB-1W 77233/N6466D/N5237V	DSPLY, ENGLAND
44-83872*	B-17G-95-DL	PB-1W 77235/N7227C	OPRTNL, TX
44-83873	B-17G-95-DL	PB-1W 77236/CF-JJH	S. JAN 1962
44-83874	B-17G-95-DL	PB-1W 77237/N6467D/N5236V	S. 1963
44-83875	B-17G-95-DL	PB-1W 77238/N6468D/N5231V/CP-640	D. AUG 1967
44-83877	B-17G-95-DL	PB-1W 77240/N6469D/N5232V	S. DEC 1961
44-83883	B-17G-95-DL	PB-1W 77243/N6470D/N5229V	S. DEC 1961
44-83884*	B-17G-95-DL	PB-1W 77244/N6471D/N5230V	DSPLY, LA
44-85507	B-17G-95-VE	N5116N	D. NOV 1952
44-85583*	B-17G-95-VE	FAB 5402	RSTOR, BRAZIL
44-85594	B-17G-95-VE	F-BGSQ	S. 1972
44-85599*	B-17G-95-VE		DSPLY, TX
44-85600	B-17G-95-VE	N3696G/N3701G (#1)	D. FEB 1960
44-85643	B-17G-100-VE	F-BEEA	D. JUL 1989
44-85679	B-17G-100-VE	PB-1W 77138/N6460D/N5225V	D. MAR 1964
44-85706	B-17G-105-VE	N7045C	S. 1959
44-85718*	B-17G-105-VE	F-BEEC/ZS-EEC/G-FORT/N900RW	OPRTNL, TX
44-85728	B-17G-105-VE	N4600/N1B/EP-HIM	S. UNKN
44-85733	B-17G-105-VE	F-BEEB	D. MAR 1949
44-85734*	B-17G-105-VE	N5111N	STORAGE, CT
44-85738*	B-17G-105-VE		DSPLY, CA
44-85740*	B-17G-105-VE	N5017N	OPRTNL, WI
44-85741	B-17G-105-VE	N5110N	S. UNKN
44-85774	B-17G-105-VE	CP-621/N621L	D. JUL 1975
44-85778*	B-17G-105-VE	N3509G	STORAGE, CA
44-85784*	B-17G-105-VE	F-BGSR/N17TE/G-BEDF	OPRTNL, ENGLAND
44-85790*	B-17G-105-VE		DSPLY, OR
44-85806	B-17G-110-VE	PB-1G 77245/N7739B/N117W/CP-762	S. DEC 1964
44-85812	B-17G-110-VE	PB-1G 77246/N4710C	D. AUG 1976
44-85813*	B-17G-110-VE	N6694C	PARTIAL, STORAGE
44-85817	B-17G-110-VE	CP-622	D. FEB 1957
44-85821	B-17G-110-VE	PB-1G 77247/N2873G/OB-SAA-532/OB-R-532	UNKN
44-85823	B-17G-110-VE	PB-1G 77249/N3192G/N8055E	D. MAR 1960
44-85824	B-17G-110-VE	PB-1G 77250/N4711C/N8055E/N9347R/CP-694	D. DEC 1963
44-85825	B-17G-110-VE	PB-1G 77251/N7901C	D. OCT 1959
44-85827	B-17G-110-VE	PB-1G 77253	S. 1962
44-85828*	B-17G-110-VE	PB-1G 77254/N9323R	DSPLY, AZ
44-85829*	B-17G-110-VE	PB-1G 77255/N3193G	RSTOR, MI
44-85840	B-17G-110-VE	CP-620/N620L	D. JUL 1973

APPENDIX FOUR: CIVIL REGISTRATION OF B-17S

The following listing is of civil registrations as applied to individual B-17s. Further information can be gleaned by cross-indexing to the military serial number in Appendix 2.

AN-	**NICARAGUA**	**N-**	**UNITED STATES**	N6470D	44-83883
AN-AMI	42-3470	N1B	44-85728	N6471D	44-83884
CB-	**BOLIVIA** (LATER CP-)	N1098M	44-83851	N66568	43-38322
CB-70	42-3360	N117W	44-85806	N66570	43-37650
CB-71	42-30921	N1212N	44-83842	N66571	44-83814
CB-79	41-24434	N131P	44-83439	N66573	42-102715
CB-80	43-38322	N1340N	42-6107	N66574	42-3470
CB-88	44-6332	N17TE	44-85784	N6694C	44-85813
CB-97	43-37650	N17W	42-29782	N67974	42-3360
CF-	**CANADA**	N207EV	44-83785	N68269	44-83735
CF-HBP	44-83814	N2873G	44-85821	N7040C	44-83778
CF-ICB	41-9210	N3192G	44-85823	N7041C	44-83763
CF-JJH	44-83873	N3193G	44-85829	N7042C	44-83634
CP-	**BOLIVIA**	N3509G	44-85778	N7043C	43-39281
CP-570	42-3360	N3678G	44-8990	N7044C	44-83600
CP-571	42-30921	N3696G	44-85600	N7045C	44-85706
CP-579	41-24434	N3701G(#1)	44-85600	N7046C	44-83587
CP-580	43-38322	N3701G(#2)	44-8543	N7227C	44-83872
CP-588	44-6332	N3702G	43-38635	N7228C	44-83857
CP-597	42-37650	N3703G	44-83546	N73648	44-83864
CP-620	44-85840	N3713G	44-83684	N7712M	44-83842
CP-621	44-85774	N39356(1)	43-39356	N7726B	44-83538
CP-622	44-85817	N4520	44-83525	N7739B	44-85806
CP-623	44-83750	N4600	44-85728	N7901C	44-85825
CP-624	44-6556	N4710C	44-85812	N7942A	42-6073
CP-625	43-39307	N4711C	44-85824	N8WJ	41-9210
CP-626	44-83809	N47780	44-83663	N8055E	44-85824
CP-627	44-6393	N4960V	43-38978	N809Z	44-83785
CP-633	42-3470	N5014N	44-83811	N83525	44-83525
CP-640	44-83875	N5017N	44-85740	N900RW	44-85718
CP-686	42-6073	N5024N	44-83753	N93012	44-83575
CP-694	44-85824	N5110N	44-85741	N9323R	44-85828
CP-741	44-83861	N5111N	44-85734	N9323Z	44-83514
CP-742	44-83858	N5116N	44-85507	N9324Z	44-83542
CP-753	41-9210	N5198N	44-83757	N9347R	44-85824
CP-762	44-85806	N5225V	44-85679	N9407H	43-39304
CP-767	44-83859	N5226V	44-83858	N9563Z	44-83563
CP-891	44-6393	N5227V	44-83861	N9720F	41-9210
CP-936	43-38322	N5228V	44-83859	N9814F	44-83811
EP-	**IRAN**	N5229V	44-83883	N9815F	42-3470
EP-HIM	44-85728	N5230V	44-83884	**OB-**	**PERU**
F-	**FRANCE**	N5231V	44-83875	OB-LIN-623	44-83859
F-AZDX	44-8846	N5232V	44-83877	OB-R-532	44-85821
F-BDAT	43-39304	N5233V	44-83863	OB-R-623	44-83859
F-BDRR	44-83757	N5234V	44-83864	OB-RAN-346	42-3470
F-BDRS	44-83735	N5235V	44-83538	OB-SAA-532	44-85821
F-BEEA	44-85643	N5236V	44-83874	OB-SAB-576	44-83538
F-BEEB	44-85733	N5237V	44-83868	OB-SAC-623	44-83859
F-BEEC	44-85718	N5842N	41-9210	**OY-**	**DENMARK**
F-BEED	44-83729	N5845N	42-102542	OY-DFA	42-32706
F-BGOE	44-83728	N6015V	42-29782	OY-DFE	42-107067
F-BGSH	42-32076	N60475	41-24434	**SE-**	**SWEDEN**
F-BGSG	42-30177	N6180C	44-83439	SE-BAH	42-3543
F-BGSO	44-8889	N620L	44-85840	SE-BAK	42-30661
F-BGSP	44-8846	N621L	44-85774	SE-BAM	42-31163
F-BGSQ	44-85594	N6460D(2)	44-85679	SE-BAN	42-3490
F-BGSR	44-85784	N6461D	44-83858	SE-BAO	42-97115
G-	**UNITED KINGDOM**	N6462D	44-83859	SE-BAP	42-32076
G-BEDF	44-85784	N6463D	44-83861	SE-BAR	42-107067
G-FORT	44-85718	N6464D	44-83863	**XB-**	**MEXICO**
HK-	**COLOMBIA**	N6465D	44-83864	XB-BOE	44-83864
HK-580	42-3470	N6466D	44-83868	**ZS-**	**SOUTH AFRICA**
LV-	**ARGENTINA**	N6467D	44-83874	ZS-DXM	44-8846
LV-RTO	41-2438	N6468D	44-83875	ZS-EEC	44-85718
LV-RTP	41-9142	N6469D	44-83877		

NOTES: 1) N39356 was never assigned to a B-17, though this registration was applied to 43-39356 while still carrying its military markings. Purpose of the this aircraft carrying the bogus registration is not known. 2) The series of numbers between N6460D and N6471D were never actually assigned to these aircraft. Apparently both an aircraft broker and the new aircraft owner applied for registration numbers simultaneously and this series was tentatively reserved for these aircraft but later withdrawn with the assignment of the N5225V through N5237V series.

APPENDIX FIVE: AIR TANKER CIVIL REGISTRATIONS

■■■■■■

A total of twenty-three B-17s were converted to air tankers for use, under contract, by the U.S. Forest Service and various state agencies. Other B-17s were converted for use as agricultural sprayers but were not assigned USFS tanker codes.

REGISTRATION	USFS TANKER CODES	DISPOSITION
N1340N	A34, E34, 35	DESTROYED, 1970
N17W	04, 44, C44, C84, E84	OPERATIONAL, WA
N207EV (N809Z)	22, 71, B71, C71	RESTORATION, AZ
N3193G	34, C34	RESTORATION, MI
N3509G	16, E16, 42, F42, 97, 102	STORAGE, CA
N3678G	15	DESTROYED, 1962
N3702G	61, E61	DISPLAY, CA
N3703G	68, E68, E75, E78	DISPLAY, CA
N5230V	C19, E19	DISPLAY, LA
N5233V	D1, E18	DISPLAY, FL
N5237V	65	DISPLAY, UK
N620L	54, C54	DESTROYED, 1973
N621L	64, C64	DESTROYED, 1975
N66571	09, C13, 18, A18	STORAGE, WASHINGTON D.C.
N66573	10, A10, B10, 33, E85	DESTROYED, 1979
N6694C	12, C12	STORAGE, FL (PARTIAL)
N7228C	B31	DESTROYED, 1967
N73648	B11, E56	DESTROYED, 1972
N93012	99	RESTORATION, PA
N9323Z	C17, E17	OPERATIONAL, AZ
N9323R	30, B30, 37	DISPLAY, AZ
N9324Z	C18, E18	STORAGE, CA (PARTIAL)
N9563Z	24, C24, E24, 89	OPERATIONAL, NY

AIR TANKER USFS REGION/NUMBER DECODE LIST

Air Tankers were marked with large coded numbers for ease of identification. Prior to 1975, tankers were assigned by regions and a letter prefix or suffix was used for region identification. Regions were as follows:

Code Letter	Region	States
A	1	Idaho, Montana, Washington
B	2	Colorado,Kansas, Nebraska, South Dakota, Wyoming
C	3	Arizona, New Mexico
D	4	Idaho, Nevada, Utah
E	5	California
F	6	Oregon, Washington

After 1975, a standardized, nationwide system of numbering air tankers was employed. Following is a list of USFS tanker codes with corresponding civil registration numbers. For ease of use, the prefix/suffix code has been standardized as a prefix.

USFS NBR	REG NBR	USFS NBR	REG NBR	USFS NBR	REG NBR	USFS NBR	REG NBR
A10	N66573	E15	N5237V	04	N17W	99	N93012
A18	N66571	E16	N3509G	09	N66571	102	N3509G
A34	N1340N	E17	N9323Z	10	N66573		
		E18	N9324Z	12	N6694C		
B10	N66573	E18	N5233V	15	N3678G		
B11	N73648	E24	N9563Z	16	N3509G		
B30	N9323R	E34	N1340N	18	N66571		
B31	N7228C	E56	N73648	22	N207EV		
B71	N809Z	E61	N3702G	24	N9563Z		
		E68	N3703G	30	N9323R		
C12	N6694C	E75	N3703G	32	N66573		
C13	N66571	E78	N3703G	34	N3193G		
C17	N9323Z	E84	N17W	35	N1340N		
C18	N9324Z	E85	N66573	37	N9323R		
C19	N5230V			42	N3509G		
C24	N9563Z	F15	N5237V	44	N17W		
C34	N3193G	F42	N3509G	54	N621L		
C44	N17W	F71	N5233V	61	N3702G		
C54	N620L			64	N62IL		
C64	N621L			65	N5237V		
C71	N809Z			68	N3703G		
C84	N17W			71	N207EV		
				89	N9563Z		
D1	N5233V			97	N3509G		

APPENDIX SIX: SELECTED POST-WAR FOREIGN MILITARY SERIAL LISTING AND MISCELLANEOUS LISTING

■■■■■■

BOLIVIA

Bolivia was the second largest civil operator of B-17s after the United States. A total of 26 were utilized in their civil aviation fleet by several users. Most were purchased on the civil market but of interest are the eight B-17s transferred by the U.S. government in 1956. Assigned Bolivian civil registrations between CP-620 and CP-627, these aircraft were transferred directly from USAF surplus stocks at Davis-Monthan AFB. Hamilton Aircraft at nearby Tucson Municipal Airport was contracted by the Civil Aeronautics Administration to prepare the eight aircraft for delivery to the Bolivian government. In addition, Hamilton was also given 7 B-17 airframes to salvage for parts, which were also transferred to Bolivia. The seven aircraft were issued civil registrations but were never flown. They were trucked out in 1956, salvaged for useful parts, and scrapped by 1959.

1956 TRANSFERS FROM USAF TO BOLIVIA THROUGH CAA:

CP-620	44-85840	returned to U.S. 1968; D. 1975
CP-621	44-85774	returned to U.S. 1968; D. 1973
CP-622	44-85817	D. 1957
CP-623	44-83750	D. 1958
CP-624	44-6556	D. 1963
CP-625	43-39307	D. 1957
CP-626	44-83809	D. 1959
CP-627	44-6393	returned to U.S. 1981; display USAF

AIRCRAFT SALVAGED FOR PARTS BY HAMILTON AIRCRAFT FOR BOLIVIA IN 1956

N7040C	44-83778
N7041C	44-83763
N7042C	44-83634
N7043C	43-39281
N7044C	44-83600
N7045C	44-85706
N7046C	44-83587

BRAZIL

Brazil was provided with a total of thirteen B-17s under the auspices of the Rio Pact as established in 1947. Six aircraft were transferred in April and May of 1951. Five were SB-17Gs and the sixth was an RB-17G. Seven additional aircraft were transferred in late 1954 and early 1955. All were used for search and rescue or photo-reconnaissance. In 1955 the twelve surviving aircraft were assigned Forca Aerea Brasileira serial numbers between 5400 and 5411. Following is a listing of aircraft assigned:

5400	44-83663	TO USAFM OCT 1968/DISPLAY HILL AFB
5401	44-85567	WITHDRAWN 1967
5402	44-85583	WITHDRAWN 1968/DISPLAY RECIFE
5403	44-85602	WITHDRAWN 1966
5404	44-85836	CRASHED 1959
5405	43-39246	CRASHED 1962
5406	43-39335	WITHDRAWN 1966
5407	44-8891	WITHDRAWN 1967
5408	44-83718	WITHDRAWN 1968/UNDER RESTORATION
5409	44-83764	CRASHED 1964
5410	44-83378	WITHDRAWN 1965
5411	44-85494	WITHDRAWN 1968
NONE	44-85579	CRASHED 1952

FRANCE — INSTITUT GEOGRAPHIQUE NATIONAL

The French Institut Geographique National is a world ranging survey company which operated thirteen B-17s during the post-war years, and owned an addditional Fortress for use as a spares source.

S/N	FRENCH REG	MISCL
42-30177	F-BGSG	SPARES, S. 1973
42-32076	F-BGSH	RESTORED USAFM
43-39304	F-BDAT	D. 1950
44-8846	F-BGSP	OPERATIONAL, FRANCE
44-8889	F-BGSO	MUSEE DE L'AIR, FRANCE
44-83728	F-BGOE	S. 1970
44-83729	F-BEED	S. 1962
44-83735	F-BDRS	IMPERIAL WAR MUSEUM, BRITAIN
44-83757	F-BDRR	S.
44-85594	F-BGSQ	S. 1972
44-85643	F-BEEA	D. 1989
44-85718	F-BEEC	LONE STAR FLIGHT MUSEUM, TEXAS
44-85733	F-BEEB	D. 1949
44-85784	F-BGSR	B-17 PRESERVATION, BRITAIN

ISRAEL

Israel acquired a total of four B-17s in 1948 for their war of independence. All were bought on the American civil market and ferried to Europe one step ahead of American customs officials. One Fortress was interned by the Portugese when it landed at the Azore Islands for fuel. The other three aircraft made it through to Czeckhoslovakia where they were loaded with bombs and armed with hand-held machine guns. Their final leg of the ferry flight included bomb runs over Egyptian targets. The three B-17s were successfully employed by the Israeli Air Force in the 1948 and 1956 Middle East wars. They were withdrawn from service in the late fifties and scrapped in 1961.

44-83753	(ex N5024N)
44-83811	(ex N5014N)
44-83842	(ex N7712M, interned in Portugal)
44-83851	(ex N1098M)

OPERATION CROSSROADS

A total of sixteen B-17s were converted in the late spring of 1946 for use in Operation Crossroads. Six were used as mother ships for control of the B-17 drones. The other ten were used as "babies" and carried the actual cameras and research equipment. The mother ships were marked with large Roman numerals on the tail. The babies were marked with large stripes on the fuselage waist and vertical tail. Back-up babies were marked identically.

Mother Ships:		Babies:	
I	44-85818	One stripe:	44-85820
II	44-85815		44-83560
III	44-85752		unknown
IV	44-85738	Two stripes:	44-85819
V	44-85690		44-83553
VI	44-83646 (super mother)		unknown
		Three stripes:	44-83528
			44-83603
		Four stripes:	44-83519
			44-83588

SELECTED BIBLIOGRAPHY

■■■■■■

Books

Aderton, David A. *History of the United States Air Force*, New York: Crescent Books, 1981

Bowers, Peter M. *Fortress in the Sky*, Canoga Park, CA: Sentry, 1976

Bowers, Peter M. *50th Anniversary, Boeing B-17 Flying Fortress, 1935-1985*, Seattle: Museum of Flight, 1985.

Caidin, Martin. *Everthing But the Flak*, New York: Duell, Sloan, and Pearce, 1964.

Farmer, James H. *Celluloid Wings*, Blue Summit Ridge, Pennsylvania: Tab Books, 1985.

Edmonds, Walter D. *They Fought With What They Had*, Washington, D.C.: Zenger Publishing Company, 1951.

Futrell, Robert Frank. *The United States Air Force in Korea 1950-1953*, New York: Duell, Sloan, and Pearce, 1961.

Garber, Paul E. *The National Aeronautical Collections*, Washington, D.C.: Smithsonian Institution, 1956.

Goldberg, Alfred, ed. *History of the United States Air Force*, Princeton, New Jersey: D. Van Nostrand Company, Inc., 1957.

Gougon, Malcolm. *Fortress Survivors*, (mimeographed), 1987.

Johnsen, Frederick, ed. *Winged Majesty*, Tacoma, WA: Bomber Books, 1980.

Leary, William F. *Perilous Missions-Civil Air Transport and CIA Covert Operations in Asia*, Montgomerey, Alabama: University of Alabama Press, 1984.

Lloyd, Alwyn T. *B-17 Flying Fortress in Detail and Scale, Part 2* Fallbrook, CA: Aero Publishers, 1983.

Lloyd, Alwyn T. *B-17 Flying Fortress In Detail and Scale, Part 3*, Blue Ridge Summit, PA: Tab Books, Inc., 1986.

McPearson, Lee; Van Fleet, Clarke; and Van Wyen, Adrian. *United States Naval Aviation, 1910-1970*, U.S. Office of Naval Operations, Department of the Navy, U.S. Government Printing Office, 1971.

Miller, Richard L. *Under the Cloud*, New York: Free Press, 1986.

Olsen, Jack. *Aphrodite: Desparate Mission*, New York: G.P. Putnam and Sons, 1970.

Orriss, Bruce W. *When Hollywood Ruled The Skies*, Hawthorne, CA: Aero Associates, 1984.

Robins, Christopher. *Air America*, New York: Putnam, 1979.

Robins, Christopher. *The Invisible Air Force-CIA's Secret Airlines*, London: McMillan, 1979.

Vincent, Carl. *Canada's Wings, Volume 2: Consolidated Liberator and Boeing Fortress*, Stittsville, Ontario: Canada's Wings, 1975.

White, W.L. *Queens Die Proudly*, New York: Harcourt, Brace, and Company, 1943.

Operation Crossroads, The Official Pictorial History, New York: Wm.H. Wise and Co., 1946.

Periodicals

Babcock, Jim. "Restoring the Mighty Fortress," *Air Classics*, October 1980, pp. 48-53.

Blandin, Serge, "French Fortresses," *FlyPast*, November 1986, pp. 46-47.

Evans, Stuart. "Aphrodite II," *FlyPast*, November 1986, p. 20.

Farmer, James H. "The Making Of Twelve O'Clock High," *Journal of the American Aviation Historical Society*, Vol. 19 (Winter 1974) pp. 257-258.

Farmer, James H. "Saga Of The Civil Forts," *Journal of the American Aviation Historical Society*, Part 1: Vol 22 (Winter 1977) p. 292-302. Part 2: Vol 23 (Fall 1978) p. 162-167.

Farmer, James H. "Santa Maria Diary," *Journal of the American Aviation Historical Society*, Vol. 14 (Winter 1969) pp. 178-182.

Holder, William G. and Siuru, William D.; "The Final Mission," *Air Classics*, Volume 8 (December 1971), pp 48-51.

Larkins, William T. "Kingman Army Air Field, Arizona," *Aerophile*, Vol. 2, (June 1979), pp. 18-19.

Mikesh, Robert C. "The Boeing PB-1," *The Journal of the American Aviation Historical Society*, Volume 9 (Spring 1964) pp. 42-44.

Minnich, Mike. "Shoo Shoo Baby," *FlyPast*, January 1977, pp. 41-43.

Myers, Julian. "Kingman," *Flying*, February 1989, pp. 70-75.

O'Leary, Michael. "The Last Great Warbird Auction," *Warbirds International*, Summer 1986, pp. 38-43.

Ramey, General Roger M. "Phantom Fortresses Vs. The Atom Bomb, *Saturday Evening Post*, June 22, 1946, pp. 9-13.

Sherman, Gene. "Warplanes Go To Arizona Desert To Die," *Los Angeles Times*, April 1, 1946, p. 1.

"Air Research and Development Command," *Aviation Week*, August 17, 1953.

"B-17 Damaged In Accident," *Tulare Advanced-Register*, August 28, 1982, p. 1.

"Flying Fortress Was An Afterthought," *Tulare Advanced-Register*, October 31, 1981, p. 6.

"Largest Remote Controlled Drones," *Radio And Television News*, August 1956, p. 18.

"Last B-17 Drone Killed," *Holloman Rocketeer*, August 14, 1959, p. 1.

"War-Scarred Swoose Turned Over To City," *Los Angeles Times,* April 6, 1946, p. 5.

"Yes, We Have No Marana's," *New Times*, July 12, 1974.

Reports

Surplus Property Administration, *Annual Report*, Government Printing Office, 1945.

Surplus Property Administraton, *Quarterly Progress Reports By the Surplus Property Administration to Congress*, Government Printing Office, 1945, 1946, and 1947 (various).

United States Air Force, *Appendix No. 2, Air Materiel Command Regulation No. 20-307*, dated 09 April 1946, as provided by the Office of History, Headquarters, Air Force Logistics Command, Wright-Patterson AFB.

United States Air Force, *Brief History of Flight Testing At WPAFB*, not dated, as provided by the Office of History, Headquarters Air Force Logistics Command, Wright-Patterson AFB.

United States Air Force, *The Modification of Army Aircraft in the United States, 1939-1945*, Army Air Force Historical Studies No. 62, Air Historical Office.

United States Air Force, *Redeployment and Demobilization*, USAF Historical Study No. 77, USAF Historical Division, Air University, June 1953.

United States Air Force, *Air-Sea Rescue 1941-1952*, USAF Historical Study No. 95, USAF Historical Division, Research Studies Institute. Air University, August 1954.

United States Navy, Naval Historical Center, *Airborne Early Warning Squadron TWO Report for the period 1 January 1952 to 1 July 1952*.

United States Navy, Naval Historical Center, *Historical Report of Airborne Early Warning Squadron ONE (VW-1) covering period of 18 June 1952 through 31 December 1952*.

ABOUT THE AUTHOR

Scott Thompson has long held an interest in the B-17 and, in particular, its post-war use. He has written numerous articles for various publications including Warbirds International and Air Classics, and maintains an extensive aviation slide collection. He has worked in the aviation industry for fifteen years and holds Airline Transport Pilot and Flight Instructor certificates. He has worked for the Federal Aviation Administration since 1984, first as an Air Traffic Controller and now as an Airspace System Inspection Pilot. He lives in Manteca, California with his wife, Lisa, and their three sons. This is his first book.